Your P

HORO

— 1996 —

Your Personal
HOROSCOPE
——1996——

*Month-by-month Forecasts
for Every Sign*

Joseph Polansky

Thorsons
An Imprint of HarperCollinsPublishers

Thorsons
An Imprint of HarperCollins*Publishers*
77–85 Fulham Palace Road,
Hammersmith, London W6 8JB
1160 Battery Street,
San Francisco, California 94111–1213

Published by Thorsons 1995
1 3 5 7 9 10 8 6 4 2

Joseph Polansky asserts the moral right to
be identified as the author of this work

A catalogue record for this book
is available from the British Library

ISBN 1 85538 445 0

Printed in Great Britain by
HarperCollinsManufacturing Glasgow

Contents

Acknowledgements 7

Introduction 9

Glossary of Astrological Terms 11

Aries

    Personality Profile 18

    Horoscope for 1996 – Major Trends 24

    Month-by-month Forecasts 32

Taurus

    Personality Profile 51

    Horoscope for 1996 – Major Trends 57

    Month-by-month Forecasts 64

Gemini

    Personality Profile 83

    Horoscope for 1996 – Major Trends 89

    Month-by-month Forecasts 96

Cancer

    Personality Profile 116

    Horoscope for 1996 – Major Trends 122

    Month-by-month Forecasts 130

Leo

    Personality Profile 150

    Horoscope for 1996 – Major Trends 156

    Month-by-month Forecasts 163

Virgo

Personality Profile   182

Horoscope for 1996 – Major Trends   188

Month-by-month Forecasts   195

Libra

Personality Profile   215

Horoscope for 1996 – Major Trends   221

Month-by-month Forecasts   228

Scorpio

Personality Profile   248

Horoscope for 1996 – Major Trends   254

Month-by-month Forecasts   261

Sagittarius

Personality Profile   280

Horoscope for 1996 – Major Trends   286

Month-by-month Forecasts   293

Capricorn

Personality Profile   312

Horoscope for 1996 – Major Trends   318

Month-by-month Forecasts   325

Aquarius

Personality Profile   344

Horoscope for 1996 – Major Trends   350

Month-by-month Forecasts   357

Pisces

Personality Profile   376

Horoscope for 1996 – Major Trends   382

Month-by-month Forecasts   391

ACKNOWLEDGEMENTS

The author wishes to give special
thanks to STAR★DATA, who originally
commissioned this work. Without their
help – both financial and technical
– this book could not have been written.

Introduction

Welcome to the fascinating and intricate world of astrology!

For thousands of years the movements of the planets and other heavenly bodies have intrigued the best minds of every generation. Life holds no greater challenge or joy than this: knowledge of ourselves and the universe we live in. Astrology is one of the keys to this knowledge.

Your Personal Horoscope 1996 gives you the fruits of astrological wisdom. In addition to general guidance on your character and the basic trends of your life, it shows you how to take advantage of planetary influences so you can make the most of the year ahead.

The section on each Sign includes a Personality Profile, a look at general trends for 1996 and in-depth month-by-month forecasts. The Glossary on page 11 explains some of the astrological terms with which you may not be familiar.

One of the many helpful features of this book is the 'best' and 'most stressful' days section at the beginning of each monthly forecast. Read these sections to learn which days in each month will be good overall, good for money and good for love. Mark them on your calendar – they are your best days. Similarly, make a note of the days that will be stressful for you. It is best to avoid important meetings or taking major decisions on these days, as well as on those days when important planets in your Horoscope are *retrograde* (moving backwards through the Zodiac).

The Major Trends section for your Sign lists those days when your vitality is strong or weak, or when relationships with your co-workers or loved ones may need a bit more effort on your part. If you are going through a difficult time,

9

take a look at the colour, metal, gem and scent listed in the 'At a Glance' section of your Personality Profile. Wearing a piece of jewellery that contains your metal and/or gem will strengthen your vitality; just as wearing clothes or decorating your room or office in the colour ruled by your Sign, drinking teas made from the herbs ruled by your Sign or wearing the scents ruled by your Sign will sustain you.

Another important virtue of this book is that it will help you to know not only yourself but those around you: your friends, co-workers, partners and/or children. Reading the Personality Profile and forecasts for their Signs will provide you with an insight to their behaviour that you won't get anywhere else. You will know when to be more tolerant of them and when they are liable to be difficult or irritable.

I consider you – the reader – to be my personal client. By studying your Solar Horoscope I gain an awareness of what is going on in your life – what you are feeling and striving for – and the challenges you face. I then do my best to address these concerns. Consider this book the next best thing to having your own personal astrologer!

It is my sincere hope that *Your Personal Horoscope 1996* will enhance the quality of your life, make things easier, illuminate the way forward, banish the obscurities and make you more aware of your personal connection to the universe. Astrology – understood properly and used wisely – is a great guide to understanding yourself, the people around you and the events in your life – but remember that what you do with these insights – the final result – is up to you.

Glossary of Astrological Terms

Ascendant

We experience day and night because the Earth rotates on its axis once every 24 hours. It is because of this rotation that the Sun, Moon and planets seem to rise and set. The Zodiac is a fixed belt (imaginary, but very real in spiritual terms) around the Earth. As the Earth rotates, the different Signs of the Zodiac seem to the observer to rise on the horizon. During a 24-hour period every Sign of the Zodiac will pass this horizon point at some time or another. The Sign that is at the horizon point at any given time is called the Ascendant, or Rising Sign. The Ascendant is the Sign denoting a person's self-image, body and self-concept – the personal ego, as opposed to the spiritual ego which is indicated by a person's Sun Sign.

Aspects

Aspects are the angular relationships between planets, the way in which one planet stimulates or influences another. If a planet makes a harmonious aspect (connection) to another, it tends to stimulate that planet in a positive and helpful way. If it makes a stressful aspect to another planet, the stimulation is stressful and uneasy, causing disruptions in the planet's normal influence.

Astrological Qualities

There are three astrological qualities into which all the 12 Signs are divided: *cardinal*, *fixed* and *mutable*.

The cardinal quality is the active, initiating principle. Cardinal Signs (Aries, Cancer, Libra and Capricorn) are good at starting new projects.

Fixed qualities are stability, persistence, endurance and perfectionism. Fixed Signs (Taurus, Leo, Scorpio and Aquarius) are good at seeing things through.

Mutable qualities are adaptability, changeability and balance. Mutable Signs (Gemini, Virgo, Sagittarius and Pisces) are creative, if not always practical.

Direct Motion

When the planets move forward – as they normally do – through the Zodiac they are said to be going 'direct'.

Houses

There are 12 Signs of the Zodiac and 12 Houses of experience. The 12 Signs are personality types and ways in which a given planet expresses itself. The Houses show 'where' in your life this expression takes place. Each House has a different area of interest (see the list, opposite). A House can become potent and important – a House of power – in different ways: if it contains the Sun, the Moon or the Ruler of your chart, if it contains more than one planet, or if the Ruler of the House is receiving unusual stimulation from other planets.

1st House of Body and Personal Image

2nd House of Money and Possessions

3rd House of Communication

4th House of Home and Family, Domestic Life

5th House of Fun, Entertainment, Creativity, Speculations and Love Affairs

6th House of Health and Work

7th House of Love, Romance, Marriage and Social Activities

8th House of Elimination, Transformation and Other People's Money

9th House of Travel, Education, Religion and Philosophy

10th House of Career

11th House of Friends, Group Activities and Fondest Wishes

12th House of Spiritual Wisdom and Charity

Karma

Karma is the law of cause and effect which governs all phenomena. We are all in the situation in which we find ourselves because of Karma – because of actions we have performed in the past. The universe is such a balanced instrument that any unbalanced act immediately sets corrective forces into motion – Karma.

Long-term Planets

The planets that take a long time to move through a Sign are considered long-term planets – these planets are Jupiter (which stays in a Sign for about a year), Saturn (which stays in a Sign for two and a half years), Uranus (seven years), Neptune (14 years) and Pluto (15 to 30 years). These planets show the long-term trends in a given area of life and thus they are important when astrologers forecast the prolonged view of things. Because these planets stay in one Sign for so long, there are periods in the year when the faster-moving (short-term) planets will join them, further activating and enhancing the importance of a given House.

Lunar

Relating to the Moon.

Natal

Literally means 'birth'. In Astrology this term is used to distinguish between planetary positions that occurred at birth (natal) and transiting (current) ones. For example, Natal Sun refers to where the Sun was when you were born; the transiting Sun refers to where the Sun's position is currently at any given moment – which usually doesn't coincide with your birth, or Natal, Sun.

Out of Bounds

The planets move through our Zodiac at various angles relative to the celestial equator (if you draw an imaginary extension of the Earth's equator out into the universe you will have the celestial equator). The Sun – being the most dominant and powerful influence in the Solar system – is the measure astrologers use as a standard. The Sun never goes more than approximately 23 degrees north or south of this celestial equator. At the winter solstice the Sun reaches its maximum southern angle of orbit (declination) and at the summer solstice it reaches its maximum northern angle. Any time a planet exceeds this Solar boundary – and occasionally planets do – it is said to be 'out of bounds'. This means that the planet exceeds or trespasses into strange territory – beyond the limits allowed by the Sun, the Ruler of the Solar system. The planet in this condition becomes more emphasized and exceeds its authority, becoming an important influence in a forecast.

Phases of the Moon

After the full Moon, the Moon seems to shrink in size (as perceived from the Earth), gradually growing smaller until it is virtually invisible to the naked eye – at the time of the next new Moon. This is called the *waning* Moon phase – or the waning Moon.

After the new Moon, the Moon gradually gets bigger in

size (as perceived from the Earth), until it reaches its maximum size at the time of the full Moon. This period is called the *waxing* Moon phase – or waxing Moon.

Retrogrades

The planets move around the Sun at different speeds. Mercury and Venus move much faster than the Earth, while Mars, Jupiter, Saturn, Uranus, Neptune and Pluto move more slowly. Thus there are times when, relative to the Earth, the planets appear to be going backwards. In reality they are always going forward, but relative to our vantage point on Earth they seem to go backwards through the Zodiac for a period of time. This is called 'retrograde' motion and it tends to weaken the normal influence of a given planet.

Short-term Planets

These are the fast-moving planets: the Moon (which stays in a Sign for only two and a half days), Mercury (20 to 30 days), the Sun (30 days), Venus (approximately a month) and Mars (approximately two months). Since these planets move so quickly through a Sign their effects are generally of a short-term nature. They show the immediate, day-to-day trends in a Horoscope.

Transits

This refers to the movements or motions of the planets at any given time. Astrologers use the word 'transit' to make the distinction between a birth or Natal planet and its current movement in the heavens. For example, if at your birth Saturn was in the Sign of Cancer in your 8th House, but is now moving through your 3rd House, it is said to be 'transiting' your 3rd House. Transits are one of the main tools with which astrologers forecast trends.

Aries

♈

THE RAM

Birthdays from
21st March
to 20th April

Personality Profile

ARIES AT A GLANCE

Element – Fire

Ruling Planet – Mars
    Career Planet – Saturn
    Love Planet – Venus
    Money Planet – Venus
    Planet of Home and Family Life – Moon
    Planet of Wealth and Good Fortune – Jupiter

Colours – carmine, red, scarlet

Colours that promote love, romance and social harmony – green, jade green

Colour that promotes earning power – green

Gem – amethyst

Metals – iron, steel

Scent – honeysuckle

Quality – cardinal (= activity)

Quality most needed for balance – caution

Strongest virtues – abundant physical energy, courage, honesty, independence, self-reliance

Deepest need – action

Characteristics to avoid – haste, impetuousness, over-aggressiveness, rashness

Signs of greatest overall compatibility – Leo, Sagittarius

Signs of greatest overall incompatibility – Cancer, Libra, Capricorn

Sign most helpful to career – Capricorn

Sign most helpful for emotional support – Cancer

Sign most helpful financially – Taurus

Sign best for marriage and/or partnerships – Libra

Sign most helpful for creative projects – Leo

Best Sign to have fun with – Leo

Signs most helpful in spiritual matters – Sagittarius, Pisces

Best day of the week – Tuesday

Understanding the Aries Personality

Aries is the activist *par excellence* of the Zodiac. The Arien need for action is almost an addiction and those who do not really understand the Arien personality would probably use this hard word to describe it. In reality 'action' is the essence of the Arien psychology – the more direct, blunt and to-the-point the action, the better. When you think about it, this is the ideal psychological makeup for the warrior, the pioneer, the athlete or the manager.

Ariens like to get things done and in their passion and zeal often lose sight of the consequences for themselves and others. Yes, they often *try* to be diplomatic and tactful, but it is hard for them. When they do so they feel that they are being dishonest and phony. It is hard for them even to understand the mind-set of the diplomat, the consensus builder, the front office executive. These people are involved in endless meetings, discussions, talks and negotiations – all of which seem a great waste of time when there is so much work to be done – so many real achievements to be gained. An Aries can understand, once it is explained to him to her, that talks and negotiations – the social graces – lead ultimately to better, more effective actions. The interesting thing is that an Aries is rarely malicious or spiteful – even when waging war. Aries people fight without hate for their opponents. To them it is all good-natured fun; a grand adventure; a game.

When confronted with a problem many people will say 'Well, let's think about it, let's analyse the situation.' But not an Aries. An Aries will think 'Something must be done. Let's get on with it.' Of course neither response is the total answer. Sometimes action is called for, sometimes cool thought. But an Aries tends to err on the side of action.

Action and thought are radically different principles. Physical activity is the use of brute force. Thinking and deliberating require one not to use force – to be still. It is not good for the athlete to be deliberating the next move; this will only slow down his or her reaction time. The athlete must act instinctively and instantly. This is how Aries people tend to behave in life. They are quick, instinctive decision-makers and their decisions tend to be translated into actions almost immediately. When their intuition is sharp and well tuned, their actions are powerful and successful. When their intuition is off, their actions can be disastrous.

Do not think this will scare an Aries. Just as a good warrior knows that in the course of combat he or she might acquire a few wounds, so too does an Aries realize – somewhere deep down – that in the course of being true to oneself, one might incur a disaster or two. It is all part of the game. An Aries feels strong enough to weather any storm.

There are many Aries people who are intellectual: Ariens make powerful and creative thinkers. But even in this realm they tend to be pioneers – outspoken and blunt. These types of Ariens tend to elevate (or sublimate) their desire for physical combat with intellectual, mental combat. And they are indeed powerful.

In general, Aries people have a faith in themselves that others could learn from. This basic, rock-bottom faith carries them through the most tumultuous situations of life. Their courage and self-confidence make them natural leaders. Their leadership is more by way of example than by actually controlling others.

Finance

Aries people often excel as builders or estate agents. Money in and of itself is not as important as are other things – action, adventure, sports, etc. They are motivated by the need to support their partners and to be well thought of by partners. Money as a way of attaining pleasure is another important motivation. Ariens function best in their own businesses or as managers of their own departments within a large business or corporation. The fewer orders they have to take from higher up the better. They also function better out in the field rather than behind a desk.

Aries people are hard workers with a lot of endurance; they can earn large sums of money due to the strength of their sheer physical energy.

Venus is their Money Planet, which means that Ariens need to develop more of the social graces in order to realize their full earning potential. Just getting the job done – which is what an Aries excels at – is not enough to create financial success. The co-operation of others needs to be attained. Customers, clients and co-workers need to be made to feel comfortable. Many people need to be treated properly in order for success to happen. When Aries people develop these abilities – or hire someone to do this for them – their financial potential is unlimited.

Career and Public Image

One would think that a pioneering type would want to break with the social and political conventions of society. But this is not so with the Aries-born. They are pioneers within conventional limits, in the sense that they like to start their own businesses within an established industry rather than to work for someone else.

Capricorn is on the 10th House (of Career) cusp of Aries' solar horoscope. Saturn is the planet that rules their life's work and professional aspirations. This tells us some interesting things about the Arien character. First off, it shows that in order for Aries people to reach their full career potential they need to develop some qualities that are a bit alien to their basic nature. They need to become better administrators and organizers. They need to be able to handle details better and to take a long-range view of their projects and their careers in general. No one can beat an Aries when it comes to a short-range objective, but a career is long term, built over time. You cannot take a 'quickie' approach to it.

Some Aries people find it difficult to stick with a project until the end. Since they get bored quickly and are in constant pursuit of new adventures, they prefer to pass the old project or task to somebody else in order to start something new. Those Ariens who learn how to put off the search for something new until the old gets done will achieve great success in their careers and professional lives.

In general, Aries people like society to judge them on their own merits, on their real and actual achievements. A reputation acquired by 'hype' feels false to them.

Love and Relationships

In marriage and partnerships Ariens like people who are more passive, gentle, tactful and diplomatic – people who have the social grace and skills they sometimes lack. Our partners always represent a hidden part of ourselves – a self that we cannot express personally.

An Aries tends to go after what he or she likes aggressively. The tendency is to jump into relationships and marriages. This is especially true if Venus is in Aries as well as the Sun. If an Aries likes you, he or she will have a hard time taking no for an answer; many attempts will be made to sweep you off your feet.

Though Ariens can be exasperating in relationships – especially if they are not understood by their partners – they are never consciously or wilfully cruel or malicious. It is just that they are so independent and sure of themselves that they find it almost impossible to see somebody else's viewpoint or position. This is why an Aries needs someone with lots of social grace to be his or her partner.

On the plus side, an Aries is honest, someone you can lean on, someone with whom you will always know where you stand. What he or she lacks in diplomacy is made up for in integrity.

Home and Domestic Life

An Aries is of course the ruler at home – the Boss. The male will tend to delegate domestic matters to the female. The female Aries will want to rule the roost. Both tend to be handy around the house. Both like large families and both believe in the sanctity and importance of the family. An Aries is a good family person, although he or she does not especially like being home a lot, preferring instead to be roaming about.

For natures that are so combative and wilful, Aries people can be surprisingly soft, gentle and even vulnerable with their children and partners. The Sign of Cancer, ruled by the Moon, is on the cusp of their Solar 4th House of Home and Family. When the Moon is well aspected – under favourable influences – in the birth chart an Aries will be tender towards the family and want a family life that is nurturing and supportive. Ariens like to come home after a hard day on the battlefield of life to the understanding arms of their partner and the unconditional love and support of a family. An Aries feels that there is enough 'war' out in the world – and he or she enjoys participating in that. But when Aries comes home, comfort and nurturing are key.

Horoscope for 1996

Major Trends

1995 was a kind of 'cosmic holiday' time for most of you. It was a year of increased fun, pleasure, foreign travel and tremendous intellectual expansion. It was a year for expanding your mental horizons either through the study of foreign cultures, higher education or deep philosophical studies. Many of you had opportunities to become more cultured and refined. In 1996 you will take what you have learned and apply it to your career and outward objectives. It will be a banner career year, so enjoy it. Moreover, whatever new knowledge you gained in the past is now going to be recognized by the outer world, by superiors and elders, and by those who have authority over you.

For those of you who are born early in the Sign of Aries (21st to 28th March), the education process is far from over. In fact it is just beginning in a much deeper, more profound way. The insights of 1995 now must be forged into a long-term, workable philosophy of life. Many of you will break with the religions you were born into. Others will enter into them in a new way. Many of you will even be called to change your place of worship, be it church, synagogue or mosque.

For those of you born later in the Sign of Aries (29th March to 20th April) this process will come later – perhaps a few years from now. In 1996, as you have been doing in the past, you are working to break habit-patterns and psychological barriers that obstruct your present progress. You are still learning to re-invent yourself by understanding how to 'die daily', as St Paul wrote. True transformation of personality and life does not necessarily come by 'adding' to your life but by a process of removal – of ridding yourself of obstructions. When this is done your personality automatically transforms and you become the person that you desire to be.

Saturn, the great Cosmic Tester and giver of long-term boons, is moving into your Sign in April and will stay there for the next two years or so. All of you will feel the impact of this move in one way or another, but those born early in the Sign (21st to 28th March) will feel it more acutely this year. Those of you born later in the Sign (29th March to 20th April) will feel the full impact in 1997 – but it is still good to understand what is going on so that you can co-operate with the process.

Saturn is going to give you a 'reality check' – an adjustment, a correction. If your self-esteem is overblown and unrealistic, Saturn will knock you down a peg or two to make it more realistic. On the other hand, if your self-esteem is too low Saturn will raise it. Saturn loves reality and truth. Many of you will feel the limits of your physical energy this year. You just cannot do everything, be everywhere, solve all of the world's problems and waste energy this year. You have to focus on what is important to you and eliminate the unnecessary. Though cosmic energy is in essence unlimited, our capacity to absorb it at any given time *is* limited. Respect those limits.

Saturn is going to make you more serious, more dutiful, and bless you with a long-term perspective on things. The short-term view no longer suffices. And, since Saturn also happens to be your Career Planet, the obvious scenario here is that your career success and expansion brings added burdens and responsibilities which force you to limit your personal desires and interests and to focus on what is important to you over the long term. No matter what your age, this is the year to think about your old age, your retirement and the kind of lifestyle you want to live many years from now.

Health

Your House of Health is not especially active in 1996, Aries, and thus the Cosmos is neither impelling you in one direction nor the other. Astrologers consider an 'inactive' 6th House to be a good thing, so there is no special need to pay attention to your health because it is basically good. You can more or less take it for granted. Yet, in spite of this, the Saturn transit mentioned earlier is having some impact on you – first off in feelings of 'lack of energy'. Of course, there is no real lack of energy – you have enough to do what you need to do and what you are supposed to do – but not too much for extraneous, unnecessary things. Stick to what is important and in line with your life's work and you will have plenty of energy. Stray into areas that have no bearing on your real goals and you will feel the lack very acutely.

Saturn moving through your 1st Solar House from mid-April onwards suggests a need for moderate exercise programmes, weight-loss programmes, and watching your diet more. Those of you born early in the Sign *will* lose weight this year – practically effortlessly. Those of you born later in the Sign will see it happen in 1997.

On a psychological level, the Saturn trait often creates a feeling of 'carrying burdens and responsibilities'. One feels the weight of the whole world upon one's shoulders. Of itself this is good, but do not overdo it. It is one thing to bear one's rightful responsibilities – these burdens make us stronger and benefit ourselves and others. It is the 'false burdens' – the unrealistic ones – that cause the problems and make us feel that we are crushed beneath them. Distinguish between true and false responsibilities and you will get through the year with flying colours. Remember, the Cosmos never holds you responsible for things that are not in your power.

Home and Domestic Life

Your 4th House of Home and Family is not especially active this year, thus you pretty much have a free hand to create your domestic situation, to mould home and family relationships according to your will. But your home life, though not active, can and probably will be indirectly affected. For your career is ultra-important this year (as it has been for many years now) and the changes that are made – the attention you give to career matters – probably detracts from your attention to your family and home base. Career changes (as well as pressure from your spouse or romantic partner) could very well cause a move. Career responsibilities leave you with less time to spend with your family. Emotional security and harmony are much less important to you than is outward achievement. Your spouse, on the other hand, seems more interested in home, family and the pleasures of the hearth.

One of your parents (or parental figures) – which one depends on whether you are male or female – places extra burdens on you this year, in effect restricting your freedom. But there is a strong positive side to this, as this parent (or parental figure) is also very generous towards you.

Your spouse's family (or the family of your business partner/s) increases this year either by birth or marriage.

Your enthusiasm for the pleasures of home and hearth, for mingling with family members and for doing domestic chores waxes and wanes with the Moon – your Family Planet. When the Moon waxes you have more enthusiasm for these things; when it wanes you have less. When the Moon waxes it is good to start domestic projects, to purchase furniture and accessories for the home, to add more rooms or make other extensions to your domestic sphere; when it wanes it is good to finish projects, to get rid of excess possessions, old furniture or old belongings that are rotting in your attic or basement. When the Moon waxes it is a good time to buy a new home or move into a new apartment. When the Moon wanes it is a good time to sell your home.

The two lunar eclipses of 1996 – one in April and the second in September – do show long-term changes in the home and with family members. These will bring up vulnerabilities and weaknesses in your domestic and family situation so that you can deal with them. Whatever you have been ignoring or sweeping under the carpet will now come to light so that you can deal with it.

Love and Social Life

Although your love life will be tumultuous this year – two eclipses will occur in your House of Marriage – there are no major trends in this area. Love and romance seem less important to you this year as you focus on things such as friendships and career. This does not mean you will have no love life – of course you will. It only means that you have more freedom to shape it as you will. But can increased freedom make up for lack of interest?

Singles will tend to stay single; marrieds (if it is your first marriage) will tend to stay married. For those working on a second or third marriage, however, the situation is different. First off, this marriage is more volatile this year than last year. Major changes are happening within the relationship. If the relationship is basically sound the marriage will survive and the changes and experimentation craved will occur within the marriage. If the relationship is not sound then the marriage is in very real danger in 1996. But have no fear, there are other prospects waiting in the wings – especially for those of you who are on the third go round. You meet the special someone suddenly and unexpectedly. There is great freedom in the relationship and a great feeling of equality. Your lover is more like a friend and a companion than a spouse.

Singles (those who have never been married) will have marriage opportunities from 3rd April to 7th August. But there is no special push from the Cosmos saying that you must marry. This period may merely bring a hot affair. This occurs with someone in your neighbourhood or someone you meet at a school/education centre or seminar. More marriage opportunities come from 22nd September to 23rd November. These are people you meet at parties, art galleries or through other artistic endeavours.

Now romance is one thing and friendship another. This is

a year for making new friends, joining groups and mingling with those who are like-minded. These relationships are more fun than highly-charged romances because there is more freedom involved and a greater appreciation of other people's intellectual gifts. Also, cool friendships are less painful, therefore more attractive. You are meeting true friends this year – friends who want (and are able) to make your fondest dreams come true.

Career and Finance

This is a major interest – especially your career – this year, just as it has been for many years now. Most of you are more settled in your life's work and more sure of what it is by now. You have been experimenting for the past seven years and by now have learned what you needed to learn. Now is the time for expanding your career, and you are getting a lot of help. Last year was a good money year, and this year continues this trend. More pay-rises and promotions are likely. More-business related travel is also on the cards. Superiors recognize your worth, your knowledge and optimistic attitude. You are asked to teach or coach other employees. Your scope of power within the corporate structure is expanded. But with this, as mentioned earlier, comes increased responsibility and the need to limit your activities. Be careful of overwork.

On a personal level you seem more interested in status, prestige and your public image than you are in mere money-making. Given the choice between glory and money you will choose glory.

Though 1995 was a year for much travel, this year too much travel can put you into debt, so be careful.

Your spouse or partner can increase his or her income through advertising, sales and marketing. He or she must focus on getting the word out about a product or service. Your partner also earns more by getting better interest or dividends from present investments (interest rates are of major concern for your partner this year).

One of your parents (or parental figure) is prospering greatly this year. A move or renovation of his or her home is likely – an enlarging of his or her personal room or personal quarters. This parent needs to be careful not to put too much weight on, nor to over-indulge too much. He or she is very involved in science, engineering or high-tech industries or stocks.

Your personal investment philosophy will tend to be more conservative this year. Normally a risk-taker, you are more calculated now – thinking of the long term, investing in areas that have good long-term, stable value. Of course, with Venus as your Money Planet your investment philosophy and strategies tend to change from month to month, but this year there is a conservatism in spite of the changes.

Self-improvement

Your career and friendships are going to improve this year almost by themselves. Career opportunities will come from foreign lands, in the publishing area, and from academia. Friendships will come naturally as a result of joining groups and professional organizations. As long as you do not obstruct things, these areas of your life will improve.

But your spiritual life seems to demand more work and effort on your part. Pluto moving through your 9th House forces you to purify your religious attitudes and personal philosophy of life. Saturn moving through your 12th House forces you to confront unconscious fears and complexes that obstruct your spiritual progress. You must allow more time for introspection and self-analysis in spite of a busy career schedule. Seek out a teacher or therapist who can assist you in these areas, and work out a programme that fits in with your career demands.

Month-by-month Forecasts

January

Best Days Overall: 7th, 8th, 16th, 17th, 18th, 25th, 26th

Most Stressful Days Overall: 5th, 6th, 12th, 13th, 19th, 20th

Best Days for Love: 2nd, 3rd, 12th, 13th, 14th, 23rd, 24th

Best Days for Money: 1st, 2nd, 3rd, 10th, 11th, 12th, 13th, 14th, 19th, 20th, 23rd, 24th, 27th, 28th

This is a major, tumultuous month, Aries, which sets the stage for the rest of the year. On the 3rd Jupiter makes a major move from Sagittarius into Capricorn – enhancing your career prospects, expanding career horizons and bringing pay-rises, promotions, recognition and outward success. Moreover, this month there are many other planets activating your 10th House of Career as well. By all means focus on this area – push ahead boldly. The lunation of 20th January is going to clarify career doubts and anxieties – showing you exactly what you need to do step by step. Do not worry too much about mundane domestic affairs now, focus on your career. Achieve domestic goals on the 15th when the Moon is full in your 4th House. Sudden wealth or a 'big-ticket' (expensive, long-lasting) item comes to you from the family. The wealth of a family member increases.

With all of this career action going on it is understandable that you are working unusually hard. Take time to rest and relax. Take time for leisure activities and for mingling with friends. This is not one of your better health months.

On 13th January Uranus makes a major – long-term – move into Aquarius. Thus your social life starts to become very exciting and fulfilling. You are meeting all kinds of new friends – some of whom want to be more than that. New friends come and go seemingly endlessly. Those that depart are replaced by new ones.

After the 20th the planetary power shifts into your 11th House. Your health and vitality immediately improve. Your focus is on happiness and in making fondest hopes and wishes come true. With Uranus now helping you great progress will be made – wishes manifest suddenly and unexpectedly.

Mercury is retrograde (moving backwards) from the 9th to the 30th, so be more careful about communication. Avoid doing mass mailings or signing important contracts then. Do these things either before or after this period.

Earnings are strong this month. Social contacts provide earning opportunities. Networking helps you enhance your 'bottom line'. After the 15th your financial intuition is ultra-powerful – if you listen, every financial need will be met. A second of true intuition is often the equivalent of months – even years – of hard labour.

February

Best Days Overall: 3rd, 4th, 5th, 13th, 14th, 21st, 22nd

Most Stressful Days Overall: 1st, 2nd, 8th, 9th, 10th, 15th, 16th, 28th, 29th

Best Days for Love: 1st, 2nd, 8th, 9th, 10th, 13th, 14th, 21st, 22nd

Best Days for Money: 1st, 2nd, 6th, 7th,

13th, 14th, 15th, 16th, 21st, 22nd, 23rd, 24th, 25th

With all of the planets moving forward this month, and with 80 to 90 per cent of them in the eastern sector of your horoscope, you are in a month of action, achievement and forward momentum. The pace is probably even too fast for you, Aries – a person who normally likes speed. All I can say is 'go for it.' You get your way this month and the planetary momentum is behind you.

Your ability to create your own conditions – a situation that you especially enjoy – is getting stronger day by day as the planets shift ever more eastward. Those involved with an Aries should either help or get out of their way – it is unwise to play the obstructer right now.

Career progress is swift and spectacular now. You achieve work goals with confidence and speed – last month you experienced some delays in this area. Especially favourable events happen around the 15th and 16th. Foreign travel related to business is likely to happen as well – though your partner or lover may object. Your financial intuition is strong and if followed will bring lucrative windfalls very swiftly. Watch your dreams and hunches. You are getting your way both in love and in finance.

Your love nature changes very radically this month. As the month begins you are altruistic and idealistic. You love everybody and are very giving. After the 9th, Venus moves into your own Sign and you become more self-centred, self-assertive and demanding in love. Your attitude switches from universal, unconditional love to 'me first – 'I'm going to get mine and that's all there is to it.' In spite of this, romance blooms. Your lover or partner goes out of his or her way to please you – putting your interests and desires ahead of his or her own. After the 9th, with Venus in your own Sign, you project a more glamorous image and become more attractive to the opposite sex. This is a good time to buy clothing or jewellery or to have your hair styled. Your aesthetic sense is super.

Health is good all month. After the 19th people around you may seem more depressed, weepy and hopeless. They will turn to you to lift their spirits. You have enough optimism for the world.

Though you are busy with work and career issues, do not forget your spiritual life this month. Set aside some quiet moments every day for meditation and contemplation. Donate some time – without stressing yourself out – to charitable activities.

March

Best Days Overall: 1st, 2nd, 3rd, 11th, 12th, 19th, 20th

Most Stressful Days Overall: 6th, 7th, 8th, 13th, 14th, 26th, 27th, 28th

Best Days for Love: 1st, 2nd, 3rd, 6th, 7th, 8th, 13th, 14th, 22nd, 23rd

Best Days for Money: 1st, 2nd, 3rd, 4th, 5th, 13th, 14th, 22nd, 23rd

Always independent, self-directed and self-motivated, this month you are 100 times more so – especially after the 20th. The planetary concentration in the eastern half of your horoscope along with the power in the Sign of Aries reinforce these natural traits in you. You are self-assertive, self-confident, bold, aggressive and likely to get your way. Now, getting your way can either be a blessing or a curse depending on what your way is. Use the early part of the month – from the 1st to the 20th – to clarify your goals and ideals. Try to make sure that your goals are legitimate and in line with the greatest good for all concerned. Then, when the Sun moves into your own Sign after the 20th, you will be ready to put your plans into action. Objectives are achieved easily this month as you are filled with unusual vitality and strength – especially after the 20th. The opposition melts away.

This month is important in other ways as well, Aries. After the 20th planetary power is starting to shift to the bottom half of your horoscope. They are not all there yet – but they are headed there. Thus you are shifting focus from outward, career-orientated objectives to home and family interests. This will be a gradual process for the next few months. This month, however, is very much a 'me-first' month. You are into pleasing yourself, your own personal and sensual pleasures, and your own interests.

Until the 24th you have a more spiritual – impersonal – perspective on life. You see the Divine Hand and Plan in almost everything. You see it in history, politics, economics, in your relationships and especially in the nitty-gritty details of everyday life. The world and all its workings are merely the manifestation of Great Spiritual Laws. Those of you involved in yoga and meditation make great progress this month.

After the 24th your perspective becomes more 'ego-centred'. You see the world and its workings in terms of your own self-interest. World and political events are judged as to how they affect you personally here and now. There is nothing wrong with this – this too is a valid way of seeing things – and it enables you to act more effectively in the world.

Wealth is super this month and will get even better next month. A conservative investment philosophy helps you. Real estate and agricultural industries are sources of profit. Your partner, spouse or lover is supportive and co-operative financially.

April

Best Days Overall: 7th, 8th, 16th, 17th, 25th, 26th, 27th

Most Stressful Days Overall: 3rd, 4th, 9th, 10th, 23rd, 24th, 30th

Best Days for Love: 1st, 2nd, 3rd, 4th, 11th, 12th, 20th, 21st, 30th

Best Days for Money: 1st, 2nd, 3rd, 9th, 10th, 11th, 12th, 18th, 19th, 20th, 21st, 29th, 30th

This is an important yet highly tumultuous month, Aries. The two eclipses of the month – on the 3rd and the 17th – occur on the angles of your chart. This makes them more powerful than normal. They occur in your 1st and 7th Houses, signifying long-term changes in your personality, body and personal image (1st House) and in your marriage, love life and social relationships (7th House). The unfolding of these events has various scenarios. Many of you will be forced by events to redefine your personality – perhaps you will be subjected to some unfair verbal attacks. You either define and become clear as to who you are, or others will define your personality for you – probably not in flattering ways. It is as if you are making a new introduction to the people around you or to a new circle of friends. Those of you who have not been watching your diet or health might find that repressed, hidden toxins or irregularities come to the surface so that you have to deal with them. Those of you who do watch your diet and health will merely change your lifestyle, mode of dress and the way you accessorize yourself. Many of you will move house. Single women may marry – thus causing a change in their name. Marrieds in stressful relationships might find this is the time to call it quits – thus again causing a redefinition of your self-image from married person to single person. Disciples of spiritual teachers are given new spiritual names. Creative people change their mode and style of expression.

As if all of this were not enough, Saturn, the Cosmic Tester, moves into your own Sign on the 7th forcing more long-term changes to your personality and self-image and compelling you to become more careful about your physical energy for the next two years. Do your best to enjoy the changes now. Flow with them rather than try to resist. Fortunately you have plenty of energy, vitality and self-confidence in spite of all that is going on – you will prevail and prosper. There is brief period of adjustment which you need to get used to.

In spite of all this – perhaps because of all this – continue to design your life as you would like it to be. What you cannot do physically and materially you can still do in your mind – through visualization and affirmation.

May

Best Days Overall: 5th, 6th, 13th, 14th, 23rd, 24th

Most Stressful Days Overall: 1st, 2nd, 7th, 8th, 20th, 21st, 22nd, 27th, 28th, 29th

Best Days for Love: 1st, 2nd, 9th, 10th, 18th, 19th, 27th, 28th, 29th

Best Days for Money: 1st, 2nd, 7th, 8th, 9th, 10th, 15th, 16th, 17th, 18th, 19th, 25th, 26th, 27th, 28th, 29th

The fallout from the two eclipses last month now suggest a period of caution, introspection and review. This is hard for an action-orientated person like you, Aries; particularly because, with most of the planets in your eastern sector, you want to do and get things over with.

Keep in mind that for most of the month 50 to 60 per cent of the planets are retrograde – including your Money and Love Planet, Venus. Thus people in general are more cautious and have perhaps changed many of their opinions and plans since last month. It is as if the cosmic movements themselves are checked – hesitant – while in the process of reviewing its actions. Do not let frustration get you down. Use any delays to improve your product and/or service. Allow yourself more time to get things done. Be extra careful with communications from the 3rd to the 27th, when Mercury is retrograde – and it might be a good idea to have your car and telephone equipment checked over. Though sales and marketing projects are very interesting to you this month, it is better to prepare rather than actually release them into the world. If you must do mass mailings or release books, newsletters or periodicals this coming month, do so on the 27th, 28th and 29th.

This same caution applies to your financial life and your love life – though both are inherently sound. If you are going to make purchases, investments or long-term financial commitments, do so from the 1st to the 3rd and from the 17th to the 20th. After that, hold off. Venus goes retrograde on the 20th. After the 20th is a time for reviewing and evaluating past investments and financial strategies. Rash financial moves after the 20th can take you backwards instead of forwards. Your financial judgement tends to be unrealistic when your Money Planet is retrograde. Though your love life is good – your appeal to the opposite sex is strong – a marriage or business partnership should not be entered into after the 20th. Wait till July, when Venus starts to go forward again. Your judgement about people tends to be unrealistic after the 20th – either over-optimistic or over-pessimistic.

You feel strongly speculative in your financial life now,

but cool it. If you must speculate do with only a small – harmless – percentage of your money. Intellectual interests go well and singles find hot romance right in the neighbourhood – or with neighbours. Health is good all month.

June

> Best Days Overall: 1st, 2nd, 9th, 10th, 19th, 20th, 29th, 30th
>
> Most Stressful Days Overall: 3rd, 4th, 16th, 17th, 18th, 24th, 25th
>
> Best Days for Love: 5th, 6th, 14th, 15th, 24th, 25th
>
> Best Days for Money: 3rd, 4th, 5th, 6th, 12th, 13th, 14th, 15th, 22nd, 23rd, 24th, 25th

While the short-term, fast-moving planets are now moving more and more towards the bottom of your chart, the long-term, slow-moving planets are still very much at the top. Thus, over the long haul you are very much focused on career activities and outward achievements – but for now you need to get your emotional and domestic life in order. This is all the more true now that these 'upper planets' are retrograde. You are in a 'pause and review' stage in your career. You are taking a 'cosmic breather' – much needed – in your outer life.

This is also a month to pursue intellectual interests and tune up your communication abilities. If you need new phones, faxes, modems and the like, this is the month to get them. If you need a new car or to repair your present one, this is the time to do it. The New Moon of the 15th is going to clarify and resolve any questions you might have. You will be shown exactly what you need to do – on a very personal and specific level.

Fifty per cent of the planets – like last month – are still retrograde in June. This kind of thing does not sit well with action-orientated Fire-types like you, for whom inaction is a slow form of torture. Yet there is great wisdom in inaction now – especially in areas where you are not clear about what to do next. In spite of your frustrations you will find that things sometimes get done just as efficiently by inaction as by action. Like a seed developing beneath the soil, your projects are making progress in the unseen, invisible realms. Trying to force growth now is counter-productive. Let patience do her perfect work.

On the financial front you are still in a period of sitting tight. Study new investments very carefully. Read the fine print in all new purchases. Rethink investments and investment strategies. When in doubt, do nothing. Interest and dividend income increase this month. High-yielding investments appeal to you more than aggressive investments.

Singles find love close to home – at schools, in the neighbourhood and with neighbours. Siblings play a role in your love life. Your lover is more like a brother/sister than a partner. Do not send out wedding invitations just yet. Your judgement on social issues is not realistic now.

July

> Best Days Overall: 6th, 7th, 8th, 16th, 17th, 26th, 27th
>
> Most Stressful Days Overall: 1st, 14th, 15th, 21st, 22nd, 28th, 29th
>
> Best Days for Love: 2nd, 3rd, 11th, 12th, 21st, 22nd, 30th, 31st

Best Days for Money: 1st, 2nd, 3rd, 9th,
10th, 11th, 12th, 19th, 20th, 21st, 22nd,
28th, 29th, 30th, 31st

Career and family obligations place great demands on your normally superabundant physical energy this month. Make sure to rest and relax more – especially until the 22nd. Visits to a chiropractor or massage therapist would not hurt, either.

The challenge this month is to balance your career and family obligations without unduly denying yourself. You are going to have to curb some of your personal interests and personal desires in order to fulfil the demands of superiors at work and the family – but do not go too far and completely deny yourself.

For most of the year you have been able to sweep family obligations and domestic duties under the carpet, but not now. The neglect has caught up with you and this is the month to deal with it. You seem overly assertive and wilful with the family this month, but this will not work – compromise and balance are key here.

On the financial level things are finally straightening out and moving forward again. Venus, which has been retrograde for the past two months, is now going direct. This is the month to release those sales and marketing projects into the world. Mail those letters, place those advertisements, make those calls. They pay off now. This is the month to implement your investment plans and sign those contracts. The New Moon of the 15th brings a happy – and substantial – financial surprise. It is either a 'big-ticket' item for the home or some financial bonanza that comes through your family or family connections. A financial speculation works out favourably this month.

Your love life is also starting to straighten out. Those of you involved in a serious relationship now know more or less where you stand. Those planning to marry can schedule the marriage now. Those already married see their relationship progress. The need in love this month is for good communication and intellectual harmony. You are attracted to people you can talk to and share ideas with. You are attracted to 'brainy' types. Unattached singles find love in the neighbourhood and with the boy or girl next door. Married Ariens can strengthen their relationships by taking domestic and neighbourhood jaunts – go to that tourist spot in your neighbourhood, or take a romantic holiday in a neighbouring city.

August

Best Days Overall: 3rd, 4th, 12th, 13th, 14th, 22nd, 23rd, 30th, 31st

Most Stressful Days Overall: 10th, 11th, 17th, 18th, 19th, 24th, 25th

Best Days for Love: 10th, 11th, 17th, 18th, 19th, 20th, 21st, 28th, 29th

Best Days for Money: 5th, 6th, 10th, 11th, 15th, 16th, 20th, 21st, 24th, 25th, 28th, 29th

When Saturn moves over someone's Sun Sign – as is the case with you since April – it usually casts a serious, stern and perhaps pessimistic outlook on life. Usually this produces many good things – a sense of duty and responsibility, physical resilience and an appreciation for the long-term good. But it can be a downer to friends and associates. It makes a person seem cold and aloof – separate from others and very conscious of his or her sense of separation. But this month you can take a break from all this seriousness and have some fun. Saturn is retrograde and therefore weaker, and the Sun moves through the glorious fun-loving

Sign of Leo. People in general are not interested in the long term but want to enjoy life in the here and now. And so should you. Oh, later on in the month you can pick up your burdens and cares if you like – and will probably handle them better – but now the rapture of life calls to you. You need a little holiday. You need some rest and recreation. So take a break, get involved in creative hobbies, spend some time with children and go to parties and places of entertainment. This is also a good month to get involved in sports or vigorous physical exercise.

Your finances are good this month with a few challenges thrown in to make things interesting. Until the 7th, sales, marketing and advertising projects are still important to your 'bottom line'. Getting the word out to customers and clients is the number-one priority. After the 7th you are faced with an ethical problem in your finances. You must somehow choose between profits and ethics – profits and your personal philosophy. The need is to feel that your earnings are not hurting others. Money comes to you through real estate investments, family connections, buying and selling of homes, and people from your past. Your financial intuition is strong after the 7th – but you must be in a calm state of mind to receive it. Avoid taking financial decisions when you are upset or in a bad mood. Sleep on things.

Your love life is becoming more interesting. Someone from your past – an old boyfriend or girlfriend – comes back on the scene. Unresolved issues between you get resolved one way or another. Singles are not sure whether they want intellectual communion – the sharing of minds – or the sharing of feelings and nurturing. Both seem important this month.

Your health is excellent.

September

> Best Days Overall: 9th, 10th, 18th, 19th,
> 27th, 28th
>
> Most Stressful Days Overall: 6th, 7th, 8th,
> 14th, 15th, 20th, 21st
>
> Best Days for Love: 8th, 9th, 14th, 15th,
> 18th, 19th, 27th, 28th
>
> Best Days for Money: 1st, 2nd, 3rd, 8th, 9th,
> 11th, 12th, 18th, 19th, 20th, 21st, 27th,
> 28th, 29th, 30th

September is an active and tumultuous month during which your courage gets tested. Thus there are many opportunities for spiritual growth now. But let's start at the beginning: the planets have now shifted to the western part of your horoscope, forcing you to learn lessons of diplomacy, adaptability and how to depend on others. Though you are always a self-reliant type, this month you need to lean on others a little more than you are accustomed to. Your good comes to you through the good graces of other people and you must learn to get along with them and see their points of view.

Issues of personal health become important this month. Those of you in good health should perhaps be more careful about dietary issues, as the lunar eclipse of the 26th is going to bring up impurities in the body. The New Moon of the 12th is going to guide you in these areas, bringing you all the information you need. The field of diet is like a vast jungle with no consensus among the authorities – thus we need all the personal guidance that the Moon can give us.

The lunar eclipse has a tremendous impact on both your career and personal image. It will in many cases force a career change. In other cases it will create a shake-up in the corporate hierarchy – leaving your personal status up in the air for a while. A legal matter suddenly confronts you or does not turn out the way you expected. Your personal philosophy changes. When the dust settles you will be in better shape than before. But while the dust is still in the air be courageous, stand firm and have faith.

In spite of all the tumult and shake-ups going on, your love life and financial life are solid. Love is fun and playful. You manage to have fun amidst all of the uncertainty. Speculations are favourable, too. Personal creativity is strong. Money is earned in pleasurable ways. There are more parties and social gatherings in your life this month. Singles have ample romantic opportunities. Marrieds are more in synch with their partners, with almost no divergent interests.

October

Best Days Overall: 6th, 7th, 16th, 17th, 24th, 25th

Most Stressful Days Overall: 4th, 5th, 11th, 12th, 18th, 19th, 31st

Best Days for Love: 8th, 9th, 11th, 12th, 18th, 19th, 27th, 28th

Best Days for Money: 9th, 10th, 18th, 19th, 26th, 27th

With 90 per cent of the planets all in forward motion by the end of the month there is a lot of action and forward progress going on. And though this is the kind of celestial environment that you like, this month it is a bit uncomfortable – for you are not the one causing the actions; the changes happening in your life (for good or ill) are coming from others. You are merely reacting to events. Still, there is a beautiful plan working out beneath it all, and when the dust settles you will see it.

To add to the sense of dramatic change there is a solar eclipse on the 12th – more powerful in your chart than in most. It occurs in your 7th House of Love and Marriage, showing that long-term changes are occurring *vis à vis* your marital status; that your partner or spouse is redefining his or her personality – and this will always change a relationship. He or she might redefine the personality to such an extent that it is no longer that of the person you married or fell in love with. In effect you are with someone new – someone you have to become acquainted with all over again. In many cases this could make the relationship stronger, in others it could destroy it. It all depends on how well you like this 'new' partner. Singles are likely to marry now. Social and love decisions can no longer be postponed and you are forced to act one way or another.

The eclipse of the Sun, Lord of your Solar 5th House, also shows long-term changes in your creative life, in your relations with children (they are redefining themselves and making major life-changing decisions) and in a current love affair. Avoid speculations this month.

This eclipse makes a stressful aspect to Jupiter, Lord of your 9th House. For those of you attending college or university it shows a major change in your education – perhaps you change schools, or change subjects, or perhaps you find that the school you are attending is redefining itself in such a way as to be totally different from the one you thought you enrolled in. Religious and philosophical attitudes are also shaken and tested this period. Your faith in whatever 'ism' you subscribe to is tested now.

Definitely rest and relax more this month – especially around the time of the solar eclipse (12th).

November

Best Days Overall: 2nd, 3rd, 4th, 12th, 13th, 20th, 21st, 30th

Most Stressful Days Overall: 1st, 7th, 8th, 14th, 15th, 27th, 28th

Best Days for Love: 7th, 8th, 16th, 17th, 27th, 28th

Best Days for Money: 5th, 6th, 7th, 8th, 14th, 15th, 16th, 17th, 23rd, 24th, 27th, 28th

With both your Personal Solar Cycle and the Universal Solar Cycle waning now – and with many planets moving through your 8th House – this is a good month to get rid of the unnecessary in your life. Life is an alternation between positive and negative – getting and giving, building up and tearing down. Both sides of life are necessary to achieve our goals, maintain happiness and foster a balanced, healthy being.

Right now you are in a 'tearing down' phase. On a financial level this means reducing debt and expenses and getting rid of possessions that are no longer needed and perhaps bog you down and drain your resources. On a domestic level it means doing a thorough house-cleaning, getting rid of old furniture, old appliances and the like that merely collect dust and take up space. On a psychological level it means getting rid of character traits, emotional reaction-patterns and unresolved traumas that merely sap your energy and are no longer helping you move forward. On a physical level it means detoxifying the body and ridding it of things that are no longer useful – such as extra pounds – and getting rid of old clothing and accessories that you never wear or have no use for. On a spiritual level, rid yourself of thoughts, ideas and concepts that block your Unity with the All.

Less is more this month. Acquire by eliminating. Expand by first contracting. Much good that wants to come to you cannot because there is no room for it. Empty yourself so that you can be filled.

Your health is excellent all month but gets even better after the 22nd. Your love and social life should also be going well. Love is romantic, flowery and harmonious most of the month. There is a great sense of fairness and consideration in your relationships – and until the 23rd this is what you really want most. Neither side must give too much or too little. Singles are probably romantically involved this month.

December

Best Days Overall: 1st, 9th, 10th, 18th, 19th, 27th, 28th

Most Stressful Days Overall: 5th, 6th, 11th, 12th, 25th, 26th

Best Days for Love: 5th, 6th, 7th, 8th, 15th, 16th, 17th, 27th, 28th

Best Days for Money: 2nd, 3rd, 7th, 8th, 11th, 12th, 15th, 16th, 17th, 20th, 21st, 27th, 28th, 30th, 31st

Until the 21st you are still in one of your best health and pleasure periods of the year, Aries. You have a lot of energy with which to achieve work goals, but the problems arise from distractions. Higher education, reading and perhaps travel conflict with your work goals. You must balance all these interests, not going too far in any one direction.

The planets are now mostly above the horizon of your chart, once again fostering your career and the need for outward achievement. Be sure to have some fun before the 21st, as after that things become more serious – more work-, career- and duty-orientated. Happy career surprises – advancements, promotions, recognition, pay-rises and the like – are coming after the 21st.

Love is physical, intense and single-minded until the 17th. You seem focused on one person exclusively. You need to be careful of being overly intense – trying to make your partner over and otherwise trying to control behaviour. Jealousy can be a problem this period as well. But after the 17th you lighten up and your social horizons widen. You are more philosophical about love and love is happier and freer for it. Singles and the uninvolved will want to date more and play the field after the 17th. Marrieds and the involved will become less obsessive.

Your Money Planet in the Sign of Scorpio until the 17th shows that you have opportunity either to make or pay debts rather easily. Better though to pay them now. Needless (unnecessary) expenses should be trimmed. Get rid of possessions and investments that are no longer needed.

Your diligence and hard work all year are paying off in your career after the 21st. Do not be shy about promoting yourself.

Opportunities for foreign travel come this month, but see if you can integrate these trips with your career or job. Travelling for pleasure enhances love but conflicts with your work goals.

Rest and relax more – where possible – after the 21st. This will be difficult because you seem very busy, but you must discern between the essential and the inessential.

Taurus

☉

THE BULL
*Birthdays from
21st April to
20th May*

Personality Profile

TAURUS AT A GLANCE

Element – Earth

Ruling Planet – Venus
   Career Planet – Uranus
   Love Planet – Pluto
   Money Planet – Mercury
   Planet of Home and Family Life – Sun
   Planet of Wealth and Good Fortune – Jupiter

Colours – earth tones, green, orange, yellow

*Colours that promote love, romance and social
harmony* – red-violet, violet

Colours that promote earning power – yellow,
yellow-orange

Gems – coral, emerald

Metal – copper

Scents – bitter almond, rose, vanilla, violet

Quality – fixed (= stability)

Quality most needed for balance – flexibility

Strongest virtues – endurance, loyalty, patience, stability, a harmonious disposition

Deepest needs – comfort, material ease, wealth

Characteristics to avoid – rigidity, stubbornness, tendency to be overly possessive and materialistic

Signs of greatest overall compatibility – Virgo, Capricorn

Signs of greatest overall incompatibility – Leo, Scorpio, Aquarius

Sign most helpful to career – Aquarius

Sign most helpful for emotional support – Leo

Sign most helpful financially – Gemini

Sign best for marriage and/or partnerships – Scorpio

Sign most helpful for creative projects – Virgo

Best Sign to have fun with – Virgo

Signs most helpful in spiritual matters – Aries, Capricorn

Best day of the week – Friday

TAURUS

Understanding the Taurus Personality

Taurus is the most earthy of all the Earth Signs. If you understand that Earth is more than just a physical element, that it is a psychological attitude as well, you will get a better understanding of the Taurus personality.

A Taurus has all the power of action that an Aries has. But Taureans are not satisfied with action for its own sake. Their actions must be productive, practical and wealth-producing. If Taureans cannot see a practical value in an action they will not bother taking that action.

Taureans' forte lies in their power to make real their own or other people's ideas. They are generally not very inventive but they can take another's invention and perfect it, make it more practical and useful. The same is true for all projects. Taureans are not especially keen on starting new projects, but once they get involved they will bring these projects to completion. A Taurus carries everything through. He or she is a finisher and will go the distance as long as no act of God intervenes.

Many people find Taureans too stubborn, conservative, fixed and immovable. This is understandable, because Taureans dislike change – in their environment or in their routine. Taureans even dislike changing their minds! On the other hand, this is their virtue. It is not good for a wheel's axle to waver. The axle must be fixed, stable and unmovable. Taureans are the axle of the wheel of society and the heavens. Without their stability and so-called stubbornness, the wheels of the world (and especially the wheels of commerce) would not turn.

Taureans love routine. A routine, if it is good, has many virtues. It is a fixed – and, ideally, perfect – way of taking care of things. When one allows for spontaneity mistakes can happen, and mistakes cause discomfort and uneasiness – something almost unacceptable to a Taurus. Meddling with Taureans' comfort and security is a sure way to irritate and anger them.

While an Aries loves speed, a Taurus likes things slow. They are slow thinkers – but do not make the mistake of assuming they lack intelligence. On the contrary, Taureans are very intelligent. It is just that they like to chew on ideas, to deliberate and weigh them up. Only after due deliberation is an idea accepted or a decision taken. Taureans are slow to anger – but once aroused, take care!

Finance

Taureans are very money-conscious. Wealth is more important to them than it is to many other Signs. Wealth to a Taurus means comfort and security. Wealth means stability. Where some Zodiac Signs feel that they are spiritually rich if they have ideas, talents or skills, Taureans only feel their wealth when they can see and touch it. Taurus' way of thinking is 'What good is a talent if it has not been translated into a home, furniture, car and swimming pool?'

These are all reasons why Taureans excel in estate agency and agricultural industries. Usually a Taurus will wind up owning land. They love to feel their connection to the Earth. Material wealth began with agriculture, the tilling of the soil. Owning a piece of land was humanity's earliest form of wealth: Taureans still feel that primeval connection.

It is in the pursuit of wealth that Taureans develop their intellectual and communication abilities. Also, in this pursuit of wealth and need to trade with others Taureans are forced to develop some flexibility. It is in the quest for wealth that they learn the practical value of the intellect and come to admire it. If it were not for the search for wealth and material things Taureans might not try to reach a higher intellect.

Some Taureans are 'born-lucky' people who usually win in any gamble or speculation they make. This luck is due to other factors in their Horoscope and is not part of their essential nature. By nature they are not gamblers. They are hard workers and like to earn what they get. Taureans' innate conservatism makes them abhor unnecessary risks in finance and in other areas of their lives.

Career and Public Image

Being essentially down-to-earth people, simple and uncomplicated, Taureans tend to look up to those who are original, unconventional and inventive. Taureans like their bosses to be creative and original – since they themselves are content to perfect their superiors' brain-waves. They admire people who have a wider social or political consciousness and they feel that someday (when they have all the comfort and security they need) they too would like to be involved in these big issues.

In business affairs Taureans can be very shrewd – and that makes them valuable to their employers. They are never lazy; they enjoy working and getting good results. Taureans do not like taking unnecessary risks and do well in positions of authority, which makes them good managers and supervisors. Their managerial skills are reinforced by their natural talents for organization and handling details, their patience and thoroughness. As mentioned, through their connection with the earth Taureans also do well in farming and agriculture.

In general a Taurus will choose money and earning power over public esteem and prestige. A position that pays more – though it has less prestige – is preferred to a position with a lot of prestige but fewer earnings. Many other Signs do not feel this way, but a Taurus does, especially if there is nothing in his or her personal birth chart that modifies this. Taureans will pursue glory and prestige only if it can be shown that these things have a direct and immediate impact on their wallet.

Love and Relationships

In love, the Taurus-born likes to have and to hold. They are the marrying kind. They like commitment and they like the terms of a relationship to be clearly defined. More importantly, Taureans like to be faithful to one lover and they expect that lover to reciprocate this fidelity. When this does not happen the whole world comes crashing down. When they are in love Taureans are loyal, but they are also very possessive. They are capable of great fits of jealousy if they are hurt in love.

Taureans are satisfied with the simple things in a relationship. If you are involved romantically with a Taurus there is no need for lavish entertainments and constant courtship. Give them enough love, food and comfortable shelter and they will be quite content to stay home and enjoy your company. They will be loyal to you for life. Make a Taurus feel comfortable and – above all – secure in the relationship and you will rarely have a problem.

In love, Taureans can sometimes make the mistake of trying to take over their partners, which can cause great pain on both sides. The reasoning behind their actions is basically simple. Taureans feel a sense of ownership over their partners and will want to make changes that will increase their own general comfort and security. This attitude is OK when it comes to inanimate, material things but it can be dangerous when applied to people, so Taureans should be careful and attentive.

Home and Domestic Life

Home and family are vitally important to Taureans. They like children. They also like a comfortable and perhaps glamorous home – something they can show off. They tend to buy heavy, ponderous furniture – usually of the best quality. This is because Taureans like a feeling of substance in their environment. Their house is not only their home but their place of creativity and entertainment as well. The Taureans' home tends to be truly their castle. If they could choose, Taureans would prefer living in the countryside to being city-dwellers. If they cannot do so during their working lives, many Taureans like to holiday in or even retire to the country, away from the city and closer to the land.

At home a Taurus is like a country squire – the lord of the manor. They love to entertain lavishly, to make others feel secure in their home and encourage them to derive the same sense of satisfaction as they do from it. If you are invited for dinner at the home of a Taurus you can expect the best food and best entertainment. Be prepared for a tour of the house – which the Taurus treats as a castle – and expect to see your Taurus friend exhibit a lot of pride and satisfaction in his or her possessions.

Taureans like children but they are usually strict with them. The reason for this is they tend to treat their children – as they do most things in life – as their possessions. The positive side to this is that their children will be well cared for and well supervised. They will get every material thing they need to grow up properly. On the down-side, Taureans can get too repressive with their children. If a child dares to upset the daily routine – which Taureans love to follow – he or she will have a problem with a Taurus parent.

Horoscope for 1996

Major Trends

Last year was a time of great psychological progress. It was a year for breaking addictions, getting at the root of psychological problems and otherwise eliminating the unnecessary from your life and character; for paying off debts, making money for others and putting other people's financial interests ahead of your own. Most of you made great progress.

This year is much happier and less serious for you, Taurus – something like a 'cosmic holiday'. Expansive Jupiter's move into Capricorn makes beautiful aspects to you, bringing more money, recognition, self-esteem and what the world calls 'lucky breaks'. It brings foreign travel, opportunities for higher education and a general widening of your horizons.

But do not think that 1996 will be a total bowl of cherries. The Cosmos has thrown in a few challenges to keep things interesting. Uranus' move into Aquarius – which has tremendous implications for the world as a whole – has special meaning for you. For this movement brings accelerated change, modernism and 'avant-gardism' to the world. Conservative types like you are challenged by this. Your happiness for the coming seven or so years depends on your ability to embrace change and to make it your friend. This ability will not come overnight, but it will come – you have got seven years to learn.

Health

Your ability to cope with change and to handle it in positive ways will have special impact on your health. Too much internal resistance could cause unnecessary problems. Remember that it takes life-force to set up psychological resistance and that the root of most diseases – from the cosmic perspective – comes from wasting precious life-force.

But what does it mean to embrace change? Does it mean that you have to change principles that you know are right? Does it mean that you have to follow the world into not-so-honourable actions in the name of 'change' or 'modernism'? Of course not. On issues of honour and principle, do not budge. But on subsidiary issues – like using that new computer system in your home or office, or embracing new and better technology – by all means go along. This is the trend now. You are about to witness a technological explosion of such magnitude that the advances of the past 10 years or so seem like the works of a child playing with a toy science kit. 'Techno-phobes' are going to have a rough time of it.

So how do you go about dealing with change? One way is to think of yourself as a Solar Centre – a Cosmic Solar Being (this is what you are in your true nature anyway). You are a fixed point around which a constantly changing universe revolves. The landscape shifts and changes constantly, but you are 'centred' in who you are, in your goals, life work and in your morals and ethics. You are the unchanging within the change. The movement on the periphery brings new opportunities, some you can take and some you can let go. But do take the things that further your goals and life-purposes.

Otherwise, your health is basically good this year. Pluto has moved away from its stressful aspect to you, and most of the major long-term planets are making harmonious aspects with you. Moreover, your relatively inactive 6th House this year shows that health is not a big priority, that you have much freedom in this regard and that you have no need to pay too much attention to it.

The health of your partner, spouse or lover becomes more delicate after April. There is a need for your partner to get his or her health in order – to exercise regularly, watch the diet and in general purify the body. Your partner's approach to health seems very orthodox and traditional. There is an unwillingness to experiment with new methods or new technologies. Your partner's conservatism comes from a desire for long-term health and long-term well-being. Health fads are therefore mistrusted. Your partner can overcome health problems through long-term changes in lifestyle and diet. Magic fads and other quick solutions are not the way to go here.

Home and Domestic Life

Your 4th House of Home and Family Life is not particularly active this year, Taurus. Thus you attach no special importance to it on an overall level. A move or change of residence (perhaps a major renovation of your home) could come – not from your own personal desires but as a result of pressure from your spouse and sudden career changes. Your spouse, partner or lover feels itchy for a move, and is generally more concerned with domestic issues than you. You are more focused on outward and career achievement.

One of your parents (which depends on whether you are male or female) is very restless, moving from house to house and from place to place. This parent (or parental figure) is redefining his or her personality this year and is not sure of the next step to take – and is thus in a 'transient' state. He or she experiments with one image, then another, with one home, then another, seeking through these actions to find out who he or she really is. Do not let these things stress you. Keep plenty of room in your phone directory for your parent's many changes of phone number and address. Keeping track of people who are under the influence of Uranus can be a trying experience.

Love and Social Life

For many years now your love life has been undergoing purification and renewal. There was a constant balancing act going on between your interests and desires and those of your spouse or lover – as if your interests were at odds and incompatible. The lessons of compromise, though difficult, were called for. But this is over with now. Your love life/marriage has stabilized. Moreover, since the 7th House of Marriage is relatively inactive this year, 1996 seems a year that fosters the status quo. Singles will tend to remain single, marrieds will tend to remain married.

Love and social interests will become more prominent from 23rd October to the end of the year. Singles are most likely to meet that special someone during this period. Marriage is possible but not an imperative, however.

All the above refers to those of you who have never been married. Those of you looking to make a second marriage have very good prospects this year. Someone prominent, well educated, refined and wealthy – or who at least lives a wealthy lifestyle – comes into your life. He or she may be a guide or teacher, someone you can look up to and admire. This person earns his or her income through science, technology, the media or other high-tech fields. Sounds wonderful? It is. But do not rush headlong into anything. The relationship will be sternly tested come April. If it survives that – and the tests of June and October – you are home free.

Those working on a third marriage also face slow going. There is a need for great caution here. The urge is for long-term, stable and enduring love. This can only happen by being patient and observant. The feeling that both of you have is 'better no marriage than the wrong one', 'better no love than wrong love'.

This attitude of caution and testing applies to your friendships as well. Disappointments with friends are wake-up calls forcing you to re-evaluate your notions of friendship. Is any mere acquaintance a friend? Just because someone belongs to the same group or organization that you do, does that make him or her your friend? Real friends are people who want you to achieve your fondest hopes and wishes – and who are willing to make this happen, each according to his or her ability. Such friends want for you what you want for yourself. When in doubt about a friend, apply this test to him or her. It is an unerring guide.

The trend of weeding out false friends from the true ones has been going on for some years now and continues this year. Better fewer friends but real ones, rather than hosts of lukewarm ones.

A sibling's marriage is undergoing crisis and testing this year. Survival is iffy.

Career and Finance

Financial affairs are always important to you, Taurus, but like last year the emphasis seems less on personal earning power and more on shared resources, investments and the use of other people's money. Pluto, now firmly established in your 8th House, shows profits from bankrupt or defunct companies or enterprises, from waste management and recycling industries, from publishing houses and travel companies, from royalties, tax refunds and legal battles. Your credit line seems unusually good – but this is a double-edged sword. Yes, you have greater access to other people's money, but if you overdo it you run the danger of rampant debt. Debts are most easily made or paid from 20th March to 20th April, 23rd July to 23rd August, and from 22nd November to 21st December.

Yet, though your personal earning power is less emphasized and less important you nevertheless prosper greatly this year. Your wealth increases. Your partner is unusually generous with you – for he or she is prospering this year as well. Investors believe in your projects and are easily attracted, you are remembered in someone's will, and global investments also work well for you.

On a philosophical level your prosperity can be explained in this way: Jupiter increases your sense of self-esteem and self-worth, leading to added recognition and greater earning power. Your loose and relaxed attitude towards money also helps.

Your partner is very focused on financial affairs this year and for many years to come – with an almost single-minded, laser-like concentration on amassing wealth. Very little can distract him or her from this quest – therefore success is likely. Life always honours commitment and concentration. Where the attention is, there flows the cosmic energy. But your partner can enhance his or her income through advertising, good public relations and expanded use of the media. It is very important for your partner to get the word out about his or her product or service. Your partner seems poised to acquire new communication equipment as well – a good investment.

You, on the other hand, are more focused on career and public prestige and status this year. With Uranus right on the Midheaven of your chart all year you can expect many sudden changes here – all leading to better prospects. Changes in the corporate hierarchy leave room for your advancement and offers from other companies at better salaries. You seem restless in your career, looking for the ideal and not satisfied until you find it. Thus serial career changes are likely now. And, though this goes against your innately conservative nature, it seems necessary. It is just as important to find out what you do not want as what you do want. Look in high-tech industries for your advancement.

Self-improvement

Come April of 1996 Saturn makes a major, long-term move into your 12th Solar House. Those of you born early in the Sign of Taurus will feel the impact of this most dramatically. Those of you born later in the Sign will feel minor twinges of this energy, not feeling the full brunt until next year. This Saturn transit forces you to confront deep psychological issues – fears and unconscious blockages that obstruct your happiness and spiritual advancement. These irrational fears may come from your 'past lives'. These must be brought up, recognized and dealt with appropriately. Give yourself more time for introspection, and seek the guidance of a trained teacher.

Jupiter will be in your Solar 9th House all year bringing opportunities for foreign travel and higher education. By all means take these opportunities. The results will pay off in your career next year. Opportunities to study foreign cultures and religions should also be taken. You will need this knowledge in the future.

Month-by-month Forecasts

January

Best Days Overall: 1st, 10th, 11th, 19th, 20th, 27th, 28th

Most Stressful Days Overall: 7th, 8th, 14th, 15th, 21st, 22nd

Best Days for Love: 2nd, 3rd, 7th, 8th, 12th, 13th, 14th, 15th, 16th, 17th, 23rd, 24th, 25th

Best Days for Money: 2nd, 3rd, 10th, 11th, 12th, 13th, 19th, 20th, 27th, 28th

A very active and exciting month. Your health and vitality are simply super and you have abundant energy to achieve whatever you will. After the 20th, however, rest and relax more. You seem torn between the opportunities that are opening for higher education and foreign travel and the new career choices presenting themselves. See if you can satisfy both these urges. Look for the educational opportunities that do not interfere with your career. Choose a career path that lets you travel and study. Merge these twin urges into a cohesive whole.

Your Money Planet, Mercury, goes retrograde from the

9th to the 30th. Thus it will seem to you that you are going backwards instead of forwards in earnings. But this is only temporary. Avoid making major investments, trades or purchases ('big-ticket' items) during this period. Be patient with your self financially. Use delays to improve your product or service. When in doubt during a Mercury retrograde period it is best to do nothing. Things clarify when it starts going forward again. Use this period to study potential investments and purchases rather than actually to indulge in them.

Major and happy changes are happening in your career this month. Barriers to progress fall suddenly and unexpectedly. Yet you feel restless about your present position. This is as it should be, for you seem to be moving from position to position for a long time. Career fantasies are being fulfilled this month and for years to come – some of these fantasies might not actually be good for you, but you need to go through them to find this out. Only then can you create healthier and more realistic career fantasies. You are just as ambitious for family members as you are for yourself. In turn the family supports your career aspirations. Nitty-gritty domestic details seem unimportant to you and you are probably ignoring them. A family member wants to move.

Your love life is stable this month.

February

Best Days Overall: 6th, 7th, 15th, 16th, 23rd, 24th, 25th

Most Stressful Days Overall: 3rd, 4th, 5th, 11th, 12th, 17th, 18th

Best Days for Love: 1st, 2nd, 3rd, 4th, 13th, 14th, 21st, 22nd

Best Days for Money: 6th, 7th, 15th, 16th, 17th, 23rd, 24th, 25th, 26th, 27th

Day by day you are getting stronger, more self-directed and more in control of conditions. Day by day the planetary power is swinging eastward in your chart. So start making plans for the kind of conditions that you would like to create. When the planetary powers are fully eastward you will be ready to act and to set your plans in motion.

All the planets are moving forward this month, Taurus, so you are in a period of action and achievement. Perhaps things are moving too fast for you – especially in your career. Try to flow with it. If you feel tired, rest and relax more. Your vitality is going to improve after the 19th.

With 90 to 100 per cent of the planets still at the top half of your chart, career and outward objectives are the focus for now. Let domestic duties slide for a while – do only what is absolutely essential. It is not that your family is unimportant to you – quite the contrary – but you will better satisfy them and fulfil domestic goals by focusing on your career. Career months like this one do not happen all the time. For singles the pursuit of career goals brings romantic opportunities. People involved in your career are either interested romantically or introduce you to romantic prospects.

The 15th brings an opportunity to impress superiors with your creativity. You mingle socially with superiors. Be careful of rash speculation around that time.

Finances are much better this month than last. The delays and frustrations are over as Mercury moves forward at a rapid clip. Your financial confidence is back. Financial and investment goals are achieved swiftly, and money is earned pleasurably. A sudden windfall comes around the 15th, from seeds planted in the past. One of your parents (which one depends on whether you are male or female) and superiors are supportive financially and provide opportunities. Your professional prestige has a direct impact on your 'bottom line' now – this is not always the case, but this month it is.

March

Best Days Overall: 4th, 5th, 13th, 14th, 22nd, 23rd

Most Stressful Days Overall: 1st, 2nd, 3rd, 9th, 10th, 15th, 16th, 29th, 30th

Best Days for Love: 1st, 2nd, 3rd, 9th, 10th, 11th, 12th, 13th, 14th, 19th, 20th, 22nd, 23rd, 29th, 30th

Best Days for Money: 4th, 5th, 9th, 10th, 13th, 14th, 17th, 18th, 22nd, 23rd, 24th, 25th, 29th, 30th

With 80 to 90 per cent of the planets still above the horizon, the focus this month continues to be on your career and outward achievement. Home and family issues still take a back seat and are de-emphasized. The majority of the planets – though not an overwhelming majority – are now in the eastern half of your horoscope, making you more self-directed, aggressive and interested in pleasing yourself.

As the month begins you are involved with group work and group activities. You are searching for 'happiness' but of a deeper sort – a personal happiness that is balanced with a happiness for all people, a kind of trans-personal happiness. Much progress is made here and your fondest hopes and wishes are being fulfilled.

Later on in the month you are more focused on spiritual, altruistic activities – charitable, philanthropic and meditation activities. Your dream life is active, ESP experiences multiply and much guidance is given to you regarding love and finance. This is a good period to review the past year, evaluate past performance and set goals for your coming Solar cycle (Personal Solar Cycle) which will begin on your birthday. When your birthday comes round you will be in a position to execute new plans and projects.

Your overall health and vitality are excellent all month. You have plenty of energy to accomplish what you will. Meditation and metaphysical techniques enhance your health until the 6th. After that health is enhanced through physically means – diet, sports and exercise regimes.

Mercury, your Money Planet, moves through three different Signs this month – and moving pretty quickly at that. Thus your approach to finances needs to be more flexible – financial strategies that seem right at the beginning of the month are not right towards the end of the month. Keep alert to changing markets and conditions. Those of you who are investors – and what Taurus is not an investor? – will have more of the 'trader' than the 'investor' mentality this month. You seem to prosper by playing the short-term trends rather than 'having and holding' for the long haul. Until the 7th you see opportunities in scientific and high-tech products. From the 7th to the 24th you see opportunities in shipping, oil and perhaps tobacco. After the 24th you become interested in steel, sporting goods and military contractors. Financial confidence is strong and your judgement is sound. You should prosper now.

April

> Best Days Overall: 1st, 2nd, 9th, 10th, 18th, 19th, 28th, 29th

> Most Stressful Days Overall: 5th, 6th, 11th, 12th, 25th, 26th, 27th

> Best Days for Love: 1st, 2nd, 3rd, 5th, 6th, 7th, 8th, 11th, 12th, 16th, 17th, 20th, 21st, 25th, 26th, 30th

TAURUS

The planets are mostly eastward now, energizing you and your personal interests and desires. Initiative, independence and self-motivation are strong now, but before you can fully apply them you need to do some psychological and spiritual 'housecleaning'. Your 12th House of Spiritual Wisdom is the main headline this month and is the scene of most of the planetary action.

Four powerful planets move through this House this month – and as if this were not enough there is a solar eclipse here on the 17th. Before you can start creating conditions you have to get your spiritual life in order. The 12th House is the place where the soul finds atonement and Divine Grace. It has a need to rid itself of obstructions to this process. It usually makes a person more charitable and philanthropic so that karmic debris – fears, false racial conditioning, false views of people and society – can be cleared away. The soul needs to renew itself at the source so it can be properly reborn in the 1st House. Thus your dream life is overactive. There is great psychological disturbance and uneasiness as old fears, ideas and complexes come up to be dissolved. As the process continues you will get closer to your Inner Source and have a clearer understanding of where to go from here. Your biggest need this month is for clear spiritual guidance.

Secret enemies – actual people as well as internal subconscious fears and drives – are revealed this month. And though it is not the most pleasant process, it is good. In this revelation lies the cure. Once you know about these enemies they cannot hurt you – it was their secrecy that made them dangerous.

Meditation, psychological therapies, prayer, contemplation and going off to retreats and ashrams are all good activities during this period. They boost – though indirectly – your wealth, love life and higher mind. As you dissolve your complexes and fears, financial ideas come along with your new sense of financial clarity. And though these activities seem to conflict with your career or disturb a parental specure they are still good – only you will have to integrate these projects with career demands.

Your health is good but that of your spouse or partner is more delicate. Let him or her rest and relax more.

May

Best Days Overall: 7th, 8th, 15th, 16th, 17th, 25th, 26th

Most Stressful Days Overall: 3rd, 4th, 9th, 10th, 23rd, 24th, 30th, 31st

Best Days for Love: 1st, 2nd, 3rd, 4th, 5th, 6th, 9th, 10th, 13th, 14th, 18th, 19th, 23rd, 24th, 27th, 28th, 29th, 30th, 31st

Best Days for Money: 7th, 8th, 15th, 16th, 17th, 18th, 19th, 25th, 26th

Though many of the people around you are upset, chafing at the bit and restless because of the delays, the prudence, caution and slowness of people and events – you sail through with it with ease and equanimity. No one loves the status quo more than you. No one better appreciates the virtues of prudence and caution. And few understand the wisdom of 'making haste slowly' better than you. You are in excellent shape this month.

Your virtues are appreciated by others. Your attitude to life is better understood by others. Your counsel is taken.

Forty to 60 per cent of the planets are in the element of

Earth this month. And 50 to 60 per cent of the planets are at one time or another retrograde this month. All of this suggests caution, review, re-evaluation, a down-to-earth practicality and the virtues of inaction. The buccaneers and swashbucklers are in a state of disarray – stymied. The prudent and the conservative are thriving.

Your health is excellent all month and you are in a personal 'pleasure period', seeking good food, good wines, good restaurants and other bodily delights. Sexual and sensual fantasies are fulfilled. A bit of hedonism is no bad thing now while the Cosmos is pausing to decide what to do next. Athletes perform at their peak now. Even non-athletes are more interested in sports and athletics and perform above their normal abilities. You Taureans are unusually physical. The only health problem that could arise would be from over-indulgence – too much food (too much of the wrong food), sex and the like.

Your financial life is stable, but Mercury's retrograde suggests more caution in financial affairs. Avoid making major purchases, investment decisions or financial commitments from the 3rd to the 27th. This is a period for reviewing investment strategies and philosophy. It is a good time to make improvements in your product or service. Payments due to you or deals yet to be completed could be delayed during Mercury's retrograde, but this is short term – they will come through in due course. If there is nothing for you to do objectively – in the outer world – to improve finances, you can always work subjectively by visualizing your cherished financial goals as 'here-and-now' realities.

Your love life, too, warrants caution this month as Pluto (your Love Planet) is retrograde now and for many months to come. Your social judgement may not be realistic. Do not jump too quickly into marriage or serious relationships. Take your time.

June

Best Days Overall: 3rd, 4th, 12th, 13th, 22nd, 23rd

Most Stressful Days Overall: 5th, 6th, 19th, 20th, 26th, 27th

Best Days for Love: 1st, 5th, 6th, 9th, 14th, 15th, 19th, 24th, 25th, 26th, 27th

Best Days for Money: 3rd, 4th, 12th, 13th, 14th, 15th, 22nd, 23rd, 24th, 25th

Like Aries, for you there is a split between the long-term, slow-moving planets and the short-term, fast-moving ones this month. The slow-moving ones are all at the top half of your Horoscope while the fast-moving ones are at the bottom. This shows many things – first, that though your long-term goals are 'outward', career-orientated, in the short term you are more focused on the home and emotional harmony. And since the long-term planets are mostly retrograde now you need to take a breather from career activities and get your personal and emotional life more in order. Secondly, you need to balance long-term and short-term goals and interests. Thirdly, you need to harmonize your career drives with your family obligations and emotional needs. The middle way is always the answer, but for now focus on emotional serenity and creating a stable home base. Venus (your Ruling Planet) is still retrograde, and thus you have a wonderful opportunity to think these things through.

This is also the month to get your financial life in order. Finances are much better than they were last month. Mercury (your Money Planet) is moving forward quickly and will go through your Money House as of the 15th. Your financial judgement is sound and financial confidence has returned. Until the 15th you are both the 'trader' and the

72

'haver and holder' – though having and holding seem to work better. After the 15th you become more of the 'trader', capitalizing on your acute awareness of short-term trends and tendencies. You are in a period where your image and personal appearance are big factors in your earning ability. Dress for success. Fashion models, manual workers, sales and marketing people – people who earn their living through their bodies and appearance – do better this month. The New Moon of the 15th occurs in your Money House – a happy occurrence as it will clarify both your real financial status and the next steps to take. Sales and marketing projects prosper all month. Interest and dividend income increases after the 21st. Your partner's income is at a temporary lull but your earning power more than makes up for it. Tension could develop between you and your spouse or partner over finances. You need to balance your own financial interests with those of your partner – you seem pulled in opposite directions.

Love and social activities seem on hold. A current relationship seems to go backwards instead of forwards, but do not make any rash moves yet. Inaction is the path of wisdom. Long-term love is good.

July

Best Days Overall: 1st, 9th, 10th, 19th, 20th, 28th, 29th

Most Stressful Days Overall: 2nd, 3rd, 16th, 17th, 24th, 25th, 30th, 31st

Best Days for Love: 2nd, 3rd, 6th, 11th, 12th, 16th, 21st, 22nd, 24th, 25th, 26th, 30th, 31st

Best Days for Money: 1st, 4th, 5th, 9th, 10th, 11th, 12th, 14th, 15th, 16th, 19th, 20th, 26th, 27th, 28th, 29th

With your career and outer life on hold for a while – it still needs more planning and re-evaluation – this is a good month to focus on the domestic sphere, spending time with your family, taking care of household and domestic projects and further stabilizing your home base. Perfect your living quarters and your emotional life. Remember: your moods and emotional patterns are your true spiritual home – the physical home merely reflects that. When the former is put in order the latter more or less falls into place. Great psychological progress is made now.

Old unconscious fears and blockages are being brought to the surface this month so that you can become aware of them. They are stimulated from a variety of sources – parents, siblings, neighbours and perhaps schoolmates and priests. What causes these things to be stimulated is of little importance, but what gets triggered in you is *very* important. Watch your dreams and feelings now.

Your financial life gets better every day. Venus (your Ruling Planet) is now moving forward in your Money House, showing that you are very focused on financial issues and feel confident about them. Being a Taurus, when you focus on wealth it usually happens for you – you are one of the best wealth-creators in the Zodiac. Your investment philosophy continues (as it was last month) to be that of the 'trader' rather than the 'haver and holder' (your normal approach). You have a special talent now for discerning short-term, fluctuating trends, and capitalizing on them. Money is earned through advertising, sales and marketing projects and good communication. The pursuit of your intellectual interests and schooling also helps your 'bottom line' in a dramatic way this month. The 13th, 14th and/or 15th (perhaps even all these days) bring happy financial surprises to you. The Full Moon of the 1st also brings a financial surprise. What you get will depend on your need. If it is money or an object that you need, that is what you will get. If it is ideas or right connections, you will get those.

TAURUS

Your partner still needs to be cautious in financial matters and to re-evaluate investments and his or her investment philosophy. This is the time for your partner to be forming investment and financial plans to carry out at a later date. The general trend, though, is towards prosperity.

Singles still need to be cautious in love. A current relationship should be given time. Marriages and/or divorces should not be scheduled right now. Yet, in the current lull, there will be periods of increased social activity and opportunity for singles – this comes after the 22nd.

August

> Best Days Overall: 5th, 6th, 15th, 16th, 24th, 25th

> Most Stressful Days Overall: 12th, 13th, 14th, 20th, 21st, 26th, 27th

> Best Days for Love: 3rd, 10th, 11th, 12th, 20th, 21st, 22nd, 28th, 29th, 30th

> Best Days for Money: 5th, 6th, 7th, 8th, 9th, 15th, 16th, 24th, 25th, 26th

Though your career continues to be important and you should by no means abandon it, there is nevertheless a lull there and you should use the opportunity to get your house, family and domestic life in order. Mend fences with family members, embark on psychological therapies, re-decorate or refurnish now. And when you work on your domestic life, always keep your career needs in mind. The home base must support your career if it is to last.

Rest and relax more until the 23rd. Your health seems to be bound up with your sense of financial health until the

7th. When you feel financially healthy and strong you feel physically healthy and strong. You seem more concerned with financial health than physical health. After the 7th watch your words and thoughts. Negative words and ideas have an unusual impact on your health (this is true for everyone but right now even more so for you). Speak words of health and think thoughts of health. Health improves dramatically after the 23rd.

Personal finances are strong most of the month. Until the 7th you are good at discerning short-term trends and capitalizing on them. Speculations are favourable. Personal creativity brings money. Financial opportunities come to you from the sports, nutrition and health industries. Those of you looking for a job or career should look to these industries. Those of you looking to invest should also look here. After the 26th social networking brings profits. The income of your partner seems much delayed this period. Patience and caution are necessary. Financial goals and investments need to be reviewed. Your partner is perhaps less generous with you now – not out of malice but more from a feeling of lack of resources.

After the 7th pursue intellectual interests – education and the like. Short domestic trips seem like fun. After the 23rd give yourself more pleasure. Attend parties, take a holiday and go out more.

Singles find that their love life starts straightening out this month, as Pluto (your Love Planet) starts moving forward on the 10th. This will come as a relief for many of you, as it has been retrograde for many months. Your social life progresses. A backwards-moving relationship starts moving forward again. Physical passion and intimacy are renewed in a current relationship.

September

Best Days Overall: 1st, 2nd, 3rd, 11th, 12th, 20th, 21st, 29th, 30th

Most Stressful Days Overall: 9th, 10th, 16th, 17th, 23rd, 24th

Best Days for Love: 8th, 9th, 16th, 17th, 18th, 19th, 27th, 28th

Best Days for Money: 1st, 2nd, 4th, 5th, 11th, 12th, 20th, 21st, 29th, 30th

By the 10th all of the short-term planets will be in the western sector of your horoscope, forcing you to become more adaptable to situations and to rely on others more. You are becoming less interested in pleasing yourself and more interested in gaining the good opinion of others.

Though there are still four planets retrograde this month you are mostly unaffected – except for the retrograde of Mercury from the 4th to the 26th. The retrograde of Mercury is worth mentioning as it affects your financial life – creating delays, apparent reverses (temporarily) and the general feeling that you are going backwards instead of forwards on the road to your financial dreams. You have been through this sort of thing before and have weathered it. You can make positive use of these delays to re-evaluate your finances, spending and investments. Improve your product or service. Work towards financial goals subjectively – through meditation, visualization and positive thinking. Avoid signing contracts, making long-term financial commitments, investing or buying 'big-ticket' (expensive and long-lasting) purchases. While Mercury is retrograde your normally astute and shrewd financial judgement is not what it should be – and things that seem certain and sure now are likely to change when

Mercury goes forward. Study and plan but do not execute.

The lunar eclipse of the 26th seems to deal kindly with you. It will cause major shifts in spiritual attitudes and personal philosophy. Your view of the world is not what you thought it to be and you will be forced to revise it. You see the fragility of governments and bureaucracies – solid though they have always seemed to be. Your partner is hit with a short-term expense or financial reversal but will emerge from it in due course.

Your health is excellent all month. Most of the planets are still in the bottom half of your chart, showing that you still need to work on creating emotional harmony and a solid home base. This is a good month to redo or redecorate your home. Your personal creativity is strong and your aesthetic sense is good. Take a reduced schedule on the day of the eclipse.

October

Best Days Overall: 9th, 10th, 18th, 19th, 26th, 27th

Most Stressful Days Overall: 6th, 7th, 13th, 14th, 20th, 21st

Best Days for Love: 6th, 8th, 9th, 13th, 14th, 16th, 17th, 18th, 19th, 24th, 27th, 28th

Best Days for Money: 1st, 2nd, 9th, 10th, 11th, 12th, 18th, 19th, 20th, 21st, 26th, 27th, 29th, 30th, 31st

Another active and tumultuous month, during which great progress takes place and needed changes – though disruptive – occur.

Day by day as the short-term planets move ever westward you are becoming more socially conscious, more other-orientated and more dependent on the good will and grace of others. Goals are being achieved through other people now, so treat them right. Social miscues made when the planets are in the west have greater impact than when the planets are in the east.

After many months of retrograde motion, Uranus (your Career Planet) is starting to move forward again, signifying forward momentum and career progress. And if this were not enough, there is a powerful solar eclipse on the 12th in your 6th House, showing a shake-up at the workplace and perhaps a change of job or career. This change could be within your current place of work or take you somewhere else. It should be viewed as a positive step forward. Employers lose employees during this period and otherwise have to revamp working conditions. Strikes and slowdowns are possible now. The good news is that these things bring up hidden resentments and problems so that they can be dealt with.

The Sun is your Home and Family Planet. Its eclipse shows that a move or major renovation of your home is taking place. If you own your home you are likely to be personally involved in these issues. If you rent, the landlord is making major changes. Flaws and festering resentments with family members now surface and need to be dealt with. When the dust settles you will be in a happier, more harmonious home environment.

The solar eclipse makes a stressful aspect to Jupiter and Neptune. Thus there is some financial upheaval affecting your partner's income and earning ability as well as your own. An unexpected expense reveals flaws in his or her current financial plan. Monies that were due to you from your partner, a shared investment or insurance claim are either delayed or not as big as you thought. A legacy gets temporarily halted or stalled. But hang in there, Taurus, it is all going to work out in the end. In the mean time you will have to realize the true source of your earning ability – the Spiritual Power within you.

November

> Best Days Overall: 5th, 6th, 14th, 15th, 23rd, 24th
>
> Most Stressful Days Overall: 2nd, 3rd, 4th, 10th, 11th, 16th, 17th, 30th
>
> Best Days for Love: 2nd, 7th, 8th, 10th, 11th, 12th, 16th, 17th, 20th, 27th, 28th, 30th
>
> Best Days for Money: 1st, 5th, 6th, 10th, 11th, 14th, 15th, 20th, 21st, 23rd, 24th, 25th, 26th, 30th

There are many factors contributing to your social popularity this month. First off, most of the planets are in the western half of your horoscope – stimulating your social urges and making you more reliant on other people. Secondly, there are many planets moving through your House of Love and Marriage. Thirdly, the lunation of the 11th occurs in your 7th House of Love and Marriage. This is the major headline for the month. For singles it signals a new social cycle and new guidance and information in the governance of your love life and current relationships. As the Moon makes its cycle through the various Houses it will show where improvements can be made, and the nature of these improvements. As it waxes through your 8th House on the 12th and 13th it will show you what obstructs love and what you need to do to get rid of the obstructions. As it goes through your 9th House (14th and 15th) it will show you the correct philosophical concepts to hold about love so that you can view it more meaningfully and cosmically. As the Moon then moves through your 10th House it will show you your duties and responsibilities in love – and so on and so forth through the Zodiac.

For singles there are romantic opportunities with nurturing types, with people from your childhood or distant past and with people involved in your financial life. Family introductions and family gatherings play a role in love this month. Moods in general are more romantic and this of course always furthers love. Serious commitment is likely. Marrieds are working to bring more romance into their marriage and into their day-to-day lifestyle.

Your financial progress this month hinges very much on your social charisma and social contacts. Partners and or lovers are financially supportive. Debts are easily paid and easily made this month – though you should work on paying them rather than making them. Still, your credit line is increased and you have greater access to other people's money. Your ability to attract investors to your projects is greatly increased after the 15th. Write those proposals and business plans this month.

Rest and relax more until the 22nd.

December

> Best Days Overall: 2nd, 3rd, 11th, 12th, 20th, 21st, 30th, 31st
>
> Most Stressful Days Overall: 1st, 7th, 8th, 13th, 14th, 27th, 28th
>
> Best Days for Love: 1st, 7th, 8th, 9th, 15th, 16th, 17th, 18th, 27th, 28th
>
> Best Days for Money: 1st, 2nd, 3rd, 11th, 12th, 20th, 21st, 22nd, 23rd, 30th, 31st

Both the Universal and your Personal Solar Cycles continue to wane through the 8th House until the 21st. Continue to wind down activities, finish up old projects, tie up loose ends, pay debts and clear the decks for the new cycle that begins after the 21st. This is one of the best periods of the year for psychological therapies, losing weight and breaking habits and addictions. The force of the Cosmos aids you mightily in these efforts.

Most of the planets are now firmly established in the top half of your Horoscope (above the horizon), making you less interested in family and domestic issues and more focused on career progress. Your work should be geared towards eliminating things that obstruct your career progress.

Your social urges are unusually strong now as well. Love is both romantic/flowery and passionate/physical. There is a sense of possessiveness with your lover – and perhaps jealousy. Singles do not look like being single for long. Serious romance – committed romance – is in the stars now. Marrieds and those of you involved in an established relationship are more romantic and intense. Your passionate desires and fantasies are being fulfilled.

Health is excellent all month but gets even better after the 21st. Your health can be enhanced by dropping pounds, detoxifying your system and achieving adequate (not too much and not too little) sexual expression.

Enhance your wealth by helping your partner/spouse and others to prosper. Resist the temptation to create new debt – though it is very easy now as your line of credit is probably increased. As mentioned earlier, create future wealth by reducing debt and unnecessary expenses. Your financial judgement could be overly optimistic until the 23rd. With your Money Planet (Mercury) in Sagittarius you tend to see only 'best-case scenarios'. After the 23rd Mercury goes retrograde, making your financial judgement unrealistic in other ways. Avoid major purchases after the 23rd. Your normally acute financial insight will return to you in January of 1997.

Gemini

♊

THE TWINS
Birthdays from
21st May
to 20th June

Personality Profile

GEMINI AT A GLANCE

Element – Air

Ruling Planet – Mercury
   Career Planet – Neptune
   Health Planet – Pluto
   Love Planet – Jupiter
   Money Planet – Moon

Colours – blue, yellow, yellow-orange

Colour that promotes love, romance and social harmony – sky blue

Colours that promote earning power – grey, silver

Gems – agate, aquamarine

Metal – quicksilver

Scents – lavender, lilac, lily of the valley, storax

Quality – mutable (= flexibility)

Quality most needed for balance – deep rather than superficial thought

Strongest virtues – great communication skills, quickness and agility of thought, ability to learn quickly

Deepest need – communication

Characteristics to avoid – gossiping, hurting others with harsh speech, superficiality, using words to mislead or misinform

Signs of greatest overall compatibility – Libra, Aquarius

Signs of greatest overall incompatibility – Virgo, Sagittarius, Pisces

Sign most helpful to career – Pisces

Sign most helpful for emotional support – Virgo

Sign most helpful financially – Cancer

Sign best for marriage and/or partnerships – Sagittarius

Sign most helpful for creative projects – Libra

Best Sign to have fun with – Libra

Signs most helpful in spiritual matters – Taurus, Aquarius

Best day of the week – Wednesday

Understanding the Gemini Personality

Gemini is to society what the nervous system is to the body. It does not introduce any new information but is a vital transmitter of impulses from the senses to the brain and vice versa. The nervous system does not judge or weigh these impulses – this function is left to the brain or the instincts. The nervous system only conveys information. And does so perfectly.

This analogy should give you an indication of a Gemini's role in society. Geminis are the communicators and conveyors of information. To Geminis the truth or mendacity of the information is irrelevant, they only transmit what they see, hear or read about. They teach what the textbooks say or what their managers tell them to say. Thus they are capable of spreading the most outrageous rumours as well as conveying truth and light. Geminis sometimes tend to be unscrupulous in their communications and they can do great good or great evil with their power. This is why the Sign of Gemini is called the Sign of the Twins. They have a dual nature.

Their ability to convey a message – to communicate with such ease – makes Geminis ideal teachers, writers and media and marketing people. This is helped by the fact that Mercury, the Ruling Planet of Gemini, also rules these activities.

Geminis have the gift of the gab. And what a gift this is! They can make conversation about anything, anywhere, at any time. There is almost nothing that is more fun to Geminis than a good conversation – especially if they can learn something new as well. They love to learn and they love to teach. To deprive a Gemini of conversation, or of books and magazines, is cruel and unusual punishment.

Geminis are almost always excellent students and take well to book learning. Their minds are generally stocked with all kinds of information, trivia, anecdotes, stories, news items, rarities, facts and statistics. Thus they can support any intellectual position that they care to take. They are awesome debaters and, if involved in politics, make good orators.

Geminis are so verbally smooth that even if they do not know what they are talking about they can make you think that they do. They will always dazzle you with their brilliance.

Finance

Geminis tend to be more concerned with the wealth of learning and ideas than with actual material wealth. As mentioned they excel in professions that involve writing, teaching, sales and journalism – and not all of these professions pay very well. But to sacrifice intellectual needs merely for money is unthinkable to a Gemini. Geminis strive to combine the two.

Cancer is on Gemini's Solar 2nd House (of Money) cusp, which indicates that Geminis can earn extra income (in a harmonious and natural way) from investments in residential property, restaurants and hotels. Given their verbal skills, Geminis love to bargain and negotiate in any situation, but especially when it has to do with money.

The Moon rules Gemini's 2nd Solar House. The Moon is not only the fastest-moving planet in the Zodiac but actually moves through every Sign and House every 28 days. No other heavenly body matches the Moon for swiftness or the ability to change quickly. An analysis of the Moon – and lunar phenomena in general – describes Gemini's financial attitudes very well. Geminis are financially versatile and flexible. They can earn money in many different ways. Their financial attitudes and needs seem to change daily. Their moods about money change. Sometimes they are very enthusiastic about it; sometimes they could not care less.

For a Gemini, financial goals and money are often seen

only as means of supporting a family; they have little meaning otherwise.

The Moon, as Gemini's Money Planet, has another important message for Gemini financially: in order for Geminis to realize their financial potential fully they need to develop more of an understanding of the emotional side of life. They need to combine their awesome powers of logic with an understanding of human psychology. Feelings have their own logic; Geminis need to learn this and apply it to financial matters.

Career and Public Image

Geminis know that they were given the gift of communication for a reason, that it is a power that can achieve great good or cause unthinkable distress. They long to put this power at the service of the highest and most transcendental truths. This is their primary goal, to communicate the eternal verities and prove them logically. They look up to people who can transcend the intellect – to poets, artists, musicians and mystics. They may be awed by stories of religious saints and martyrs. A Gemini's highest achievement is to teach the truth, whether it is scientific, inspirational or historical. Those who can transcend the intellect are a Gemini's natural superiors – and a Gemini realizes this.

The Sign of Pisces is in Gemini's Solar 10th House of Career. Neptune, the planet of spirituality and altruism, is Gemini's Career Planet. If Geminis are to realize their highest career potential they need to develop their transcendental – their spiritual and altruistic – side. They need to understand the larger cosmic picture, the vast flow of human evolution – where it came from and where it is heading. Only then can a Gemini's intellectual powers take their true position and he or she can become the 'messenger of the Gods'. Geminis need to cultivate a facility for 'inspiration', which is something that does not originate *in* the intellect but which comes *through* the intellect. This will further enrich and empower a Gemini's mind.

Love and Relationships

Geminis bring their natural garrulousness and brilliance into their love and social life as well. A good talk or a verbal joust is an interesting prelude to romance. Their only problem in love is that their intellect is too cool and passionless to incite passion in others. Emotions sometimes disturb them, and their partners tend to complain about this. If you are in love with a Gemini you must understand why this is so. Geminis avoid deep passions because these would interfere with their ability to think and communicate. If they are cool towards you, understand that this is their nature.

Nevertheless, Geminis must understand that it is one thing to talk about love and another to actually love – to feel it and radiate it. Talking about love glibly will get them nowhere. They need to feel it and act on it. Love is not of the intellect but of the heart. If you want to know how a Gemini feels about love you should not listen to what he or she says but rather observe what he or she does. Geminis can be quite generous to those they love.

Geminis like their partners to be refined, well educated and well travelled. If their partners are more wealthy than them, that is all the better. If you are in love with a Gemini you had better be a good listener as well.

The ideal relationship for the Gemini is a relationship of the mind. They enjoy the physical and emotional aspects, of course, but if the intellectual communion is not there they will suffer.

Home and Domestic Life

At home the Gemini can be uncharacteristically neat and meticulous. They tend to want their children and partner to live up to their idealistic standards. When these standards are not met they moan and criticize. However, Geminis are good family people and like to serve their families in practical and useful ways.

The Gemini home is comfortable and pleasant. They like to invite people over and they make great hosts. Geminis are also good at repairs and improvements around the house – all fuelled by their need to stay active and occupied with something they like to do. Geminis have many hobbies and interests that keep them busy when they are home alone.

Geminis understand and get along well with their children, mainly because they are very youthful people themselves. As great communicators, Geminis know how to explain things to children; in this way they gain their children's love and respect. Geminis also encourage children to be creative and talkative just like they are.

Horoscope for 1996

Major Trends

Last year was challenging for most Geminis. Two major long-term planets, Saturn and Pluto, were making stressful aspects to you. Saturn was placing burdens and responsibilities upon you. You felt a sense of frustration and blockage as so many obstacles were in your path. Your self-esteem was not too strong and your physical energy not what it should have been. Those of you born later in the Sign were especially prone to these feelings. You had to exercise your genius of adaptability and develop more of a 'stick-to-it' attitude in the face of adversity. You did not try to burst through obstacles but rather went above and around them. Some of you learned to make the obstacles your friends by improving your character, product or service. Those of you who worked hard probably had career advancement in 1995, as Saturn likes to reward hard work and discipline (American President Clinton was elected with Saturn transiting his Midheaven). Happily, Saturn is moving away from its long-term stressful aspect in April of 1996, making the balance of the year easier than it has been.

Now, easier does not mean easy – you still have to deal with challenges in your love life and partnerships, but still life will not be as difficult as it was. Where 1995 was a very serious and duty-orientated year, 1996 is going to be less serious – not exactly playful, but less demanding.

Health

Last year was a stressful health year. This does not mean that you were gravely ill but that there was less energy available to you. You were forced to cut back on unnecessary activities and to focus on priorities. You began to see how precious life-force really is. Healthwise, 1996 is a vast improvement. Those of you who had health problems in 1995 find that they miraculously clear up in 1996. In many cases there was never a health problem to begin with – only a lack of energy. When the cosmic energy returns there will be no more health problems.

More good news: your 6th House of Health is not especially active this year, showing that there is little need to focus on health issues. Moreover, by April Saturn is going to be making beautiful aspects to Pluto (your Health Planet) all year. You will feel more secure and stable in this department. Your natural health instincts will just express themselves, with little blockage or obstruction.

Pluto has been in your House of Marriage since 1995. It will be there for many years to come. The message here is clear: good health is connected to the health of your marriage, relationships and social life. When these are good your health will tend to be good. When there is lack of harmony in these areas it will affect your health. Thus, keep things harmonious with your beloved. If harmony is impossible, get out of the relationship – it can be dangerous to your health.

Your partner or spouse could benefit from a purer diet. He or she seems more concerned with health issues than you are, and has an increased physical drive and energy. Your spouse or partner may be contemplating some form of surgery to redo his or her image. Re-inventing the self is a major long-term goal for your partner, and these activities are merely the tools which he or she uses. The health of your children (for those of you who have them) was somewhat stressful for the past two years but will improve dramatically come April. A big part of the healing process involves the restoration of emotional harmony and the banishing of depressive tendencies.

Home and Domestic Life

Home and family issues have not been a big priority for a few years now. This is understandable. You have been so busy with career and work issues that you had little time left over for domestic and family matters – for giving these areas the attention they deserve. This trend continues in 1996. You have freedom to shape this area as you will. The Cosmos does not impel you one way or the other.

The burdens placed on you by a parent (or parental figure) are easing off this year, giving you more freedom to pursue personal interests. One of your parents (or parental figures in your life) is very experimental healthwise – probably involved in food and vitamin fads. This parent or parental figure is also changing jobs or otherwise involved in major – and sudden – changes at work.

The health of your partner or spouse is basically good,

but as mentioned earlier he or she has a strong interest in regenerating (transforming) the body and personal image. Your partner is working to break undesirable habits, be they psychological, dietary or physical. Success is likely in the long haul. At the root of all this is the perception that financial goals can only come with the right image.

Many of you reading this have older children. A happy move is likely this year for them. They move to much larger, opulent quarters than they have lived in previously. Your children are also more fertile this year; grandchildren are likely.

Love and Social Life

Last year was extraordinarily social. Many of you married or became involved in a serious relationship. All of you expanded your circle of friends – and good quality ones at that. This year is the time to trim down your social life – cutting out the excess fat. The need for this will become ever more apparent after April. Romantically you want to be focused on one person and get to know him or her ever more deeply. The sexual side of romance is probably the most important this year. This is highly unusual for you, Gemini, as you – more than most – love intellectual communion. You are lucky in that you have a partner who is a good, deep listener. Yet it is the physical side that dominates this year.

Singles will have romantic opportunities with health professionals and co-workers. The workplace, hospitals and doctors' surgeries are likely meeting grounds. You are especially attracted to sedate, corporate type – managerial – people. Current relationships become more stable after April.

Those of you working your way towards a second marriage are likely to meet that special someone suddenly and unexpectedly. This person is scientifically or astrologically inclined – unconventional, highly intellectual and perhaps a bit rebellious. Professional organizations or introductions through friends are the ways in which you are most likely to meet this special someone.

Those of you working towards a third marriage will be narrowing your social horizon this year. Someone older and more established comes into your life – a bit controlling, a bit set in his or her ways – but stable, dutiful and supportive. Give time for the relationship to mature. Let love be tested. The solar eclipse of 17th April will clarify love matters.

Those of you who have children (or know others who are like children to you) of marrying age will witness big changes. Your child's marriage is being tested this year, especially after April. If he or she is still single, someone older and more mature comes into their life – someone from the past. Your child wants stable and long-term love with lots of emotional support. The desire for commitment probably scares off many potential suitors, but will in the end prevail. Let him or her transform painful isolation into fruitful solitude. Forgiveness of past lovers is essential this year.

Career and Finance

Your career has been ultra-important for over two years now. This trend continues early in 1996 and then tapers off. By April you will have found your career niche and be sated. You will be shifting your attention from career issues to issues of 'happiness', friendship and social causes. This is especially so for those of you born early in the Sign of Gemini. Those of you born later in the Sign will still be focused on your career all year – working hard, attaining promotions and pay-rises brought about through substantive achievement and discipline. Superiors are demanding but fair. You occupy the position you earn, no more no less. Play by the rules and avoid the fast track.

This is a happy financial year, Gemini, but not so much

because of your personal earning power and ability as because you help others to prosper. By putting the financial interests of others (your partner, your spouse, or shareholders) ahead of your own, you find your own coffers miraculously filled.

Your spouse or partner prospers greatly this year and is very much focused on financial issues. And though your partner is very businesslike and controlled in the way he or she spends money there is nevertheless generosity towards you. Money or property will also come to you through inheritance (someone puts you in his or her will), through insurance claims that work out in your favour, royalties, tax refunds, and the stock-market. This is a year where you have greater access to other people's money. Watch how your line of credit effortlessly increases. People trust you more and are thus more willing to lend. Debts are, therefore, easily made but also easily paid. This is a good year for reducing your debt if you so choose, and also a good year for attracting investors to your projects.

You and your spouse or partner seem to be in financial harmony this year, as you both have similar investment strategies – the avoidance of risk and the search for long-term security.

One of your parents (or parental figures in your life) is having a rough time financially and must really cut costs and live by a budget. Better financial management is essential. This parent tends to be overly speculative in his or her investment philosophy and must avoid this in 1996. Only controlled, calculated risks are acceptable.

Those of you who have children who work should encourage them to use and develop media skills more extensively. There is nothing wrong *per se* with their product or service – they just need to get the word out. You can probably be of help here.

Your son- or daughter-in-law is very serious this year, unusually ambitious, working hard, receiving promotions, pay-rises and increased public esteem. Career in his or her case outweighs mere monetary concerns. This is probably causing some stress in the marriage – and is probably why the marriage is being tested.

With the feeling-orientated Moon as your Money Planet you need to develop – and trust – the feeling side of your nature more and follow intuitive hunches in money matters. Logic alone – though you are strong in that area – is not enough to bring about your financial objectives. A purchase or investment should 'feel' right as well as seem right to you intellectually. Then you know you are on the right track.

Self-improvement

In the early part of 1996 the need for improvement remains your career. As mentioned earlier there is a need for serious, persistent, single-minded focus – something that does not come naturally to you, Gemini. Moreover, what is demanded of you is more than just words and intellectual brilliance, but performance – tangible results. You cannot talk your way into promotions this year – though in the past you have been able to do this. Superiors are looking for results, responsibility, commitment. As the year progresses, Saturn (the Lord of your 8th House of Elimination) moves into your 11th House of Friends. Friendships will start getting tested. The wheat must be separated from the chaff, the true from the false. Disappointments will come from people you thought were your friends – the problem is that they were never real friends, they only seemed that way. The Cosmos is going to create situations where truth and reality will be revealed. Yes, the truth can sting, but better a little sting than a serious hurt later on because of your misjudgement. The astrological definition of friendship is someone who wants your fondest hopes and wishes to come to pass and who is willing to help them along. This is the Cosmic measuring rod. Use it and you will avoid a lot of heartache later on.

Month-by-month Forecasts

January

Best Days Overall: 2nd, 3rd, 12th, 13th, 21st, 22nd, 29th, 30th, 31st

Most Stressful Days Overall: 10th, 11th, 16th, 17th, 18th, 23rd, 24th

Best Days for Love: 2nd, 3rd, 10th, 11th, 12th, 13th, 14th, 16th, 17th, 18th, 19th, 20th, 23rd, 24th, 27th, 28th

Best Days for Money: 1st, 5th, 6th, 10th, 11th, 19th, 20th, 27th, 28th, 29th, 30th

Like Aries and Taurus, you are focused on the outer world and outward achievement this month. Emotions and domestic issues are less important – and this is as it should be for now. Later on in the year this will change.

Your health is excellent all month but gets even better as the month progresses – especially after the 20th. The only fly in the ointment is Mercury's retrograde (backward motion) from the 9th to the 30th. Though there is nothing intrinsically wrong you might feel that you are going backwards instead of forwards and feel that you have less power to assert yourself. But this retrograde should be considered a cosmic 'breather', a pause to enable you to re-evaluate and rethink your goals. It is good for planning how you will assert

GEMINI

yourself in the future in certain situations that confront you.

Most of the planets are still in the western part of your horoscope, so you will have to exercise your genius of adaptability. To achieve your goals you will have to adapt to the situations that confront you rather than try to face them head-on. Later on in the year you will be better able to create conditions as you like them.

Love attitudes are about to change drastically as Jupiter moves from your 7th to your 8th House on the 3rd. Physical intimacy rather than courtship and romance becomes more important. Debts are easily paid from the 3rd to the 20th. Siphon off extra earnings towards reducing debt. After the 20th you can focus more on wealth-building – investing spare cash. This is a great month for attracting investors to your projects, but do not confirm anything until after Mercury goes direct on the 30th. The New Moon of the 20th will clarify relations with investors as well.

The Full Moon of the 5th is an especially powerful financial day for you. Financial goals come true, material good comes suddenly and unexpectedly and profitable wealth ideas and contacts come to you. 'Big-ticket' (expensive, long-lasting) items come to you around this period.

February

Best Days Overall: 8th, 9th, 10th, 17th, 18th, 26th, 27th

Most Stressful Days Overall: 6th, 7th, 13th, 14th, 19th, 20th

Best Days for Love: 1st, 2nd, 6th, 7th, 13th, 14th, 15th, 16th, 21st, 22nd, 23rd, 24th, 25th

Best Days for Money: 1st, 2nd, 6th, 7th, 8th,

97

9th, 10th, 15th, 16th, 17th, 18th, 19th, 23rd,
24th, 25th, 28th, 29th

Ninety to 100 per cent of the planets are in the upper half of
your chart, so your career urges are paramount right now.
Shoot for the stars. Progress is rapid all month as all the
planets are moving forward and most of them speedily.
Mercury (your Ruling Planet) moves forward very speedily
as well. This will be a month of action, achievement and
forward momentum.

A meeting with a superior on or around the 14th (this
could also be a parent) goes well, but make sure you nail
down the details. He or she may mean something totally different from what you hear.

Seek investors and negotiate loans this month. Make
investments and important purchases before the 4th and/or
after the 18th. Pay bills (where possible) and reduce debt
from the 4th to the 18th. Substantial financial windfalls are
likely from the 15th to the 18th.

Your career is furthered through advertising, teaching,
sales and networking. Intuition is also guiding you strongly
until the 9th. Any teachers and lecturers among you are
brought before the public after the 19th.

You seem to be running away from a current love – but
not too far. The relationship is far from over. Those as yet
uninvolved seem to run from love but only run closer to it.
Romantic opportunities are abundant until the 19th. But
you have free will and there is no one forcing you to take
these opportunities.

Health is excellent and self-esteem high until the 19th.
After that rest and relax more. Your career seems to sap
your energy.

This is also an excellent month to pursue religious and
metaphysical goals, to pursue opportunities for higher education, to deal with academics and to travel. Try to avoid

religious and philosophical disputes after the 15th. The New Moon of the 18th brings religious or metaphysical illumination – suddenly and unexpectedly – stay open to it. This could happen through a teacher, priest or guru type. Educational and travel opportunities also come at this time – perhaps from different sources.

March

Best Days Overall: 6th, 7th, 8th, 15th, 16th, 24th, 25th

Most Stressful Days Overall: 4th, 5th, 11th, 12th, 17th, 18th

Best Days for Love: 1st, 2nd, 3rd, 4th, 5th, 11th, 12th, 13th, 14th, 22nd, 23rd

Best Days for Money: 4th, 5th, 9th, 10th, 13th, 14th, 18th, 19th, 22nd, 23rd, 26th, 27th, 28th, 29th, 30th

All the planets (with the exception of the Moon for certain periods) are still in the upper half of your horoscope. Thus your focus continues to be – and rightfully so – on your career and outward achievement. This outer focus makes you play down 'inner' psychological achievements and not give them much esteem. For you achievement means attaining some worldly goal – something that is recognized by the public. And, though family relations are important and a high priority this month – especially after the 7th – you fulfil your familial duties through the pursuit of career objectives. By achieving outer success you attain emotional and family harmony. Interestingly, your family seems to support you in this now.

The planets are about equally distributed between the

eastern and western halves of your horoscope, showing that you have a more balanced perspective between yourself and others. You attain your goals by a combination of personal initiative and co-operation from others. You are not as dependent on others as you have been for the past few months.

Mercury (your Ruling Planet) moves quite rapidly this month and transits three different Signs. This depicts you: you are moving forward fast, achieving things easily and quickly, and constantly shifting your point of view and perspective on the world. You are a 'Super Gemini' this month – for your Ruler is reinforcing your natural inclinations.

Until the 7th you view life from a religious and philosophical perspective. You see world events, history, economics and relationships as the outworking of religious and metaphysical concepts. Wars and conflicts are seen as essentially religious clashes. History is seen as the evolution of religion and humanity's attitude to divinity. After that you seem to view life – your personal life as well – as a power struggle. You see all your relationships, economic activities, history and world events as an expression of the urge to control. You tend to react to life that way. After the 24th you view life from a perspective of happiness – world events are seen as the outgrowth of humanity's desire to find happiness and brotherhood. Which perspective is right? They all are.

Personal earnings do not seem that important to you now, which probably means that they are stable. You are still more focused on earning money for others and enhancing the income of your partner than on your personal economic interest. Your partner prospers after the 6th and is generous with you. Pay bills and reduce debt (where possible) from the 5th to the 19th. Build wealth and make investments from the 1st to the 5th and from the 19th to the end of the month.

Pace yourself until the 20th and rest when you are tired. Vitality picks up significantly after the 20th.

April

Best Days Overall: 3rd, 4th, 11th, 12th, 20th, 21st, 30th

Most Stressful Days Overall: 1st, 2nd, 7th, 8th, 13th, 14th, 28th, 29th

Best Days for Love: 1st, 2nd, 3rd, 7th, 8th, 9th, 10th, 11th, 12th, 18th, 19th, 20th, 21st, 29th, 30th

Best Days for Money: 1st, 2nd, 7th, 8th, 9th, 10th, 16th, 17th, 18th, 19th, 23rd, 24th, 28th, 29th

This is a very important month – and a happy one. Saturn is finally leaving its two-year stressful aspect with you and moving from Pisces into Aries. What a relief! You will feel it almost immediately on a health and vitality level. Suddenly there is less resistance to you. You have more energy and self-esteem; the cords that held you back are now cut. You are free.

Most of the planetary action is taking place in your 11th House of Friends. Thus your social life becomes important but also agitated in the short term. There are conflicts with friends, and disappointments. People you thought were friends turn out not to be. You want to socialize more but yet feel inhibited – perhaps fearful – about it. An upheaval in a social, political or professional organization to which you belong sends you into a tizzy. You tend to be overly critical of your friends, seeing flaws that you never knew existed – or perhaps knew about but overlooked. Now you are confronted starkly with these flaws – and you want to run. Friends are overly critical of you as well. Something is definitely going to give – old friends are moving out of the picture and you are going to take your time about making new ones. You are becoming pickier, more quality-orientated, more careful about whom you take into your aura.

Not all of this has to do with you directly. In certain cases there are merely changes going on in the life of friends – moves, marriages, divorces and the like – and they pass out of your life. You feel a sense of being 'cut off', isolated. It is up to you to transform this into something fruitful and productive. If you have a spiritual life you will learn that you are always surrounded by invisible friends – though in a different way than you had thought. You lose a few human friends so that you can make the universe your friend (not a bad trade-off). In time you will make higher-level human contacts.

You are also revising your notions of happiness now – by experiencing things that you thought would make you happy but which, you find, do not.

Your personal Solar cycle is winding down, so it would be best to channel surplus cash into reducing debt. If you are going to make investments do so from the 1st to the 3rd and from the 17th to the 30th.

May

Best Days Overall: 1st, 2nd, 9th, 10th, 18th, 19th, 27th, 28th, 29th

Most Stressful Days Overall: 5th, 6th, 13th, 14th, 25th, 26th

Best Days for Love: 1st, 2nd, 5th, 6th, 7th, 8th, 9th, 10th, 15th, 16th, 18th, 19th, 25th, 26th, 27th, 28th, 29th

GEMINI

Best Days for Money: 7th, 8th, 15th, 16th, 17th, 20th, 21st, 22nd, 25th, 26th, 27th, 28th, 29th

You are the type who thrives in an intellectual environment. Ideas, facts and information are to you what land and property are to others. It is your coin of the realm, your genius, your key to wealth. But this month we are in an 'Earth' period – 40 to 60 per cent of the planets are in Earth Signs – so you need to adjust yourself to this. People are generally more cautious, down to earth, practical and pragmatic. They are interested in 'bottom-line' issues and less on trivia and abstract ideas. Keep your information and communications focused on useful, practical information and you will thrive.

Aside from this, 50 to 60 per cent of the planets are in retrograde motion – including your Ruler, Mercury. All of this suggests a slowing down, a reviewing and re-evaluation of past and future directions. Be patient with yourself as well. Do not let the feeling of going backwards affect your self-esteem. There is nothing wrong with you, your relationships or financial affairs. You are part of the Cosmos and you are experiencing unusual cosmic movements.

The planets are mostly eastward now so you should boldly set out to create the conditions you desire. Only, this month create the pattern, do not actually execute the plan.

Your health is better than you think. In spite of the fact that you might feel weaker and less able to assert yourself or get your own way, the planets are making nice aspects to you. As soon as Mercury goes direct (on the 27th) your self-assertion and initiative return – stronger than ever before.

After the 20th the Sun joins Venus in your own Sign. You are unusually glamorous and appealing to the opposite sex. You are charismatic and graceful. Yet, in spite of this, serious love seems on hold. A current relationship seems to go backwards instead of forwards. Those as yet uninvolved feel more cautious and inhibited about entering into new relationships. This is the time to think about what and whom you really want in love.

June

Best Days Overall: 5th, 6th, 14th, 15th, 24th, 25th

Most Stressful Days Overall: 1st, 2nd, 7th, 8th, 22nd, 23rd, 29th, 30th

Best Days for Love: 1st, 2nd, 3rd, 4th, 5th, 6th, 12th, 13th, 14th, 15th, 22nd, 23rd, 24th, 25th, 29th, 30th

Best Days for Money: 3rd, 4th, 5th, 6th, 12th, 14th, 15th, 16th, 17th, 18th, 21st, 22nd, 23rd, 26th, 27th

Your chart this month shows an interesting dichotomy between the long-term, slow-moving planets and the short-term, fast-moving ones. The slow-moving planets – they stay in a Sign for many, many years – are mostly in your western sector, while the fast-moving ones are now in your east. Thus, though you are focused on social matters over the long term, for the short term you need to focus on yourself and your personal desires. Also you have a greater need now to balance the interests of partners with your own personal interests. You need to assert yourself more.

If it were not for the fact that 50 per cent of the planets are moving backwards in June, this would be a month of great achievement and progress for you. It still is, but not to the extent it would otherwise be. Much of the progress you make now will only be seen later on – it will have a delayed reaction. In spite of this you are making more progress than most of the other Signs – everything is relative. And, as long as you realize that the obstructions you face are not due to your shortcomings, sins or character flaws – but the result of impersonal cosmic phenomenon – you can enjoy the coming month. It is a month of great personal pleasure. Your body shines, your personal charisma is high and you enjoy sports and exercise regimes. Sensual delights call to you and you will probably partake in them. You are more likely to get your way with partners this month. Health is fabulous all month. It is probably wise that you are fulfilling your sensual fantasies now with 50 per cent of the planets retrograde. When nothing else is happening you might as well enjoy life.

Finances are excellent all month. The New Moon of the 15th not only illuminates financial issues but begins a happy and prosperous monthly financial cycle for you. Pay bills and otherwise reduce debt from the 1st to the 15th. Invest and build wealth from the 15th onwards. The 15th to the 21st will be a very powerful wealth-building period for you.

Your sensual appeal is strong now and you have plenty of romantic opportunities, but serious love (for singles) seems not on the cards. Let relationships grow and develop. Do not push them too hard.

July

Best Days Overall: 2nd, 3rd, 11th, 12th, 21st, 22nd, 30th, 31st

Most Stressful Days Overall: 4th, 5th, 19th, 20th, 26th, 27th

Best Days for Love: 1st, 2nd, 3rd, 9th, 10th,
11th, 12th, 19th, 20th, 21st, 22nd, 26th,
27th, 28th, 29th, 30th, 31st

Best Days for Money: 1st, 4th, 5th, 9th, 10th,
14th, 15th, 19th, 20th, 26th, 27th, 28th,
29th

Though there are still a good number of planets retrograde this month you personally are moving forward and making progress. This cannot be said about the people around you, however – especially your partner or parents. Delays in the world are creating opportunities for your personal progress. You find yourself weaving round these obstructions and achieving your goals.

Your social life remains on hold for a while – and though it continues to be important in your life you are better off focusing on personal desires and personal happiness right now. Work on your image, your body, and having some fun. Work on making yourself more lovable and your love life will automatically improve in due course. Singles should avoid serious commitments now, as your social judgement is not realistic and is apt to change later when Jupiter (your Love Planet) starts moving forward again. Not that you are having any problem attracting members of the opposite sex. This is not the issue. Love opportunities are there – you are unusually magnetic and attractive – but they may not be the right ones.

Your career also seems to be on hold at the moment. Major moves or changes should not be made now. Think things over, make plans, set targets and goals. When Neptune (your Career Planet) starts moving forward you will be ready to move forward too.

Your finances are good this month. Wealth is increased. A sales or marketing project has a happy result. Real estate sales, especially, go well. A big sale is made. A 'big-ticket' piece of communication equipment – perhaps a car as well – comes to you this month. Your financial judgement is sound and confidence is strong. Use spare cash to reduce long-term debt from the 1st to the 15th and after the 30th. Make investments and purchases – build wealth – from the 15th to the 30th. The New Moon of the 15th occurs in your Money House and is going to bring clarity in your financial life and specific guidance just for you. A conflict with your spouse or partner on financial issues goes in your favour. You earn more than your partner this month. However, your partner receives a financial bonanza around the 1st and the 29th.

Your health is excellent all month.

August

Best Days Overall: 7th, 8th, 9th, 17th, 18th, 19th, 26th, 27th

Most Stressful Days Overall: 1st, 2nd, 15th, 16th, 22nd, 23rd, 28th, 29th

Best Days for Love: 5th, 6th, 10th, 11th, 15th, 16th, 20th, 21st, 22nd, 23rd, 24th, 25th, 28th, 29th

Best Days for Money: 3rd, 4th, 5th, 6th, 10th, 11th, 12th, 13th, 14th, 15th, 16th, 23rd, 24th, 25th

People in general are more communicative this month, so you should be enjoying things. (Mind your phone bill, though!)

Sales and marketing projects go well. Intellectual interests are fun and alluring to you – more so than usual. Good books and new magazines come into your sphere, making reading a special pleasure. This is a good time to buy that new car (or get the old one fixed up) and buy new communication equipment. The New Moon of the 14th is going to guide in these things.

Your career is still in a lull – temporarily. Use the opportunity to get your domestic life and home in order.

Your love life is beginning to pick up but is still not where it should and will be. A current relationship seems in crisis. Your spouse, partner or lover seems stressed about finances, affecting negatively his or her ability to love. You are in a period during which you need to weed out friends and unsuitable romantic prospects. Singles and those romantically uninvolved still find love opportunities at the workplace and with co-workers or employees. Health professionals continue to be appealing to you as well. You are looking for a 'healthy' relationship that is fun too; a relationship that promotes your physical and psychological health. You need someone who enjoys the same kind of dietary and exercise regimes that you do. Your local sports centre and health-food shop are other likely meeting grounds.

Your self-esteem and self-confidence are strong this period, but after the 23rd rest and relax more. You are thinking of changing your residence now but have hesitations about it. Perhaps you only need to make better use of the space you have. Give it more thought.

Pay bills and reduce long-term debt from the 1st to the 14th and from the 28th to the 31st. Build wealth and make investments from the 14th to the 28th. Money comes through spiritual activities and creative projects this month. Friends, too, provide opportunities.

September

> Best Days Overall: 4th, 5th, 14th, 15th, 23rd, 24th
>
> Most Stressful Days Overall: 11th, 12th, 19th, 25th, 26th
>
> Best Days for Love: 1st, 2nd, 8th, 9th, 11th, 12th, 18th, 19th, 20th, 21st, 27th, 28th, 29th, 30th
>
> Best Days for Money: 1st, 2nd, 3rd, 6th, 7th, 8th, 11th, 12th, 20th, 21st, 22nd, 23rd, 29th, 30th

Most of the planets are still below the horizon (the bottom half) of your chart, revealing your need to create a stable home base, instil emotional harmony and mend fences with your family. With your career still on hold for a while, these are good activities to be getting on with.

Your love life is perhaps the most interesting aspect of the month ahead. Your Love Planet (Jupiter), which has been retrograde for many months now, starts moving forward on the 3rd. Pluto in your House of Love and Marriage is also moving forward. The lunar eclipse of the 26th affects your Love Planet in a strong way. You cannot sit on the fence and be cautious any more. You are forced to act. A current relationship must go forward or be terminated. Decisions have to be made; action has to be taken. Singles are likely to see a change in their marriage status now. Marrieds in unhappy or unsatisfying relationships are likely to break up. A new social pattern is being created.

Mercury (your Ruling Planet) goes retrograde from the 4th to the 26th, making you less assertive and perhaps less self-confident. Use this time to review your goals and plans.

You are forced to backtrack and review issues that you thought you had already dealt with. You are in a period during which you can correct past mistakes. But Mercury's retrograde further thickens the Divine Plot of the month. For Mercury is also the Lord of your 4th House of Home and Family. Thus, though you are interested in redoing and redecorating your home, mending fences with your family and the like, you must proceed cautiously in these matters. Plan your redecoration or home improvement project now but wait till after the 26th (or before the 4th) to do it. Be careful of how you communicate to family members and to contractors involved with the home. Make sure your true message and intent get through, and make sure that you understand their true message. Take nothing for granted.

Rest and relax more until the 23rd. Health and vitality improves dramatically after that.

Pay bills and reduce long-term debt from the 1st to the 12th and from the 26th onwards. Build wealth and make investments from the 12th to the 26th.

October

Best Days Overall: 1st, 2nd, 11th, 12th, 20th, 21st, 29th, 30th

Most Stressful Days Overall: 9th, 10th, 16th, 17th, 22nd, 23rd

Best Days for Love: 8th, 9th, 10th, 16th, 17th, 18th, 19th, 26th, 27th, 28th

Best Days for Money: 1st, 2nd, 4th, 5th, 9th, 10th, 11th, 12th, 18th, 19th, 20th, 21st, 26th, 27th, 31st

With 90 per cent of the planets moving forward by the end of the month you are in a period of action, achievement and progress – never a dull moment. The solar eclipse of the 12th, while dramatic for others, seems kind to you. Your health and finances remain good – though your partner (and thus your marriage or relationship) gets stressed.

Though most of the planets are urging you to seek emotional tranquillity and harmony, Neptune (your Career Planet) starts to move forward this month. Interesting career developments are taking place. Stalled ambitions now move forward. Important decisions affecting you are made by your superiors or bosses. Your partner is forced to make changes in financial strategy and investments. Nevertheless, your main aim is to create and/or improve your home base and family relationships.

The solar eclipse of the 12th occurs in your 5th House and eclipses the Lord of your 3rd House. Those of you involved in the creative or performing arts begin a whole new phase of creativity. Flaws in creative style are brought up in order that they can be corrected. Those of you with children will see them redefining their personalities and making life-changing decisions this month. Cars and communication equipment should be checked out before you rely on them for important matters.

The eclipse makes some stressful aspects to Jupiter, your Love Planet. This shows a change in your current marital status. Love and social decisions must be made now; you can no longer sit on the fence. Events are forcing you to decide one way or the other. Marrieds could temporarily split up, while singles may marry. Flaws in your current social life are graphically revealed to be corrected one way or another. Your partner shifts his or her attitude towards your career.

In spite of all this the overall period is a happy one. There are fun, games, evenings out and entertainments. Personal pleasure is highlighted. Financial increase comes through your creativity and you become richer behind the scenes. Enjoy your wealth but do not flaunt it.

November

> Best Days Overall: 7th, 8th, 16th, 17th, 25th, 26th
>
> Most Stressful Days Overall: 5th, 6th, 12th, 13th, 18th, 19th
>
> Best Days for Love: 5th, 6th, 7th, 8th, 12th, 13th, 14th, 15th, 16th, 17th, 23rd, 24th, 27th, 28th
>
> Best Days for Money: 1st, 5th, 6th, 10th, 11th, 14th, 15th, 18th, 19th, 23rd, 24th, 27th, 28th, 30th

The planetary power in the western half of your horoscope shows more social activity and greater recognition of personal limits. We cannot always go it alone in life – nor were we meant to. Sometimes our good has to come from others. Your job is to keep your social channels open and in good repair.

Ninety per cent of the planets are moving forward, showing that your life is moving forward and that you are making progress in the pursuit of your goals. This will be a fast-paced month, but not as fast-paced as last month was.

The planetary power is focused in your 6th House of Health and Work for most of the month. Thus you are achieving work goals and getting your body in shape. Money will come to you through your work and through practical service to others now. You seem more efficient, more single-minded in your work – almost fanatical about it. Thus you probably achieve more. This is a good month for ridding yourself of habits or other things that obstruct either your efficiency or health. Sometimes you can do more merely by eliminating a distraction or obstruction than by actually working harder.

The focus on health this month has its up- and downside. On the upside you are more open to lifestyle changes which will foster health. On the downside you can be so attuned to your body that any little thing – any irregularity or pain – is magnified out of all proportion. Be careful of hypochondria. There are many reasons why we feel strange sensations in our bodies – at times. In most cases it has nothing to do with what is called disease. We are organisms in an environment and if the environment is disturbed – by world events, for example – we are all affected to some degree. Moreover, the planetary movements often produce temporary stresses in the body. Not to worry – these pass with time.

After the 22nd the focus shifts more to love and romance. Not only are the planets westward, but there is power in your 7th House. Romance is blooming. Singles are becoming romantically involved. There are more parties, more mingling and more dating. Your social vistas are expanded. You are popular because, in part, you go out of your way to please your beloved. You give him or her top priority. Few people can resist this.

December

Best Days Overall: 5th, 6th, 13th, 14th, 22nd, 23rd

Most Stressful Days Overall: 2nd, 3rd, 9th, 10th, 15th, 16th, 30th, 31st

Best Days for Love: 2nd, 3rd, 7th, 8th, 9th,

10th, 11th, 12th, 15th, 16th, 17th, 20th, 21st, 27th, 28th, 30th, 31st

Best Days for Money: 1st, 2nd, 3rd, 9th, 10th, 11th, 12th, 18th, 19th, 20th, 21st, 25th, 26th, 30th, 31st

Most of the planets are now in the western (social) half of your horoscope and your social life is sizzling. Perhaps overly so. Aside from your enhanced charisma and grace you are socially popular because you go out of your way to please your lover and friends. You sincerely like other people this month – to such an extent that you hardly distinguish your own interests from theirs. You need to be careful not to let others define who you are – or to derive self-esteem from other people's opinions. This is especially likely after the 23rd, when Mercury (your Ruling Planet) goes retrograde. But what you lack in self-esteem and assertiveness you make up for in popularity.

Singles are meeting significant others – perhaps more than one. After the 23rd you will have the opportunity to sort out your feelings and to see who belongs where in your life. Religious or university 'socials' are likely meeting grounds.

Social popularity and the ability to give and receive love are also important factors for your health this month. A harmonious social life enhances your physical feeling of well-being. Nevertheless, rest and relax more during this period.

Finances seem stable, though you are in a period for paying debt and reducing expenses rather than positive wealth-building. The Full Moon of the 24th occurs in your Money House, bringing financial windfalls, increased earnings, wealth ideas and connections, and greater ability, in general, to achieve financial goals.

The pace of your career is picking up day by day as more and more planets cross over to the top of your horoscope.

GEMINI

Major career boosts will take place next month.

Pause to review and re-evaluate your personal goals and desires while Mercury is retrograde from the 23rd onwards. Be patient with yourself and others. Be more careful of how you communicate. Though your life will seem to go backwards, this is only happening to enable you to correct past flaws or oversights.

Cancer

♋

THE CRAB
Birthdays from
21st June
to 20th July

Personality Profile

CANCER AT A GLANCE

Element – Water

Ruling Planet – Moon
Career Planet – Mars
Health Planet – Jupiter
Love Planet – Saturn
Money Planet – Sun
Planet of Fun and Games – Pluto
Planet of Home and Family Life – Venus

Colours – blue, puce, silver

Colours that promote love, romance and social harmony – black, indigo

Colours that promote earning power – gold, orange

CANCER

Gems – moonstone, pearl

Metal – silver

Scents – jasmine, sandalwood

Quality – cardinal (= activity)

Quality most needed for balance – mood control

Strongest virtues – emotional sensitivity, tenacity, the urge to nurture

Deepest need – a harmonious home and family life

Characteristics to avoid – over-sensitivity, negative moods

Signs of greatest overall compatibility – Scorpio, Pisces

Signs of greatest overall incompatibility – Aries, Libra, Capricorn

Sign most helpful to career – Aries

Sign most helpful for emotional support – Libra

Sign most helpful financially – Leo

Sign best for marriage and/or partnerships – Capricorn

Sign most helpful for creative projects – Scorpio

Best Sign to have fun with – Scorpio

Signs most helpful in spiritual matters – Gemini, Pisces

Best day of the week – Monday

Understanding the Cancer Personality

In the Sign of Cancer the heavens are developing the feeling side of things. This is what a true Cancerian is all about – feelings. Where Aries will tend to err on the side of action, Taurus on the side of inaction and Gemini on the side of thought, Cancer will tend to err on the side of feeling.

The Cancerian tends to mistrust logic. Perhaps rightfully so. For them it is not enough for an argument or a project to be logical – it must *feel* right as well. If it does not feel right a Cancerian will reject it or chafe against it. The phrase 'follow your heart' could have been coined by a Cancerian, because it describes exactly the Cancerian attitude towards life.

The power to feel is a more direct – more immediate – method of knowing than thinking is. Thinking is indirect. Thinking about a thing never touches the thing itself. Feeling is a faculty that contacts the thing or issue in question directly. We actually touch and experience it. Emotional feeling is almost like another sense that humans possess, a psychic sense. Since the realities that we come in contact with during our lifetime are often painful and even destructive, it is not surprising that the Cancerian chooses to erect barriers of defence – a shell – to protect his or her vulnerable, sensitive nature. To Cancerians this is only common sense.

If Cancerians are in the presence of people they do not know or in a hostile environment, up goes the shell and they feel protected. Other people often complain about this, but one must question their motives. Why does this shell disturb them? Is it perhaps because they would like to sting and feel frustrated that they cannot? If your intentions are honourable and you are patient, have no fear. The shell will go down and you will be accepted as part of the Cancerian's circle of family and friends.

Thought-processes are generally analytic and separative.

In order to think clearly we must make distinctions, separations, comparisons and the like. But feeling is unifying and integrative. To think clearly about something you have to distance yourself from it. But to feel something you must get close to it. Once a Cancerian has accepted you as a friend he or she will hang on. You will have to be really bad to lose the friendship of a Cancerian. If you are related to Cancerians they will never let you go no matter what you do. They will always try to maintain some kind of connection even in the most extreme circumstances.

Finance

The Cancer-born has a deep sense of what other people feel about things and why they feel as they do. This faculty is a great asset in the workplace and in the business world. Of course it is also indispensable in raising a family and building a home, but it also has its uses in business. Cancerians often attain great wealth in a family type of business. Even if the business is not a family operation, they will treat it as one. If the Cancerian works for somebody else then the boss is the parental figure and the fellow employees are brothers and sisters. If a Cancerian is him- or herself the boss, then all the workers are the children. Cancerians like the feeling of being providers for others. They enjoy knowing that others derive their sustenance because of what they do. It is another form of nurturing.

With Leo on their Solar 2nd House (of Money) cusp, Cancerians are often lucky speculators, especially with residential property or hotels and restaurants. Resort hotels and nightclubs are also profitable for the Cancerian. Waterside properties allure them. Though they are basically conventional people they sometimes like to earn their livelihood in glamorous ways.

The Sun, Cancer's Money Planet, represents an important financial message: in financial matters Cancerians need to be less moody, more stable and fixed. They cannot allow their moods – which are here today and gone tomorrow – to get in the way of their business life. They need to develop their self-esteem and feelings of self-worth if they are to realize their greatest financial potential.

Career and Public Image

Aries rules the 10th Solar House (of Career) cusp of Cancer, which indicates that Cancerians long to start their own business, to be more active publicly and politically and to be more independent. Family responsibilities and a fear of hurting other people's feelings – or getting hurt themselves – often inhibit them from attaining these goals. However, this is what they want and long to do.

Cancerians like their bosses and leaders to act freely and to be a bit self-willed. They can deal with that in a superior. Cancerians expect their leaders to be warriors in their defence.

When the Cancerian is in the position of boss or superior he or she behaves very much like a 'warlord'. Of course the wars they wage are not egocentric but in defence of those under their care. If they lack some of this fighting instinct – independence and pioneering spirit – Cancerians will have extreme difficulty in attaining their highest career goals. They will be hampered in their attempts to lead others.

Since they are so parental, Cancerians like to work with children and they make great educators and teachers.

Love and Relationships

Like Taurus, Cancer likes committed relationships. Cancerians function best when the relationship is clearly defined and everyone knows his or her role. When they marry it is usually for life. They are extremely loyal to their beloved. But there is a deep little secret that most Cancerians will never admit to: commitment or partnership is really a chore and a duty to them. They enter into it because they know of no other way to create the family that they desire. Union is just a way – a means to an end – rather than an end in itself. The family is the ultimate end for them.

If you are in love with a Cancerian you must tread lightly on his or her feelings. It will take you a good deal of time to realize how deep and sensitive Cancerians can be. The smallest negativity upsets them. Your tone of voice, your irritation, a look in your eye or an expression on your face can cause great distress for the Cancerian. Your slightest gesture is registered by them and reacted to. This can be hard to get used to, but stick by your love – Cancerians make great partners once you learn how to deal with them. Your Cancerian lover will react not so much to what you say but to the way you are actually feeling at the moment.

Home and Domestic Life

This is where Cancerians really excel. The home environment and the family that they create are their personal works of art. They strive to make things of beauty that will outlast them. Very often they succeed.

Cancerians feel very close to their family, their relatives and especially their mothers. These bonds last throughout their lives and mature as they grow older. They are very fond of those members of their family who become successful and they are also quite attached to family heirlooms and mementos. Cancerians also love children and like to provide them with all the things they need and want. With their nurturing, feeling nature Cancerians make very good parents – especially the Cancerian woman, who is the mother *par excellence* of the Zodiac.

As a parent the Cancerian's attitude is 'my children right or wrong.' Unconditional devotion is the order of the day. No matter what a family member does, the Cancerian will eventually forgive him or her, because 'you are, after all, family.' The preservation of the institution – the tradition – of the family is one of the Cancerian's main reasons for living. They have many lessons to teach others about this.

Being so family-orientated, the Cancerian's home is always clean, orderly and comfortable. They like old-fashioned furnishings but they also like to have all the modern comforts available. Cancerians love to have family and friends over, to organize parties and to entertain at home – they make great hosts.

Horoscope for 1996

Major Trends

Last year was a year of work and service. You prospered by being of practical service to others. You became a more valuable employee, thus setting the stage for the career success that is coming in 1996. This year is shaping up to be a mix of both career and social pursuits. There is much expansion in your social life, but you also have a growth-orientated attitude towards your career. When Saturn moves into your Career House in April you take on added job responsibilities and in general take a long-term view of your career. This is the year to forsake short-range mini-success in favour of long-term status and recognition.

Your normal interest in psychological issues, moods and emotions is very much intensified this year as Uranus begins its long-term transit of your 8th House. New ways of exploring your inner depths are revealed to you this year and for many years to come. Those of you born early in the Sign will experience this earlier than those of you born later in the Sign.

Health

Your House of Health – unusually active last year – is still active this year and for many years to come. Understand that we are dealing with long-term issues here, which will sometimes get intensified and sometimes eased depending on the actions of the short-term planets. For Pluto (the Planet of Transformation) will be in your Health House for the next 20 years or so. So your health is going to be transformed for the better over the coming years.

Those of you who have experienced good health might suddenly find that secret, hidden health problems come to light – things you might have been carrying around for years but never knew about – in order that they can be dealt with on a conscious level. Keep in mind that Pluto is not 'causing' your health problem, only 'revealing' what was always there. Pockets of potential problems are rising to the surface so that you can deal with them now and head off any future trouble. Understand these things as deeper cleansings.

Those of you who have been sick or experiencing health problems over the past few years might suddenly find that they are gone and that you are completely well now. Pluto is going to clear them out. Deep transformation of health is the keyword for the year.

Aside from the physical effects which Pluto is going to produce there will be deep psychological effects as well. Your attitude to health and to healing in general is undergoing radical transformation. Your understanding of the laws of health and disease deepens, and this allows you to apply these laws for your benefit. With Pluto in Sagittarius the metaphysics of health and disease – their philosophical and spiritual components – will become better understood.

Pluto in the 6th House often produces an over-reliance on surgical approaches to health. Many of you might be tempted to use this approach too readily or where it is not really called for. Try to get second opinions before rushing into often needless surgery.

There are two other factors influencing your health this year. Pluto, as Lord of your 5th House of Health, shows that it is important for you to have fun, to enjoy creative hobbies and have outlets for discharging negative energy. Yes, you will be working hard this year – but have some fun as well. Jupiter (your Health Planet) moves into your 7th House of Love and Marriage this year, showing that a happy social life and harmony with friends and partners are also very important in maintaining your health. Chances are that if you are having what seems to be a health problem it is really a relationship problem or problem of creative self-expression. Try to correct these areas before running to your health professional.

In April of 1996 Saturn will be making a major move into Aries – a stressful position for you. Now Saturn has many personalities. Its Universal personality is that of the Discipliner, Restricter and Cosmic Tester. Its stressful aspect to your Sun shows that you need to recognize your physical limits and not waste life-force needlessly. You are forced to rest and relax more, focus on priorities and in general rein in your personal desires. This does not mean that you go around denying yourself any pleasure, but that you discern what is needed and what is not needed. Many of you will drop the pounds this year. Eat less but eat better quality food.

In your horoscope, Saturn has another personality: it is your Love Planet. That it now comes into stressful aspect to your Sun Sign reinforces that your good health depends on good and harmonious social relationships. You need to give to your relationships the attention they deserve, even though it conflicts with your personal interests and desires. Maintain the harmony.

Home and Domestic Life

Family and domestic interests are always important to you, Cancer, but this year they seem less so. The 4th House of Home and Family is relatively inactive, showing that you have greater latitude and freedom in shaping this area as you will. The Cosmos is neither stressing you nor overly helping you.

In spite of this there will be some major changes in your domestic affairs this year – and in your relations with parents or parental figures. The four eclipses of the coming year occur either in your 4th or 10th House – the Houses that indicate parents. These eclipses will bring up weaknesses and vulnerabilities, both in relations with your parents and in your home. For example, if you have some hidden problem in the house – termites, a bad water pipe or the like – this is likely to reveal itself during the eclipses. Thus you are forced to deal with these things and correct them. If your living quarters are too small, cramped or otherwise inadequate, the eclipses will force a move. If you are married your spouse seems to push for a move, though you personally are content. The same applies to your relations with your parents. If there is some festering resentment or problem it will come to the fore during the eclipse periods and force you to mend fences or otherwise correct the problem.

One parent or parental figure (which one depends on whether you are male or female) feels very cramped in his or her present living quarters and wants to move. One of your parents could be having some problems with the government or authorities, but as the year progresses he or she will resolve them very harmoniously. If your parent or parental figure is still out in the workplace there are payrises and promotions in store – but with heavy new duties and responsibilities. Though his or her public esteem is higher, personal self-esteem seems lowered. This parent needs to be careful not to overwork. If the parent is retired there could be an increase in pension benefits from the government – but he or she must go through all kinds of bureaucracy and red tape to get it. It is not a smooth ride. If your parents are married their relationship is more stressful this year. You are caught in the middle and must be diplomatic. In family squabbles your spouse seems to support your parents, forcing you to compromise.

Relations with siblings seem stable and no more active or inactive than usual. You have a lot of freedom in how you relate to them and the Cosmos does not push you in one direction or the other. Keep in mind, however, that with Mercury being the Ruler of these relationships there could be short-term spats and periods where your relations seem to go backwards instead of forwards. These phenomena are due to Mercury's aspects at any given day and to its retrograde (backward) motion three times a year. But these are all short-term phenomena. Overall your 1996 horoscope fosters the status quo. If relations with siblings have been good they will tend to stay good; if they have been stressful they will tend to stay stressful.

Love and Social Life

Love, romance, marriage and social matters are probably the strongest interests in your life this year – and are much more active than in 1995. Yet, your social life is bittersweet. On the one hand there is a tremendous expansion in your circle of friends. Your social charisma and drawing power are very much enhanced. You attract new, more prominent types into your life both as friends and as potential mates. You attract lovers and friends who are into doing things for you, serving your interests in practical ways. You attract people who are health-conscious, perhaps even health professionals. You attract people who are ethical, educated and highly cultured. Singles and those who have never been married before are likely to marry or be involved in a significant romantic relationship during 1996. Married people will find their social circle expand and more romance within their marriage. Those working towards a second marriage will have an easier time of it this year. Higher education – especially in the arts, music or mystical fields – will provide opportunities for romance. Parties and social gatherings are also good places for romantic meetings. You are less serious and more relaxed about love this year – and thus more attractive. Those of you who are already in a second marriage should find things easier within this relationship. Your partner is less controlling, less serious and has higher self-esteem. Thus he or she is less likely to stress you. Your partner needs to be more careful financially this year, however.

For those of you working on (or into) a third marriage, the situation is different. Marriage is not a big priority this year and the status quo seems to reign. Your needs in love – and opportunities for love – will vary month to month with the transits of Venus.

Your love life or the marriage of a sibling – quite stormy and erratic of late – will settle down after April. Single siblings will have so many romantic opportunities that marriage may or may not be desired. Married siblings will be having more fun this year.

Many of you reading this have children of marriageable age. They are in a status quo period for love. Singles will tend to remain single, marrieds will tend to remain married. Your second-eldest child is the one having the most fun.

So enamoured are you with your social bliss that many of you want to make your marriage and/or social life your career. Nothing is as important to you as this. Those of you who are more worldly in your choice of career will find that these new social connections play a big role in career success. Networking becomes a viable career path this year.

However, problems may arise from too much of a good thing as your social whirl is too demanding. You seem called upon to sacrifice much of your personal freedom and inclinations in order to satisfy the demands of your lover, spouse or friends. Social burdens tax your physical energy and you must not allow this to happen. By all means pursue your social agenda, but mind your physical limits. Also watch your social spending. Spend within your limits and according to what you can afford. Spending more than you can afford on friends or your spouse is not going to endear you to them but rather the reverse. It will cause you stress and secret resentment which will further complicate any love or social relationship. Do not lose your own centre and your own sense of self-worth merely for the sake of popularity. You will, in the long run, be more popular and more loved for being true to yourself and keeping your self-esteem. Your true friends and true mate will love you all the more because of it.

Career and Finance

The hazards of overspending to gain personal popularity and in the pursuit of social goals have already been discussed. This is the main financial danger this year. Those of you married (in a first marriage) might find that your partner's spending habits are stressful. See if you can talk about this in a calm way. A compromise can and should be worked out.

On a personal level, the pursuit of wealth is not that important to you this year. Now, the Sign of Cancer does not have the reputation for wealth that other Signs have. Yet, the Cancer type (John D. Rockefeller, Ross Perot and many others) often attains great wealth. Wealth is more important to a Cancer than most astrologers give credit for – yet, this year, it is less so to you. You are much more interested in your career, social life and enhancing the income of others rather than in enhancing your own. Of course you will earn money this year – some periods more than others – but you basically have freedom to shape your financial destiny as you will. The Cosmos is not pushing you in any particular direction here. Your spouse or partner, on the other hand, is very much involved in money-making and is unusually experimental about it. Some might be pursuing any financial fad or get-rich-quick scheme that comes along, and learning big lessons (sad ones) because of it. Others will be exploring the scientific, high-tech field as both a means of income and place for investment. These latter types will fare much better, for high-tech is sweeping the world now more than ever. Your partner's generosity towards you will be sudden and unexpected – coming like a bolt from the blue. Your partner's earnings will rise in the same way. Weeks or perhaps months go by with little or mediocre earnings and then – out of nowhere, seemingly – a huge windfall. The financial highs are higher than usual, but the lows are lower.

As mentioned earlier, networking and social connections in general will be important aids to attaining your personal career goals this year. Your partner or spouse, too, seems very involved in your career – in a positive way. Superiors are stern and demanding, but fair. You might get a promotion because of whom you know, but you can only keep it by true worth. Avoid irregularities with the government or the corporate structure. Play by the book.

Big shake-ups in the corporate hierarchy are going to create career opportunities for you. Remain calm and things will happen.

Self-improvement

Your love and social life are going to improve with little or no effort on your part. Your career advancement, on the other hand, will happen because you make it happen and because you are the person most worthy to occupy a given position. You will need to learn to apply authority with fairness, love and self-control. There is a need to develop your organizational and administrative abilities this year. Not only do you need to know how to plan effectively your own time but that of other people as well. Take time to study the art of management. With Uranus moving into the Sign of Aquarius – its natural home – this year, there is a need for you to become 'friendlier' with the latest technology, computers and software, and media techniques. When you understand these fields better you will be able to make informed investments in these industries. Moreover, if you already invest in the stock- or bond-markets you might find that using the available computer and software technology will make you more effective (regardless of the industry you invest in). Make technology your friend.

Month-by-month Forecasts

January

Best Days Overall: 5th, 6th, 14th, 15th, 23rd, 24th

Most Stressful Days Overall: 12th, 13th, 19th, 20th, 25th, 26th

Best Days for Love: 2nd, 3rd, 5th, 6th, 12th, 13th, 14th, 15th, 19th, 20th, 23rd, 24th

Best Days for Money: 1st, 7th, 8th, 10th, 11th, 19th, 20th, 27th, 28th, 29th, 30th

With 90 to 100 per cent of the planets in the western half of your chart, the month is dominated by social activities and the needs of other people. Some people do not enjoy this kind of thing, but you will. Jupiter moves into your 7th House of Love and Marriage on the 3rd and stays there for the rest of the year. Your social charisma is strong, romance blooms and romantic opportunities for singles increase. It is a month for 'losing the self' so that later on you may find it. It is a month for playing down the personal ego and appreciating others. It is a month for putting other people ahead of yourself.

For singles, romantic opportunities come at the workplace or with co-workers. Parties with co-workers are fun and perhaps a bit boisterous. Other singles might find themselves attracting health professionals on a romantic level. These relationships too seem happy.

Your social life is probably confusing until the 20th – overactivity is the cause. But better a little confusion than no love life at all – count your blessings. The New Moon of the 20th, however, is going to clarify your social situation and you will be shown who is who and where each person belongs in your life.

This is also a month for a big financial surprise. Sudden material good comes to you – either money or a 'big-ticket' (expensive, long-lasting) item. Sometimes – I know this is hard to believe – money or things are not what is needed. We need ideas or contacts rather than cold cash. And this could be the way the 'financial scenario' happens for you. You will get whatever it is you really need – whether it be cash, a possession, or an idea. It will happen suddenly.

Rest and relax more until the 20th. Vitality surges after that.

The Sun is your Money Planet, Cancer. It has just begun (in the northern hemisphere) its waxing, growing cycle. Thus from now until your birthday you are in a wealth-building cycle. Spare cash should be channelled into investments which you want to see grow and increase. After your birthday, as the Sun wanes and diminishes in power, channel any spare cash towards reducing your debts. From the 20th January until the 20th February, in spite of the Sun's waxing cycle you have a brief period to reduce or consolidate debt. Take advantage of it.

February

Best Days Overall: 1st, 2nd, 11th, 12th, 19th, 20th, 28th, 29th

Most Stressful Days Overall: 8th, 9th, 10th, 15th, 16th, 21st, 22nd

Best Days for Love: 1st, 2nd, 11th, 12th, 13th, 14th, 15th, 16th, 19th, 20th, 21st, 22nd, 28th, 29th

Best Days for Money: 1st, 4th, 5th, 6th, 7th, 8th, 9th, 10th, 15th, 16th, 17th, 18th, 19th, 23rd, 24th, 25th, 28th, 29th

The planets are still very much in your western sector and at the top half of your horoscope, Cancer, making this very much a social and career month. Initiating things on your own – though possible – is more difficult. Goals are achieved with the aid of partners and superiors. Domestic goals, though always important to you, are best achieved through the pursuit of career goals. If you succeed in your career, domestic and family problems will just fade away. The former is intimately connected with the latter. Moreover, your ambitions are more than just personal right now – you are just as ambitious for your family as a whole as you are for yourself. Family members are hypersensitive until the 9th so be extra careful in your tone of voice, gestures and words – little things are blown out of proportion.

Your social life continues to be good. New friends and romantic opportunities come into life. Your circle of friends continues to expand. The need for physical intimacy dominates your romantic life until the 19th. After that you need more intellectual communion and the sharing of ideas and thoughts. Singles continue to be attracted to foreign, exotic types and many will fall in love with their teachers or professors. Your lover must be someone you can respect in order to interest you; he or she must be a guide as well as lover. Foreign trips lead to romance.

Those already in a marriage might want to take a second honeymoon in an exotic land this month. The prospects seem very happy.

On the financial front you are less concerned about personal earning than in enhancing the income of your partner or beloved. A joint investment in a high-tech company or venture is likely. Your partner is prospering and more generous with you. The credit line (yours) is stronger. This is a month for attracting outside investors to your projects and for obtaining outside capital. Debts are easily made but just as easily paid. The New Moon of the 18th brings clarification about personal finances, investments and the financial situation of your spouse. Pay bills (or set aside money for bills) and reduce debt from the 4th to the 18th. Make investments that build wealth from the 1st to the 4th and from the 18th onwards.

Your health is excellent all month but especially after the 19th.

March

Best Days Overall: 9th, 10th, 17th, 18th, 26th, 27th, 28th

Most Stressful Days Overall: 6th, 7th, 8th, 13th, 14th, 19th, 20th

Best Days for Love: 1st, 2nd, 3rd, 9th, 10th, 13th, 14th, 17th, 18th, 22nd, 23rd, 26th, 27th, 28th

Best Days for Money: 1st, 2nd, 3rd, 4th, 5th, 9th, 10th, 13th, 14th, 18th, 19th, 22nd, 23rd, 29th, 30th

With 80 to 90 per cent of the planets above the horizon of your chart you may seem to be ignoring family and family relationships. Of course, being who you are family and domestic issues will always be important, but you pursue those interests through achieving outward career success. The reasoning goes something like this: 'If I want to be really good to my family then I must succeed in my work and achieve something big in the outer world, then I will have the money, power and prestige to make their lives happy.' Your family agrees with this and is supportive of your career goals. Great career progress is made.

Your health is excellent until the 20th but afterwards you need to rest and relax more. Pace yourself and work to balance the needs of your spouse or lover with the demands of your career. Your ambitions in the world and your social urges need to be made to co-operate rather than to conflict with one another. This will take some work and compromise.

Finances are a big priority this month, but not so big that you will sacrifice prestige or your reputation. Rather the reverse is true: you will increase your income by furthering your professional and career standing. Money is likely to come through pay-rises, promotions, the government or your parents. Your spouse or partner puts some temporary financial pressure on you around the 16th, 17th or 18th –

and perhaps you feel pessimistic. But this pressure is temporary. Wealth increases after the 20th. Investors find opportunities in the global markets until the 20th, and in government securities (or government-backed securities) after the 20th.

Your love life is active this month and basically happy. Towards the end of the month it gets passionate and stormy. Your lover or spouse is upset over your career activities – or perhaps feels that he or she is neglected. Tension also arises because of your growing self-assertion. A sound relationship will weather this storm.

April

Best Days Overall: 5th, 6th, 13th, 14th, 23rd, 24th

Most Stressful Days Overall: 3rd, 4th, 9th, 10th, 16th, 17th, 30th

Best Days for Love: 1st, 2nd, 3rd, 6th, 7th, 9th, 10th, 11th, 12th, 16th, 17th, 20th, 21st, 25th, 26th, 27th, 30th

Best Days for Money: 1st, 2nd, 7th, 8th, 9th, 10th, 18th, 19th, 20th, 25th, 26th, 27th, 28th, 29th

A tumultuous, active month, Cancer, which brings many, many changes. Both of the eclipses this month occur at the angles of your chart, making them more powerful for you than for most of the other Signs. (They are also powerful for Aries, Libra and Capricorn. For Aries and Libra these eclipses – one on the 4th and the other on the 17th – bring personal and social change. For you and Capricorn they bring domestic and career changes – long-term ones.)

Thus you can expect to alter your career position – perhaps changing companies or jobs within the company. A temporary setback is later transformed into a long-term promotion – though at the time it may be difficult to recognize it as such. Many of you will move or break off with certain family members (or people who are like family to you) – all for the purpose of making both your family and career patterns fall into closer harmony with your inner Ideal. Many of you will find flaws with your present job or with superiors – these will come starkly to the fore and change will become inevitable. Flaws – perhaps structural flaws – will reveal themselves in your home so that you can either correct them or move somewhere better.

This is not one of your best health months so try to rest and relax more now. Stay calm throughout the tumult – as best you can. Be especially careful to take a nice, easy, relaxed and reduced schedule during the periods of the eclipses – from the 2nd to the 5th and from the 15th to the 18th. These are not periods when you want to make long trips, try to break some athletic record or undergo potentially dangerous surgery. Anything that requires you to be at 100 per cent capability should be rescheduled for another time – where possible. (If you have no choice, that is another story altogether – then you must allow more time for these projects and take extra precautions.)

Your financial life is also affected by these eclipses, so stay cool. The effect is only temporary. Wealth will return, greater than before. Flawed investments will reveal their flaws this month so that you can do something about them. When in doubt, do nothing. Let the dust settle first.

May

Best Days Overall: 3rd, 4th, 11th, 12th, 20th, 21st, 22nd, 30th, 31st

CANCER

Happily for you the unusual number of retrogrades this month occur with a good percentage of the planets in your eastern sector. Thus while many people are experiencing frustration, delay and non-achievement, you are moving forward and achieving personal goals. The Moon (your Ruler) never goes retrograde – though it waxes and wanes. So, on a personal level you are achieving your goals, moving forward and basically getting your way. The delays that you experience have to do with other people – in your relationships, at the workplace and the like.

Though you would benefit from a review of personal goals – especially after the 20th – you do not need to go too deeply into it. Start creating your kingdom immediately. If others do not co-operate – or are thinking about co-operating but are not sure – you can go it alone in the mean time.

Saturn is now the most elevated planet in your horoscope. For those of you born early in the Sign of Cancer it is now in your Career House. Your career and social life are the top priorities now. You are mixing with older, more established and career-orientated people. You are making friends at the top. The people you know are in a position to help you. You further your marriage by doing well in your career – thus you feel in a better position to supply your beloved with what he or she wants. The better you do in your career the more worthy you feel of love – a mistake, perhaps, but that is how you feel. Real and substantive achievement is what brings you career and social success now. Your longing now is for more than a happy marriage or happy social life, you want social status and social prominence as well. You are as ambitious for your beloved or partner as you are for yourself. Success is coming.

Your health is good all month, but better from the 1st to the 3rd and from the 17th to the 31st.

Financial judgement is especially sound and down to earth before the 20th. Wealth is increasing – though perhaps not as fast as you would like. Much financial growth is taking place behind the scenes. You are a conservative, 'have-and-hold' type of investor until the 20th. Afterwards you become more of a 'trader' type – profiting from short-term market trends and fluctuations

June

Best Days Overall: 7th, 8th, 16th, 17th, 18th, 26th, 27th

Most Stressful Days Overall: 3rd, 4th, 9th, 10th, 24th, 25th

Best Days for Love: 1st, 3rd, 4th, 5th, 6th, 9th, 14th, 15th, 19th, 24th, 25th

Best Days for Money: 3rd, 4th, 5th, 6th, 12th, 13th, 14th, 15th, 19th, 20th, 22nd, 23rd, 26th, 27th

The fast-moving, short-term planets and the slow-moving, long-term planets oppose each other this month, pulling you in opposite directions. The long-term planets pull you towards your social life, towards adapting to others and being generally 'other-orientated'. The short-term planets are pushing you towards a 'me-first' attitude, towards taking care of your own personal desires and interests. There is a need to balance these opposing forces right now. Over the short term it is safe to put your own personal interests first. This does not mean that you totally ignore the needs of others, but that you come first.

With 50 per cent of the planets moving backwards this month the people around you are experiencing delays, frustrations and uncertainty. But you make good progress. All of your important planets are moving forward, so you are unique this month.

Spiritual, philanthropic and meditation activities are important and dear to your heart now. This is the month to schedule that psychic or astrological reading, to attend lectures on the spiritual life and to remove any obstacles to your spiritual communion with the Source. It is a period of altruism with very practical consequences on a financial level. First off, financial guidance and ideas come through these activities. Philanthropic activities open the channels to new money-making opportunities and connect you to important financial contacts. You are better able to discern short-term market trends and to capitalize on them. You are better able to align yourself with the Divine Financial Plan for your life – a Plan that, by definition, means prosperity and joy. You are better able to discern investments which have stable, long-term value.

You invest and purchase behind the scenes this month, wisely taking a low profile. No need to be discussing your financial plans with others – many are 'wet blanket' types and you need all the faith and confidence you can muster.

Though over the long term your love life continues to be good, this month you are in a 'pause' phase. Do not accelerate a current relationship nor decelerate it. Be patient and allow the relationship time. Singles should avoid commitment now. Your social and romantic judgement is unrealistic at present.

July

> Best Days Overall: 4th, 5th, 14th, 15th, 24th, 25th
>
> Most Stressful Days Overall: 1st, 6th, 7th, 8th, 21st, 22nd, 28th, 29th
>
> Best Days for Love: 1st, 2nd, 3rd, 6th, 7th, 11th, 12th, 16th, 17th, 21st, 22nd, 26th, 27th, 28th, 29th, 30th, 31st
>
> Best Days for Money: 1st, 4th, 5th, 9th, 10th, 14th, 15th, 16th, 17th, 19th, 20th, 26th, 27th, 28th, 29th

Take advantage of the temporary lull in your social life to focus on personal goals and on creating conditions for your own happiness. The short-term planets are temporarily in the eastern sector of your horoscope – you have a chance to please yourself and do the things that you really want to do. Singles are better off working on their bodies and personal images – doing the things that will make them more appealing – than running after love in all the wrong places. You are in one of the best 'personal pleasure periods' of the year.

Those of you involved in sports perform much better this month than usual. Your body shines, obeys your will and is filled with superabundant energy. You are unusually attractive to the opposite sex, but the problem – for singles – is attracting the right one. Still, those who are merely after a good time will have no problem.

The Sun's cycle is particularly important in your financial life, as the Sun is your Money Planet. This month the Solar cycle begins to wane in the northern hemisphere. The days start to grow shorter and the Solar influence favours 'diminishment'. Thus for the next five or six months use spare cash to reduce debt and cut costs rather than to build wealth. Of course there will be many opportunities for investing in the coming months – and you should take advantage of them – but your primary focus should be on reducing debts. Once this is done you can channel spare cash into wealth building.

This is a particularly good month financially – especially after the 22nd. Earnings are stronger after the 22nd but your luck is stronger before then. Substantial financial (or material) surprises come around the 1st and the 15th. Your good appearance and personal charm are like money in the bank and bring financial opportunities to you. Doing what you personally love also turns out to be profitable. Dress in ways that make you feel wealthy. Wear expensive jewellery or other accessories that put you in the vibration of wealth. First impressions – always important – are especially significant in your financial dealings now.

August

Best Days Overall: 1st, 2nd, 10th, 11th, 20th, 21st, 28th, 29th

Most Stressful Days Overall: 3rd, 4th, 17th, 18th, 19th, 24th, 25th, 30th, 31st

Best Days for Love: 3rd, 4th, 10th, 11th, 12th, 13th, 20th, 21st, 22nd, 23rd, 24th, 25th, 28th, 29th, 30th, 31st

Best Days for Money: 3rd, 4th, 5th, 6th, 12th, 13th, 14th, 15th, 16th, 23rd, 24th, 25th

The short-term planets are still energizing your eastern sector, pushing you to become more 'me-orientated', independent and self-assertive. With your love life temporarily on hold now it is best to focus your energies on yourself, making yourself more lovable and more like the person you want to be. Such activities work out favourably this month.

You are in a strong financial period and have unusual control over your earnings, investments and purchases. Earning power is strong all month. You are a standard of wealth for others now. People judge how well they are doing by comparing themselves to you. You are a financial star this month, shining as a result of your financial abilities and moves. You dazzle others with your possessions. Though others see you as a speculator or risk-taker, this month the truth is that you have a shrewd sense of inherent value. You see the real value of a thing – others call it speculation. Financial opportunities come to you in the areas of sports, entertainment, casinos and telecommunications (later in the month). Those looking for work or looking to invest should check out these industries.

Your health is excellent all month. Physical energy is superabundant and you excel at sports and exercise. Personal glamour increases after the 7th – a good time to buy new clothes or accessories as your aesthetic judgement is superb. You easily attract the opposite sex, but attracting the right person is more of a problem. You are still in a period of personal pleasure and are interested in fulfilling physical and sensual desires – for good food, good sex and other sensual delights. Friends side with you in a domestic dispute; they are in your corner all month.

You have expanded much on a social level so far this year and now you must stop and review this area. You must give relationships – romantic or social – time to mature. Marriages or divorces should not be scheduled now. You are more involved with friends and acquaintances than with your marriage or romantic life.

CANCER

September

Best Days Overall: 6th, 7th, 8th, 16th, 17th, 25th, 26th

Most Stressful Days Overall: 14th, 15th, 20th, 21st, 27th, 28th

Best Days for Love: 8th, 9th, 10th, 18th, 19th, 20th, 21st, 27th, 28th

Best Days for Money: 1st, 2nd, 3rd, 9th, 10th, 11th, 12th, 20th, 21st, 22nd, 23rd, 29th, 30th

September is an active, tumultuous and memorable month for you, Cancer. Long-term progress comes through short-term crises. You cannot sit on the fence – though in certain situations you would like to – but are forced to choose, to act, to commit.

The lunar eclipse of the 26th causes you to redefine your personality – to rethink it. It creates major long-term change in your career and corporate hierarchy. Your partner's career is also changing. Relations with a parent alter – and the parent (or parental figure) looks to transform his or her residence. Your love life is shaken up and hard choices must be made. Your marital status changes. For singles this could mean a marriage or the breakup of a current relationship. For married Cancers it could mean a divorce or a further strengthening – a cleansing and/or purgation – of the current relationship. Co-workers or employees leave the scene. The physical workplace is redone. One thing is certain, things will not be dull!

Definitely rest and relax more this month – but especially around the time of the eclipse (from the 25th to the 27th).

Finances are strong this month. Sales and marketing

143

projects should be planned – but not executed – from the 4th to the 26th. These projects will ultimately be successful – profitable – but take more time with them. Friends, elders and authority figures are supporting your financial goals and showing you new opportunities. Networking within organizations to which you belong is profitable. Your fondest financial dreams are coming true this month in spite of all the confusion around you. Your world may seem like it is shaking and quaking, but your financial supply is coming in right on schedule. Your family is supportive of financial goals and they create opportunities for you as well. The 26th onwards is a good time to buy or sell your home or to make money in real estate. Interest and dividend income increase. Investment opportunities in entertainments, beauty, fashion, sports and athletic equipment come to you. There is a financial fearlessness in you this period and you get what you go after.

October

Best Days Overall: 4th, 5th, 13th, 14th, 22nd, 23rd, 31st

Most Stressful Days Overall: 11th, 12th, 18th, 19th, 24th, 25th

Best Days for Love: 6th, 7th, 8th, 9th, 16th, 17th, 18th, 19th, 24th, 25th, 27th, 28th

Best Days for Money: 1st, 2nd, 6th, 7th, 9th, 10th, 11th, 12th, 18th, 19th, 20th, 21st, 26th, 27th, 31st

Rest and relax more as this is a tumultuous, active month. Important actions and changes are taking place in your love and social life, with your family and in your career. Unusual planetary power below the horizon of your chart emphasizes the home and domestic responsibilities. But your love life and career demands conflict with these responsibilities. Your task is to harmonize all these areas, to bring them into line. Rather than have these different demands pull you in conflicting directions you have to make them all work together and support each other.

Family and domestic responsibilities become important this month in another way as well. The solar eclipse of the 12th occurs in your House of Family, signifying a move, change of residence, a renovation or home-repair job, and a change in the family pattern and relationship. Hidden flaws in these areas come to light now, compelling a correction. Plans you made based on one set of assumptions are now seen as inadequate because of new facts. Moods can be very erratic this month so do not identify with them. You are, in essence, much more than your moods or feelings.

The eclipsed planet is the Sun (your Money Planet). This shows temporary upheavals in finances, earnings, expenses and investments. An investment you thought was sound feels, for the moment, like it is unsound. A client you depended on seems, for the moment, not so dependable. A real estate deal seems temporarily disrupted. Financial corrections take place. Yet in spite of this you prosper. Domestic expenses perhaps increase, but family members are also supportive of your financial goals and create financial opportunities. Financial disruptions lead to increased earnings in the long run. Career status and public prestige lead directly to profits. Bosses and superiors bring earnings opportunities. Long-term – and positive – changes take place in your investment strategies and philosophy.

The eclipse also affects Jupiter (your Planet of Health and Work). Thus a job change is likely as well. This could occur within the same company or you could make a move to a completely new firm. Saturn (your Love Planet) is also affected. Changes occur in the marital status. Singles are likely to marry, marrieds are more likely to split up, and hard choices must be made in your social life. Again, rest and relax more this month.

November

> Best Days Overall: 1st, 10th, 11th, 18th, 19th, 27th, 28th
>
> Most Stressful Days Overall: 7th, 8th, 14th, 15th, 20th, 21st
>
> Best Days for Love: 2nd, 3rd, 7th, 8th, 12th, 13th, 14th, 15th, 16th, 17th, 20th, 21st, 27th, 28th, 30th
>
> Best Days for Money: 1st, 2nd, 3rd, 4th, 5th, 6th, 10th, 11th, 14th, 15th, 18th, 19th, 23rd, 24th, 30th

After the traumas of last month you deserve a little break and the Cosmos is giving it to you. Calm and stress, seriousness and playfulness tend to alternate (like night and day) in Nature. So if you are having fun this month you are in tune with Nature. The New Moon of the 11th is going to assist you in this as it makes its monthly round of your chart. It is going to show you how to be more creative, relate better with children and in general get more fun out of life. On the 12th and 13th it will show you the importance of being healthy – after all, it is hard to have fun when you are not feeling well. On the 14th and 15th it will show you how to have fun with others. On the 16th and 17th it will reveal ways to enhance sexual pleasures and to remove any obstacles to rapture. On the 18th and 19th it will clarify philosophical concepts about creativity and fun. On the 20th and 21st it will show you how your creativity can be used to further your career – and so on and so forth through the Houses and Signs of the Zodiac.

Most of the short-term planets have now joined the long-term planets in the western sector of your chart, emphasizing social interests and the need for community. This is not a month for power struggles or for going it alone. As much as possible, seek consensus in your major actions.

Earnings are strong this month. Debts are easily made but also easily paid. Speculations are favourable. Money is earned through creativity and in pleasurable ways. Creative approaches to earning and investing boost your 'bottom line'. Your financial confidence is so strong that you might be overspending. The entertainment industry looks especially alluring for investors. Your financial judgement is deep and on target. You see into the nature of different companies and financial opportunities. You are a difficult person to fool right now. After the 22nd money comes to you from work and practical service. Your ability to achieve work goals is increased and thus your earnings increase. Many of you will have opportunities to earn overtime pay. Others will find that co-workers lead them to financial opportunities. Foreign investments become alluring.

Your love life is improving day by day. But Saturn (your Love Planet) is the lone planet in the universe still going backwards – so you still need to be cautious. There are plenty of opportunities but you should sit on the fence for a while. The achievement of work goals towards the end of the month will make you feel more worthy of love.

December

Best Days Overall: 7th, 8th, 15th, 16th, 25th, 26th

Most Stressful Days Overall: 5th, 6th, 11th, 12th, 18th, 19th

Best Days for Love: 1st, 7th, 8th, 9th, 11th, 12th, 15th, 16th, 17th, 18th, 19th, 27th, 28th

Best Days for Money: 1st, 2nd, 3rd, 9th, 10th, 11th, 12th, 18th, 19th, 20th, 21st, 27th, 28th, 30th, 31st

The planets are still very much in the west now, emphasizing social activities and social interests. Not a month for power struggles or undue self-assertion. Put other people's interests ahead of your own and good will come to you very naturally. Your social grace is the key to success.

Your monthly cycle begins on the New Moon of the 10th. It occurs in your 6th House, showing that the general tenor of the month ahead is work- and health-orientated. The pace at work is demanding and your boss or superior is difficult to please. As the month progresses, however, you are being shown how to achieve work and health goals in specific ways. Problems with the boss will disappear. Miscommunication seems at the root of the problem. By the 17th there is harmony and fun at work. Singles even find romantic opportunities there. Serious love is manifesting for singles. Marrieds make new friends and go out more. Your social sphere expands greatly beginning the 21st. The uninvolved become involved. Lukewarm relationships become more torrid. Married life becomes more romantic.

Yet there is a practical dimension to love after the 21st. Friendships and social good will are considered assets – part and parcel of your wealth. You are allured to lovers who are wealthy. You feel a sense of ownership about your friends and your lover. If not overdone this can be endearing. Material gifts turn you on.

Work and relationships are important on a financial level as well. Until the 21st money comes from work and practical service. Overtime pay or bonuses boost earnings. Industries that deal with nutrition, vitamin supplements, pharmaceuticals, etc. are alluring investments. These investments and the workplace still bring money after the 21st, but there is an added social dimension as well. Social contacts provide financial opportunities. Your partner is supportive.

Rest and relax more after the 21st. Your feelings of financial health are related to feelings of physical well-being. If you feel a health problem, chances are it has its roots in finances (or family issues) and is not anything organic.

Leo

♌

THE LION
Birthdays from
21st July
to 21st August

Personality Profile

LEO AT A GLANCE

Element – Fire

Ruling Planet – Sun
   Career Planet – Venus
   Health Planet – Saturn
   Love Planet – Uranus
   Money Planet – Mercury

Colours – gold, orange, red

Colours that promote love, romance and social harmony – black, indigo, ultramarine blue

Colours that promote earning power – yellow, yellow-orange

Gems – amber, chrysolite, yellow diamond

LEO

Metal – gold

Scents – bergamot, frankincense, musk, neroli

Quality – fixed (= stability)

Quality most needed for balance – humility

Strongest virtues – leadership ability, self-esteem and confidence, generosity, creativity, love of joy

Deepest needs – fun, elation, the need to shine

Characteristics to avoid – arrogance, vanity, bossiness

Signs of greatest overall compatibility – Aries, Sagittarius

Signs of greatest overall incompatibility – Taurus, Scorpio, Aquarius

Sign most helpful to career – Taurus

Sign most helpful for emotional support – Scorpio

Sign most helpful financially – Virgo

Sign best for marriage and/or partnerships – Aquarius

Sign most helpful for creative projects – Sagittarius

Best Sign to have fun with – Sagittarius

Signs most helpful in spiritual matters – Aries, Cancer

Best day of the week – Sunday

Understanding the Leo Personality

When you think of Leo, think of royalty – that way you will get an idea of what the Leo character is all about and why Leos are the way they are. It is true that for various reasons some Leo-born are not always expressing this quality, but even if they are not they should like to do so.

A monarch rules not by example (as does Aries) nor by consensus (as do Capricorn and Aquarius) but by personal will. Will is law. Personal taste becomes the style that is imitated by all subjects. A monarch is somehow larger than life. This is how a Leo desires to be.

When you dispute the personal will of a Leo it is serious business. He or she takes it as a personal affront, an insult. Leos will let you know that their will carries authority and that to disobey is demeaning and disrespectful.

A Leo is king (or queen) of his or her personal domain. Subordinates, friends and family are the loyal and trusted subjects. Leos rule with benevolent grace and in the best interests of others. They have a powerful presence; indeed, they are powerful people. They seem to attract attention in any social gathering. They stand out because they are stars in their domain. Leos feel that, like the Sun, they are made to shine and rule. Leos feel that they were born to special privilege and royal prerogatives – and most of them attain this status, at least to some degree.

The Sun is the Ruler of this Sign, and when you think of sunshine it is very difficult to feel unhealthy or depressed. Somehow the light of the Sun is the very antithesis of illness and apathy. Leos love life. They also love to have fun; they love drama, music, the theatre and amusements of all sorts. These are the things that give joy to life. If – even in their best interest – you try to deprive Leos of their pleasures, good food, drink and entertainment, you run the serious risk of depriving them of the will to live. To them life without joy is no life at all.

LEO

Leos epitomize humanity's will to power. But power in and of itself – regardless of what some people say – is neither good nor evil. Only when power is abused does it become evil. Without power even good things cannot come to pass. Leos realize this and are uniquely qualified to wield power. Of all the Signs, they do it most naturally. Capricorn, the other power Sign of the Zodiac, is a better manager and administrator than Leo – much better. But Leo outshines Capricorn in personal grace and presence. Leo loves power where Capricorn assumes power out of a sense of duty.

Finance

Leos are great leaders but not necessarily good managers. They are better at handling the overall picture than the nitty-gritty details of business. If they have good managers working for them they can become exceptional executives. They have vision and a lot of creativity.

Leos love wealth for the pleasures it can bring. They love an opulent lifestyle, pomp and glamour. Even when they are not wealthy they live as if they are. This is why many fall into debt, from which it is sometimes difficult to emerge.

Leos, like Pisceans, are generous to a fault. Very often they want to acquire wealth solely so that they can help others economically. Wealth to Leo buys services and managerial ability. It creates jobs for others and improves the general well-being of those around them. Therefore – to a Leo – wealth is good. Wealth is to be enjoyed to the fullest. Money is not to be left to gather dust in a mouldy bank vault but to be enjoyed, spread around, used. So Leos can be quite reckless in their spending.

With the Sign of Virgo on Leo's 2nd House (of Money) cusp, Leo needs to develop some of Virgo's traits of analysis, discrimination and purity when it comes to money matters. They must learn to be more careful with the details of finance (or to hire people to do this for them). They have to be more cost-conscious in their spending habits. Basically, they need to manage their money better. Leos tend to chafe under financial constraints, yet these constraints can help Leos reach their highest financial potential.

Leos like it when their friends and family know that they can depend on them for financial support. They do not mind – even enjoy – lending money, but they are careful that they are not being taken advantage of. From their 'regal throne' Leos like to bestow gifts upon their family and friends and then enjoy the good feelings these gifts bring to everybody. Leos love financial speculations and – when the celestial influences are right – are often lucky.

Career and Public Image

Leos like to be perceived as wealthy, for in today's world wealth often equals power. When they attain wealth they love having a large house with lots of land and animals.

At their jobs Leos excel in positions of authority and power. They are good at making decisions – on a grand level – but they prefer to leave the small details for others to take care of. Leos are well respected by their colleagues and subordinates, mainly because they have a knack for understanding and relating to those around them. Leos usually strive for the top positions even if they have to start at the bottom and work hard to get there. As might be expected of such a charismatic Sign, Leos are always trying to improve their work situation. They do so in order to have a better chance of advancing to the top.

On the other hand, Leos do not like to be bossed around or told what to do. Perhaps this is why they aspire so for the top – where they can be the decision-makers and need not take orders from others.

Leos never doubt their success and focus all their attention and efforts on achieving it. Another great Leo characteristic is that – just like good monarchs – they do not attempt to abuse the power or the success they achieve. If they do so this is not wilful or intentional. Usually they like to share their wealth and try to make everyone around them join in their success.

Leos are – and like to be perceived as – hard-working, well-established individuals. It is definitely true that they are capable of hard work and often manage great things. But do not forget that, deep down inside, Leos really are fun-lovers.

Love and Relationships

Generally, Leos are not the marrying kind. To them relationships are good while they are pleasurable. When the relationship ceases to be pleasurable a true Leo will want out. They always want to have the freedom to leave. That is why Leos excel at love affairs rather than commitment. Once married, however, Leo is faithful – even if some Leos have a tendency to marry more than once in their lifetime. If you are in love with a Leo, just show him or her a good time. Travel, go to casinos and clubs, the theatre and discos. Wine and dine your Leo love – it is expensive but worth it and you will have fun.

Leos generally have an active love life and are demonstrative in their affections. They love to be with other optimistic and fun-loving types like themselves, but wind up settling with someone more serious, intellectual and unconventional. The partner of a Leo tends to be more political and socially conscious than he or she is and more libertarian. When you marry a Leo, mastering the freedom-loving tendencies of your partner will definitely become a life-long challenge – but be careful that Leo does not master you.

Aquarius sits on Leo's 7th House (of Love) cusp. Thus if Leos want to realize their highest love and social potential they need to develop a more egalitarian, Aquarian perspective on others. This is not easy for Leo, for 'the king' finds his equals only among other 'kings'. But perhaps this is the solution to Leo's social challenge – to be 'a king among kings'. It is all right to be royal, but recognize the nobility in others.

Home and Domestic Life

Although Leos are great entertainers and love having people over, sometimes this is all show. Only very few close friends will get to see the real side of a Leo's day-to-day life. To a Leo the home is a place of comfort, recreation and transformation; a secret, private retreat – a castle. Leos like to spend money, show off a bit, entertain and have fun. They enjoy the latest furnishings, clothes and gadgets – all things fit for kings.

Leos are fiercely loyal to their family and of course expect the same from them. They love their children almost to a fault; they have to be careful they do not spoil them too much. They also must try to avoid attempting to make individual family members over in their own image. Leos should keep in mind that others also have the need to be their own people. That is why Leos have to be extra careful about being over-bossy or over-domineering in the home.

Horoscope for 1996

Major Trends

Seldom have you had a year as happy as 1995, Leo. Seldom have you been able to play, enjoy life and express yourself as you did in 1995. And, though 1996 is very blessed and fortunate in many ways, it is a more serious year.

Self-expression now gives way to service and work. The nightclub must give way to the workplace. Self-expression must be made practical and useful to others and not merely used to let off steam or show off talent. And though 1996 is more serious than 1995, this does not mean that it is *all* serious. On the contrary, make your workplace a place of joy. Find work that you love and put your heart into it. Work done well that is truly useful to others has joys not found in any night-spot. The development of a proper work ethic and philosophy of work is going to be your major task in 1996, and the Cosmos is giving you considerable help.

Health

Your health keeps getting better every year. As one helping planet moves away, another one comes and takes its place. Your already superabundant vitality is even further increased in 1996. You have all the energy and power to achieve whatever you want, and some left to spare.

Your House of Health is very powerful and active this year, Leo. Normally this could show health problems or a need to focus on your health, but with your vitality so high this year this power in the 6th House must be interpreted differently. If you are in the health profession your personal healing abilities are vastly increased and you have more patients than you know what to do with. If you are not in a health profession your personal healing abilities are still increased and people feel better just being around you – though you do nothing overtly.

By April Saturn will be out of your 8th Solar House and into your 9th – a very happy transit. Bad health habits should – over the past two years – have been broken and you are starting to feel the result. Saturn is also your Health Planet. Its move into Aries, your 9th Solar House, shows that religion, metaphysics and higher knowledge are factors in the maintenance of good health. This is a good period for reading and taking courses on the laws of health. Those of you attending medical or nursing school will find 1996 to be a particularly successful year. Saturn's transit also shows that you are evolving more realistic concepts about health and disease which positively affect your health. The spiritual component of healing is vital for you to understand.

The health of your spouse or partner seems relatively stable though he or she is making radical changes in his or her self-image. The health of one of your parents (or parental figures) is delicate and he or she must work hard to get this area in order. Diet and exercise programmes – long-term health regimes – are what is called for – not quick, magic-bullet types solutions. The health of a sibling improves this year. The health of children seems stable, though one of them may opt for some type of cosmetic surgery this year.

Home and Domestic Life

Your 4th House of Home and Family Interests is not an especially active House this year, Leo, therefore you have considerable freedom to shape this area as you will. The problem is that you are not that interested in domestic pursuits.

You are, however, very interested in children and in their domestic affairs – insuring that they have happy and harmonious living conditions and the like. Some of you are involved in buying a home for your children this year, and come April this project proceeds successfully.

Your children (especially the two eldest ones) are making major changes in their self-image and redefining their personalities. One is very restless and will probably have a series of moves in the coming year – or perhaps live in many different places – like a transient. The other wants completely to transform his or her personal environment and will probably completely redo either the home or personal living quarters (the room where he or she spends most time).

A parent or parental figure is also restless and looking to move this year. Here too there are possibly a series of moves – an experimentation when it comes to living quarters. This parent will either move or acquire new homes.

Pressure for a personal move on your part could come from your spouse or partner, but what he or she really needs is not a new home but more personal space – physical and psychological.

Love and Social Life

This is an interesting and important area this year. Uranus (your Love Planet) makes a major long-term move into your 7th House of Love and Marriage, and stays there for many years to come. This has big implications for your love life. For one thing it makes you more freedom-loving in love. You want attachment and commitment but you want a lot of space as well. Moreover, you attract partners who are like this as well. Those of you who are already married find that your partner starts to redefine his or her image and personality. They want to 'do their own thing'. If the relationship is solid to begin with it will survive and your partner will find enough change and variety within the current relationship. Affections (both yours and your partner's) change radically and erratically. One day love feelings are intense and passionate, the next day indifferent, which will make your love life interesting and exciting. Never a dull moment for the coming seven years!

Singles are likely to marry now, and married people may either separate or create new rules within their relationship. New loves and marriage prospects are met suddenly and unexpectedly. Love happens at first sight – instantaneously. Friends are made suddenly and lost just as suddenly – the aspects to Uranus will show what is happening and when.

A turbulent period for love, indeed.

Though you Leos have been experimental in love for some years now, this trend is even more pronounced now that Uranus is in the experimental Sign of Aquarius. It is as if you are completely rewriting the book on romance for the coming seven years. You seek out new and novel ways to meet people and to relate to them. The use of 'high tech' in romance is explored. We can easily imagine you Leos sending passionate messages by e-mail over the Internet or some other computer network, arranging romantic trysts through these means or even meeting your future mate this way. Astrological dating services are also valid means of meeting your beloved. Singles will be attracted to scientific, technologically literate and intellectually-orientated people. There will also be an attraction to those of foreign cultures and nationalities. In short, the new and the novel are most appealing to you.

Those of you who have your heart set on a Leo this year should take note of the above. You must present yourself as something different and fresh. Do not worry about being thought of as 'freaky' – the freakier you are the more Leo will be intrigued.

However, those of you working towards a second marriage need to avoid experimentation this year – tempting and interesting though it is. You seem to need someone stable, mature and willing to accept responsibility and serve your interests. Someone at the workplace or who is involved with your health or the health profession is just waiting in the wings and fits the bill exactly. Stress quality in your love life over quantity.

A sibling's love relationships may be in a bit of trouble this year. If the sibling is as yet unmarried, a marriage is likely – to someone older, more established and perhaps more controlling. Your sibling yearns for long-term, enduring love.

Those of you who have children of marriageable age

need to be patient. The children need to find out who they are before they can find their 'other half'.

Career and Finance

Most of you Leos seem to be following one of the dictums of the Ageless Wisdom this year – 'Be not ambitious but work as if you were ambitious.' With Jupiter in your Solar 6th House of Health and Work you are becoming more productive, working hard – yet enjoying the work – and expanding your abilities to achieve work goals. Conditions at the workplace seem much happier as well. Relations with co-workers are basically happy and harmonious. Yet, in spite of all this your motives are neither career- nor wealth-orientated. You want to do a good job for the sake of doing a good job. A good job is its own reward. The inner satisfaction that it brings means more to you than mere money or promotions.

Neither your 2nd House of Money nor your 10th House of Career are especially active this year. This shows that you have greater freedom and latitude in these areas. The Cosmos does not impel you one way nor the other. You have a free hand to shape your finances and career as you will – but will you give them the attention they need? This is up to you.

You are a valued worker this year for various reasons; the fact that you are more productive is only one of them. You bring into the workplace an 'invisible something' – a quality, a vibration – which lifts the morale and spirits of those around you. You are a joy-bringer and depression-dispeller. Those of you in managerial positions get unusual support from those who work for you. Be especially alert for ideas that come from your workers.

If you are an employer, you are enlarging your workforce this year – and probably raising wages. You are also enlarging the plant or general work area. The well-being of your employees – health benefits, pension plans and the like – is also a major concern this year.

In 1995 you were more speculative in financial matters, and though one can never expect a Leo to stop speculating completely, there is a reduction in 1996. You are much more prudent. Perhaps you invest or speculate in government (or government-backed) bonds, mortgages, and securities. Long-term bonds or securities in general seem attractive to you and you do well.

Your spouse or partner is emerging from a difficult financial period and will really start prospering later on in the year. Money is earned easily and effortlessly and there is less need for the cost-cutting and budgeting that he or she has had to do for the past few years.

The income of your children is also improving greatly this year either through shrewd land deals, the stock-market, or government securities. Those of you involved in the creative arts – painting, music, sculpture, writing – will see your creations do well financially. Hopefully you have structured things so that you share in the wealth that is coming in.

However, even with all this activity the major source of income for the overwhelming majority of you will be your job.

Self-improvement

Your personal health and your understanding of health issues and diet are going to prosper in 1996 almost by themselves. Opportunities to take seminars in these subjects will come and you should take those opportunities. There is also intense devotion to the creative life this year and for many years to come. Every Leo should have creative hobbies, but this year and for many years to come this is even more essential. You are because you can create, and if you do not express this creativity it is as if you are less. There is a diminishment of self-esteem and self-worth. Creative projects with family members are especially important. Not only do they keep domestic life more tranquil but they release repressed emotions in positive ways. Though many of you are less interested in domestic affairs this year you can kill two birds with one stone by making your home (or apartment) into a work of art – through decorating, remodelling or otherwise accessorizing it. Creativity is not limited to music, painting and dance, it can also be expressed in day-to-day life.

Month-by-month Forecasts

January

Best Days Overall: 7th, 8th, 16th, 17th, 18th, 25th, 26th

Most Stressful Days Overall: 1st, 14th, 15th, 21st, 22nd, 27th, 28th

Best Days for Love: 1st, 2nd, 3rd, 10th, 11th, 12th, 13th, 14th, 20th, 21st, 22nd, 23rd, 24th, 28th, 29th

Best Days for Money: 2nd, 3rd, 10th, 11th, 12th, 13th, 19th, 20th, 27th, 28th

You are uncharacteristically putting other people's interests and happiness above your own, and enjoying it. You go out of your way to please employers and lovers. Your social charisma is strong and your social life is unusually active.

Until the 20th focus on achieving work goals, personal book-keeping and exercise and diet regimes. After the 20th give yourself over to your social life.

A 'big-ticket' health item – perhaps an exercise machine – comes to you this month. A co-worker or health professional is the medium through which a happy financial surprise or financial opportunity comes to you.

Mercury, your Money Planet, goes retrograde (backwards) from the 9th to the 30th, and though this produces all kinds of financial delays and signals a need for financial caution it does not stop the sudden financial/material windfall that comes your way. Mercury's retrograde should make you cautious about major investments, purchases or other financial commitments. Use the retrograde period to study investments and evaluate them rather than actually making them.

Money is earned through work this month. The greater your productivity and service, the higher your earnings.

You are unusually creative and original in the way you try to please that special someone in your life. Keep on being creative; it works. If there are love problems they come from too much rather than too little. Singles are dating more and seeing a variety of people.

The Full Moon of the 5th brings not only spiritual and psychological illumination but fabulous wealth ideas as well. Use the day of the Full Moon to meditate and otherwise draw closer to your spiritual source. It has special gifts to bestow this month.

Neither your career nor the family and domestic situation is overly important this month but you might find the period after the 15th a good time to clean house and get rid of excess furniture, possessions and other useless household items. Be more sensitive with family members – especially parents – as they are more easily hurt, more tender in their feelings, after the 15th. Unconscious gestures or slight remarks have unusual consequences.

February

Best Days Overall: 3rd, 4th, 5th, 13th, 14th, 21st, 22nd

LEO

Most Stressful Days Overall: 11th, 12th, 17th, 18th, 23rd, 24th, 25th

Best Days for Love: 1st, 2nd, 8th, 9th, 10th, 13th, 14th, 17th, 18th, 21st, 22nd, 26th, 27th

Best Days for Money: 6th, 7th, 15th, 16th, 17th, 23rd, 24th, 25th, 26th, 27th

With the planets still overwhelmingly concentrated in your western sector this month you are still very much a social creature, caught up in your social whirl and loving every minute of it. This is not a month for Leonine self-assertion and dominance. It is a month for recognizing the majesty in others which you know to be true in yourself. This is the secret of social popularity. Have no fear, your self-esteem is not lowered or diminished though it may feel that way. When the Sun (your Ruling Planet) shines too brightly it obscures much of the grandeur of the universe – one cannot see the Moon and the stars because of its brilliance. But when it starts to set, to weaken in influence, we can see further into the macrocosm. So it is with you, Leo. When you are shining at your peak you tend to dominate the attention of all and sundry. The lesser lights of those around you are obscured. But when your light weakens a bit others get a chance to be recognized. Give your friends a chance to shine this month, and when your light starts to brighten back to its norm it will be all the more welcome – like the start of spring.

Rest and relax more this month. The Solar Cycle is still in its early waxing phase and you will be growing stronger day by day. Still this is not your best month for vitality. Let your partner have his or her way and avoid power struggles in romance. Put others first this month.

After the 19th focus on psychological issues. Explore

addictions, habits and character traits that obstruct you, and break with them. This is a good period to start rehabilitation regimes whether they be mental, emotional or physical. This is also a good month to lose excess weight.

After the 19th work to enhance the income of your partner or lover. Seek investors to your projects or other sources of outside capital if you need them. Your credit line is strong so it is easy both to incur debts and pay them. Money comes to you through your social contacts and the influence of your partner. A sudden financial windfall is likely around the 15th. With Mercury (your Money Planet) now moving forward fast you have great financial confidence and good financial judgement. Investments in transport or communications industries – telephone companies and the like – are likely to bring profits. These industries are stronger now. But do your homework and check out the individual companies.

March

> Best Days Overall: 1st, 2nd, 3rd, 11th, 12th, 19th, 20th, 29th, 30th

> Most Stressful Days Overall: 9th, 10th, 15th, 16th, 22nd, 23rd

> Best Days for Love: 1st, 2nd, 3rd, 6th, 7th, 13th, 14th, 15th, 16th, 22nd, 23rd, 24th, 25th

> Best Days for Money: 4th, 5th, 9th, 10th, 13th, 14th, 17th, 18th, 22nd, 23rd, 29th, 30th

The planets are still westward and above the horizon of your chart, Leo. The trend towards outward achievement continues. You achieve goals through the co-operation of others. You are more dependent on the good graces of others than usual.

Family relations, though not pronounced this month, improve as the month goes along. Personal creativity and relations with children also improve later in the month.

The Sun (your Ruling Planet) shows us your attitude and perspective on life. And since the Sun moves through every Sign of the Zodiac during the course of a year you have – as a rule – a balanced, holistic perspective on life. You see the world from more than just one perspective, or one theory, or one 'ism' – you see world events as a blending of many different forces and urges. But this month – especially until the 20th – you are looking at the dark side of life. The seamy side – death, terrorism, sexual abuse and disease, despair, hatred, serial killers and the like – comes to your attention and you must gain a deeper understanding of these things and their causes. You see the world – and perhaps your personal life and relationships – as a continual struggle for survival. Perhaps you even view history from this angle. But as you go deeper into causes you see that life is a continual process of transformation – of death and rebirth, of renewal from the ashes, of change from one state to another. To grow means, by definition, the death of the old. Death is not the enemy but the friend who liberates us from our past. Thus you gain a deeper understanding of both life and death. But this sombreness – for these are indeed sombre thoughts – does not last long. By the 20th the lessons are learned and you are ready to soar to new heights. You view life now as constant expansion – an infinite growth process. Your view of life and the world becomes more religious and philosophical and you feel that your purpose is constantly to unfold new and greater concepts.

Your health is excellent all month. Your financial confidence is strong and you take financial decisions – about investments, purchases, bank loans – with speed and surety. Your social involvements bring new earning opportunities, and partners are supportive of financial goals. Pay bills and work to reduce long-term debt from the 7th to the 24th. This is also a good period to seek investors for your projects.

April

Best Days Overall: 7th, 8th, 25th, 26th, 27th

Most Stressful Days Overall: 5th, 6th, 11th, 12th, 18th, 19th

Best Days for Love: 1st, 2nd, 3rd, 11th, 12th, 20th, 21st, 30th

Best Days for Money: 1st, 2nd, 3rd, 4th, 7th, 8th, 9th, 10th, 18th, 19th, 20th, 28th, 29th, 30th

Though the world and many of the people around you are agitated by the two eclipses this month, you seem unaffected. In fact you benefit in subtle ways as the changes in pattern create opportunities for you. It is in situations like these that we see the relativity of good and evil – and the truism that one man's meat is another's poison.

Though you should take a reduced schedule during the eclipse periods – April 3rd and 4th and April 16th and 17th – this is not because of any problems they are throwing your way. It is just that others around you may not be up to par – drivers, pilots, teammates and the like. And though your faculties could be sharp you are affected by their distress. Actually your health and vitality are super this month – though not so super on the 16th and 17th.

Opportunities for foreign travel and higher education are opening up this month – but do not fly anywhere during the eclipse periods mentioned above. Try to make it either before or after these periods. Changes in personal philosophy and within your church or religious organization work out well for you. A legal matter is coming to a head this month and it looks good for you.

Be careful of rashness and a tendency towards over-speculation until the 8th. Do not jump into investments or purchases too quickly. Wait until Mercury goes into Taurus on the 8th, when your financial judgement will be more stable and down to earth. Before the 8th you would rather have two birds in the bush than one in the hand. Afterwards you prefer the reverse. Investors should look closely at the real estate, agriculture, beauty and fashion industries.

Before the 8th, while Mercury is in Aries, you are a swashbuckling entrepreneur looking to conquer new markets and take what belongs to you. But after the 8th you are more the 'farmer', planting financial seeds and content to let them flower in due course. Financial conservatism could upset your lover or spouse but this is only temporary. Your love life is basically stable.

May

> Best Days Overall: 5th, 6th, 13th, 14th, 23rd, 24th
>
> Most Stressful Days Overall: 3rd, 4th, 9th, 10th, 15th, 16th, 17th, 30th, 31st
>
> Best Days for Love: 1st, 2nd, 9th, 10th, 18th, 19th, 27th, 28th, 29th
>
> Best Days for Money: 7th, 8th, 15th, 16th, 17th, 25th, 26th

There are various reasons why you should slow down this month, take a reduced schedule and focus on 'the art of the possible'. This is very much a month for 'shifting gears' and re-orientating yourself to new realities.

First off the planets are shifting from the western sector to the eastern sector of your chart – changing your basic focus on life – making you less socially-orientated and more 'me-orientated'. Secondly, 50 to 60 per cent of the planets are retrograde, making others more cautious and careful. Thirdly, 40 to 60 per cent of the planets will be in Earth Signs, making people more cautious still. In addition, this is not one of your best health months. The basic lesson here is the wisdom of inaction, which in its time and place is just as wise as action. Not doing, at times, can further your goals more quickly than leaping into action. It may be hard for a fiery Leo to see this, but it is true.

The pace at work seems to have slowed down but you are nevertheless very career- and money-orientated now. You are making career progress. Educational opportunities that relate to your career and life's work are coming and you should take them. Your employer might even pay for them. Knowledge gained in the past now serves you in good stead. A power struggle involving your life's work goes in your favour, though you might not see the result immediately. A delayed reaction is likely.

Be especially patient in financial matters this month, as Mercury is retrograde from the 3rd to the 27th. Your financial judgement tends to be unrealistic at these times. Avoid signing contracts or making investments or major purchases during this period. Research these things further. Make sure all the questions in your mind are answered. When communicating to people involved in your financial life – whether it be your broker, bank manager, or credit card company – make sure you nail down all the details. Do not assume that they will get the message. Make sure too that you understand what they are really saying. A little caution now can save you a lot of headaches later on.

June

Best Days Overall: 1st, 2nd, 9th, 10th, 19th, 20th, 29th, 30th

Most Stressful Days Overall: 5th, 6th, 12th, 13th, 26th, 27th

Best Days for Love: 5th, 6th, 14th, 15th, 24th, 25th

Best Days for Money: 3rd, 4th, 12th, 13th, 14th, 22nd, 23rd, 24th, 25th

Learn the wisdom of inaction this month and achieve goals through patience. Pushing forward too fast can actually make things worse. Fifty per cent of the planets are still retrograde, and people in general are not ready to make commitments.

Finances, however, are moving forward this month and are much better than they were last month. Mercury (your Money Planet) moves fast forward and enters its own Sign of Gemini on the 15th. Your financial confidence is stronger and earnings are stronger. Until the 15th Mercury is in the Sign of Taurus, making you unnaturally conservative in your spending and investing. You are 'bottom line'-orientated, and like wealth that is tangible. Real estate, agricultural commodities, copper mining and fashion are interesting investments. You spend more on promoting your career, and elders and superiors are favourably disposed to your financial goals. After the 15th you are more the 'trader', able to spot short-term trends and capitalize on them. Intellectual wealth – such as copyrights, patents, and ideas – are also perceived as affluence, though these things are more abstract. Money comes through networking and high-tech investments. Social connections and network marketing also bring profits – but you must be persistent. Your fondest financial wishes are coming to pass this month.

After the 21st you become more altruistic and spiritual. The inner life calls to you; the invisible realms appeal to you. You prefer being the power behind the throne to actually sitting on it.

Your social life is more 'friend-orientated' than romance-orientated. You seem more involved with your peers and equals than with hot romantic attachments. The status of a current relationship is uncertain. Time is the only answer here. Romantic or matrimonial commitments should be avoided for now.

Your health is excellent all month, though you should not rush into a new miracle diet or exercise regime without further research. Study the matter before embarking on it.

Career issues are still on hold. Again, study all proposals thoroughly. Wait for Venus to go direct next month before making any long-term career moves.

July

Best Days Overall: 6th, 7th, 8th, 16th, 17th, 26th, 27th

Most Stressful Days Overall: 2nd, 3rd, 9th, 10th, 24th, 25th, 30th, 31st

Best Days for Love: 2nd, 3rd, 11th, 12th, 21st, 22nd, 30th, 31st

Best Days for Money: 1st, 4th, 5th, 9th, 10th, 14th, 15th, 16th, 19th, 20th, 26th, 27th, 28th, 29th

Well, Leo, you have spent enough time 'people pleasing' this year, now you need to focus on pleasing yourself. With your social life more or less on hold this month you have more freedom to do this. This does not mean that you should start trampling on the rights of others or totally ignoring their needs, only that you should put your own needs first for a while. Remember, if you do not take periods of spiritual and physical refreshment you will have nothing left to give others.

Though your romantic life is problematic, other areas – most notably your career and financial life – are moving forward. Venus (your Career Planet) finally moves forward on the 2nd after two months of backward motion. Past networking efforts pay off now. Social contacts come through for you. Your career judgement is clear and you are in a good position to choose the best of the offers and propositions made to you. It is time to push for that change, promotion or pay-rise. Your worth is recognized.

July will prove to be an excellent financial month. Until the 16th you give generously to charitable causes and are in general working to find the Divine Plan for your financial life. This is a good use of energy for – make no mistake about it – the Divine Plan for your finances is one of prosperity, harmony and success. Getting in touch with this Plan is one of the best things you can do for your 'bottom line'. Pay attention to your dreams this month as they contain uncanny financial guidance. If in doubt as to how to interpret them seek out an astrologer or psychic who can help you. Your financial intuition is very strong until the 16th. If you are in a peaceful state – not anxious, upset or afraid – you can prosper. After the 16th your personal appearance, confidence and poise play their parts in determining your earnings. You need to dress for success, present an image of success, and otherwise create the right first impression.

Your health is excellent all month.

August

Best Days Overall: 3rd, 4th, 12th, 13th, 14th, 22nd, 23rd, 30th, 31st

Most Stressful Days Overall: 5th, 6th, 20th, 21st, 26th, 27th

Best Days for Love: 7th, 10th, 11th, 17th, 20th, 21st, 26th, 27th, 28th, 29th

Best Days for Money: 5th, 6th, 15th, 16th, 24th, 25th, 26th

The trend of last month continues: people around you are experiencing delays and frustrations but your life moves merrily forward. The indecisiveness and confusion in the air creates unique opportunities for someone like you – bold, brash, confident and willing to take a few risks. While others are wavering, you are acting – and powerfully at that. Personal desires are fulfilled now. You get your way in life and people will more or less adapt to you.

Your social life is still on hold, though, so you might as well please yourself and do what you personally enjoy doing. You may find it difficult to please your partner this month as he or she is not sure what is or is not pleasing. You are attractive to the opposite sex but the general atmosphere and vibration calls for caution in love matters.

Your health is excellent all month, your self-esteem high. With the Sun in your own Sign right now you feel your 'true self' – the star that you are and that you were born to be. You shine. You are more dramatic and entertaining than usual. You are regal and lordly and your personal creativity is strong. You are in a party mood.

Your high self-esteem naturally leads to higher earnings this month. Until the 23rd money comes through creative ideas, sales and marketing, technical writing, health, nutrition and telecommunications. Your financial judgement is sound and shrewd. You see the little details that other people miss. Though you are probably spending more this month you nevertheless are an astute and savvy shopper and investor. Interest and dividend income increases after the 26th. Social connections (and your partner) start supporting your financial goals and creating money-making opportunities. You tend to take longer making financial decisions after the 26th than before – as you see too many sides to every issue.

Your career is moving forward this month. You can further it through networking (early in the month) and through charitable and philanthropic activities. Volunteer activities for worthwhile causes attract the eye and the favour of superiors and the 'powers that be'.

September

> Best Days Overall: 9th, 10th, 18th, 19th, 27th, 28th

> Most Stressful Days Overall: 1st, 2nd, 3rd, 16th, 17th, 23rd, 24th, 29th, 30th

> Best Days for Love: 4th, 8th, 9th, 14th, 18th, 19th, 23rd, 24th, 27th, 28th

> Best Days for Money: 1st, 2nd, 4th, 5th, 11th, 12th, 20th, 21st, 29th, 30th

The short-term planets are still in the eastern sector of your horoscope, giving you more initiative, self-confidence and independence – as if you needed any more than you already have! You are having your way and having things as you like them. You shine in financial matters and in the school or lecture hall this month. Your possessions somehow add to your personal glamour. Your assets and balance sheet (or things that you own) are like baubles which ornament your personality. And though you are strong financially now – and will probably end up the month with a net increase in wealth – the retrograde of Mercury (your Money Planet) shows that you need to be more cautious. Avoid signing contracts or making major purchases or investments from the 4th to the 26th. Best to ride on the financial momentum you have created in the past few months rather than launch some new project. The improvements you make in your product and service will pay off later on. Be careful how you communicate to those involved in your financial life – to bank managers, brokers, credit card companies and the like. Take nothing for granted. Get the details in writing. Allow more time for financial projects to develop. Do not over-schedule.

The lunar eclipse of the 26th, which will dramatically affect many people around you, seems rather kind to you. The upheavals you face are more of a spiritual and creative nature. There could be a job change and, if you are an employer, a loss of certain employees. A change in the hierarchy of your church or synagogue is coming. A legal issue must be confronted. Relations with academics are temporarily thrown askew. A child changes his or her lifestyle and redefines his or her personality. A new phase of your creative life is forthcoming.

Your health is excellent all month, but take a reduced schedule on the 26th.

October

> Best Days Overall: 6th, 7th, 16th, 17th, 24th, 25th
>
> Most Stressful Days Overall: 13th, 14th, 20th, 21st, 26th, 27th

LEO

Best Days for Love: 1st, 8th, 9th, 11th, 18th, 19th, 20th, 21st, 27th, 28th, 29th

Best Days for Money: 9th, 10th, 11th, 12th, 18th, 19th, 20th, 21st, 26th, 27th, 31st

Outer ambitions take a back seat this month as the focus is on your home, family and domestic life. Finances, intellectual interests and sales projects are also priorities now – and basically go well.

You Leos know that all the world is a stage and that periodically every actor needs to change his or her costume and role. This month's solar eclipse provides the opportunities for redefining your personality and starting a new act. Every solar eclipse is significant for you, Leo, as the Sun is your Ruling Planet. But the solar eclipse of the 12th is kinder to you than most. It occurs in your 3rd House of Siblings, Intellectual Interests and Communication. Those of you still going to school experience a major change here – either you change schools or subjects, or experience some temporary disruption in your schooling. A temporary disruption occurs in relations with siblings. Hidden flaws in the relationship come to light in order to be corrected. Best to take a reduced schedule on the 10th, 11th, 12th and 13th.

The eclipse affects Jupiter, the planet that rules your creative life. Those of you involved in the creative and performing arts – and many of you are – make major long-term changes in your creativity. Flaws in recent creations or performances are brought to light for correction. Your creative style and philosophy change for the long term. Those of you who have children see them making major life-changing decisions now – redefining who they are and otherwise making long-range decisions about life. The income of your partner is temporarily disrupted. Your partner changes his or her investment philosophy and the way he or she earns money.

Uranus (your Love Planet), which has been going backwards for many months, starts moving forward again this month and receives happy aspects. Singles find that the disruptions caused by the eclipse actually help their love life and create new love opportunities. Marrieds seem more 'in synch' with their partners this month – with little of the conflict of interests seen over the past few months. People involved in your financial life and in your career are helping love along. Your social charisma is generally stronger now.

November

Best Days Overall: 2nd, 3rd, 4th, 12th, 13th, 20th, 21st, 30th

Most Stressful Days Overall: 10th, 11th, 16th, 17th, 23rd, 24th

Best Days for Love: 7th, 8th, 16th, 17th, 25th, 27th, 28th

Best Days for Money: 1st, 5th, 6th, 10th, 11th, 14th, 15th, 20th, 21st, 23rd, 24th, 30th

You are still very much in a period where you seek – and probably find – emotional harmony, domestic tranquillity and the feeling of having a solid home base. Family and family relationships are your highest priority now. You are more nurturing this month and more in need of tender loving care. You excel at giving and receiving emotional support for other people's ambitions and goals. Other people's careers (especially those of family members) come before your own right now.

As you gradually achieve domestic tranquillity you will free up much creative energy to be released later in the month – after the 22nd. This period (after the 22nd) is one of the happiest of your year – a real 'personal pleasure peak'. But you must prepare for it by getting the family and domestic situation straightened out. The New Moon of the 11th is going to show you how.

As the planets start shifting now from the eastern sector of your horoscope to the west – early in the month they are more or less on the border – you will become more socially active. Right now love is complicated as you and the beloved are in conflict – probably over personal desires which are not in synch. Compromise is the key. Your lover is concerned with his or her own personal interests while you are perhaps putting the family ahead of him or her. You want nurturing while your partner or lover wants partnership and commitment. You want emotional support in ways that your partner feels violate balance and fairness. You are more traditional while your partner wants more experimentation. You want to be a couch potato for a while (this is not your true nature) while your partner wants to go out more. You want more physical intimacy while your partner wants more intellectual communion. But these are not serious conflicts and by the 23rd they pass. Singles find love exciting and filled with changes. Fun and games interest you more than serious commitment.

Rest and relax more until the 23rd.

December

Best Days Overall: 1st, 9th, 10th, 18th, 19th, 27th, 28th

Most Stressful Days Overall: 7th, 8th, 13th, 14th, 20th, 21st

Best Days for Love: 5th, 7th, 8th, 13th, 14th, 15th, 16th, 17th, 22nd, 27th, 28th

Best Days for Money: 1st, 2nd, 3rd, 11th,
12th, 20th, 21st, 30th, 31st

Though most people are partying this month you are doing
so more than most – and probably enjoying it more. You are
in one of your best 'personal pleasure periods' of the year.

The planets are still mostly below the horizon (though
this will change by February of 1997), continuing your trend
towards seeking emotional and psychological harmony. You
would rather feel good than be famous and successful.
Success, for you, is defined in terms of how good you feel –
how comfortable you are. So, continue to focus on family
and domestic issues this month. Repairs, redecoration,
rearrangements are helped by the Cosmos. Entertain at
home this month.

Your personal creativity and interest in children are also
at a yearly high. After the 21st these interests will add to
your 'bottom line'. Performers, artists and entertainers
among you will do well during this period.

By the 21st you will be more or less partied out. You
seem more likely to celebrate the holidays by being of practical service to others and by achieving work goals.

Your health is excellent all month. Your self-esteem is
high and you feel comfortable in the general mood of optimism that abounds in the air.

After the 21st you begin a powerful cycle of wealth-
building. Thus spare cash should be 'planted' – invested, put
in high-yielding bank accounts, treasuries, stocks or bonds.
Monies planted after the 21st will tend to grow faster and to
be healthier than if planted before then. Only keep in mind
that Mercury (your Money Planet) goes retrograde on the
23rd – so study your investments carefully and avoid any
financial options that you do not completely understand.
You might want to delay your investments until next month
– also a great 'planting' period – when Mercury goes direct.

LEO

Use this month for studying possible investments. Speculations are favourable all month – but of course do not overdo it. Money is earned easily and in pleasurable ways.

Your love life is happy but you seem more in a party mode than in a romantic mode. You like relationships that are non-committal and pure fun – with no responsibilities or strings attached.

Virgo

♍

THE VIRGIN
Birthdays from
22nd August
to 22nd September

Personality Profile

VIRGO AT A GLANCE

Element – Earth

Ruling Planet – Mercury
   Career Planet – Mercury
   Health Planet – Uranus
   Love Planet – Neptune
   Money Planet – Venus
   Planet of Family and Home Life – Jupiter

Colours – earth tones, ochre, orange, yellow

Colour that promotes love, romance and social harmony – aqua blue

Colour that promotes earning power – jade green

Gems – agate, hyacinth

Metal – quicksilver

Scents – lavender, lilac, lily of the valley, storax

Quality – mutable (= flexibility)

Quality most needed for balance – seeing the big picture

Strongest virtues – mental agility, analytical skills, ability to pay attention to detail, healing powers

Deepest needs – to be useful and productive

Characteristic to avoid – destructive criticism

Signs of greatest overall compatibility – Taurus, Capricorn

Signs of greatest overall incompatibility – Gemini, Sagittarius, Pisces

Sign most helpful to career – Gemini

Sign most helpful for emotional support – Sagittarius

Sign most helpful financially – Libra

Sign best for marriage and/or partnerships – Pisces

Sign most helpful for creative projects – Capricorn

Best Sign to have fun with – Capricorn

Signs most helpful in spiritual matters – Taurus, Leo

Best day of the week – Wednesday

Understanding the Virgo Personality

The virgin is a particularly fitting symbol for those people born under the Sign of Virgo. If you meditate on the image of the virgin you will get a good understanding of the essence of the Virgo type. The virgin, of course, is a symbol of purity and innocence – not naïve, but pure. A virginal object has not been touched. A virgin field is land that is true to itself, the way it has always been. The same is true of virgin forest: it is pristine, unaltered.

Apply the idea of purity to the thought processes, emotional life, physical body and activities and projects of the everyday world, and you can see how Virgos approach life. Virgos desire the pure expression of the ideal in their mind, body and affairs. If they find impurities they will attempt to clear them away.

Impurities are the beginning of disorder, unhappiness and uneasiness. The job of the Virgo is to eject all impurities and keep only that which the body and mind can use and assimilate.

The secrets of good health are here revealed: 90 per cent of the art of staying well is maintaining a pure mind, a pure body and pure emotions. When you introduce more impurities than your mind and body can deal with, you will have what is known as 'dis-ease'. It is no wonder that Virgos make great doctors, nurses, healers and dietitians. They have an innate understanding of good health and they realize that good health is more than just physical. In all aspects of life, if you want a project to be successful it must be kept as pure as possible. It must be protected against the adverse elements that will try to undermine it. This is the secret behind Virgo's awesome technical proficiency.

One could talk about Virgo's analytical powers – which are substantial. One could talk about their perfectionism and their almost superhuman attention to detail. But this would be to miss the point. All of these virtues are manifestations of a Virgo's desire for purity and perfection – a world without Virgos would have ruined itself long ago.

A vice is nothing more than a virtue turned inside out, a virtue that is misapplied or used in the wrong context. Virgos' apparent vices come from their inherent virtue. Their analytical powers, which should be used for healing, helping or perfecting a project in the world sometimes get misapplied and turned against people. Their critical faculties, which should be used constructively to perfect a strategy or proposal, can sometimes be used destructively to harm or wound. Their urge to perfection can become worry and lack of confidence; their natural humility can become self-denial and self-abasement. When Virgos turn negative they are apt to turn their devastating criticism on themselves, sowing the seeds of self-destruction.

Finance

Virgos have all the attitudes that create wealth. They are hard-working, industrious, efficient, organized, thrifty, productive and eager to serve. A developed Virgo is every employer's dream. But until Virgos master some of the social graces of Libra they will not even come close to fulfilling their financial potential. Purity and perfectionism, if not handled correctly or gracefully, can be very trying to others. Friction in human relationships can be devastating not only to your pet projects but – indirectly – to your wallet as well.

Virgos are quite interested in their financial security. Being hard-working, they know the true value of money. They do not like to take risks with their money, preferring to save for their retirement or for a rainy day. Virgos usually make prudent, calculated investments that involve a minimum of risk. These investments and savings usually work out well, helping Virgos achieve the financial security they seek. The rich or even not so rich Virgos also like to help their friends in need.

Career and Public Image

Virgos reach their full potential when they can communicate their knowledge in such a way that others can understand it. In order to get their ideas across better, Virgos need to develop greater verbal skills and more non-judgemental ways of expressing themselves. Virgos look up to teachers and communicators; they like their bosses to be good communicators. Virgos will probably not respect a superior who is not their intellectual equal – no matter how much money or power that superior has. Virgos themselves like to be perceived by others as being educated and intellectual.

The natural humility of Virgos often inhibits them from fulfilling their great ambitions, from acquiring name and fame. Virgos should indulge in a little more self-promotion if they are going to reach their career goals. They need to push themselves with the same ardour that they would use to foster others.

At work Virgos like to stay active. They are willing to learn any type of job as long as it serves their ultimate goal of financial security. Virgos may change several occupations during their professional lives, until they find the one they really enjoy. Virgos work well with other people, are not afraid to work hard and always fulfil their responsibilities.

Love and Relationships

If you are an analyser or a critic you must, out of necessity, narrow your scope. You have to focus on a part and not the whole; this can create a temporary narrow-mindedness. Virgos do not like this kind of person. They like their partners to be broad-minded, with depth and vision. Virgos seek to get this broad-minded quality from their partners since they sometimes lack it themselves.

Virgos are perfectionists in love just as they are in other

areas of life. They need partners who are tolerant, open-minded and easy-going. If you are in love with a Virgo do not waste time on impractical romantic gestures. Do practical and useful things for him or her – this is what will be appreciated and what will be done for you.

Virgos express their love through pragmatic and useful gestures, so do not be put off because your Virgo partner does not say 'I love you' day-in and day-out. Virgos are not that type. If they love you, they will demonstrate it in practical ways. They will always be there for you; they will show an interest in your health and finances; they will fix your sink or repair your radio. Virgos deem these actions to be superior to sending flowers, chocolates or St Valentine's Day cards.

In love affairs Virgos are not particularly passionate or spontaneous. If you are in love with a Virgo, do not take this personally. It does not mean that you are not alluring enough or that your Virgo partner does not love or like you. It is just the way Virgos are. What they lack in passion they make up for in dedication and loyalty.

Home and Domestic Life

It goes without saying that the home of a Virgo will be spotless, sanitized and orderly. Everything will be in its right place – and do not you dare move anything around! For Virgos to find domestic bliss, however, they need to ease up a bit in the home, to allow their partner and kids more freedom and to be more generous and open-minded. Family members are not to be analysed under a microscope, they are individuals with their own virtues to express.

With these small difficulties resolved, Virgos like to stay in and entertain at home. They make good hosts and they like to keep their friends and families happy and entertained at family and social gatherings. Virgos love children, but they are strict with them – at times – since they want to make sure their children are brought up with the right sense of family and values.

Horoscope for 1996

Major Trends

Last year was more stressful than you have been used to, Virgo. It was a serious year filled with challenges and obstructions to be overcome. You were involved in delicate balancing acts almost all year. But 1996 is shaping up to be much happier and much less grim. There is no question that you will have more fun, be more creative and in general enjoy life more in 1996.

The first improvement comes – and you will feel it almost immediately – on 3rd January as Jupiter moves from Sagittarius into Capricorn and into harmonious aspects to you. The second improvement comes in April when Saturn – which has been troubling you for two years now – moves out of Pisces and into Aries. When this happens you will feel as if the weight of the world has just been lifted from your shoulders. Vague, formless fears, insecurities, worries and anxieties just melt away. The strength that you gained in the past two years through wrestling with various obstructions has now made you healthier and more resilient.

Yet 1996 is not all fun and games. Saturn's move into Aries, your 8th Solar House, is going to affect your love life, sexual attitudes, debts and deep psychological issues. Fears and insecurities are not merely 'handled' this year, but totally eliminated. And you alone will forge the tools by which this is done.

Health

Health is always important to you, Virgo, even when your 6th House is not active. Yet this year it is even more important as Uranus (your Health Planet) moves into its own domain – the House of Health.

First off, your health is vastly improved over last year. Jupiter moves into a harmonious alignment and Saturn moves away from a stressful alignment. This will have immediate effects on your overall health and vitality, which will increase sharply. Health problems which might have been plaguing some of you for the past two years will disappear mysteriously. Fears of health problems (which tend to afflict Virgos more than most) also diminish considerably. And you will learn a big lesson about health: energy levels are key. You might never have had a health problem *per se* – only a lack of energy. When your energy is restored – as it will be in 1996 – the so-called health problems will disappear. The relationship between overall vitality and health is not yet adequately understood by modern medicine. This surge in life-force is similar to getting a huge financial windfall. You can spend it as you like. You can use it to further enhance your vitality – invest it in yourself – or to achieve financial or career goals, or in your creative life. The idea is to invest it wisely.

Uranus has been highly stimulated for many years now. This has led to tremendous experimentation and exploration on your part regarding health, healing techniques and your attitudes towards health. It is as if you have been rewriting the book on health. This experimentation not only continues in 1996 but probably accelerates. Thus, many of the trends of last year are going to continue. So how is this likely to manifest? Some of you will be trying out every new dietary, vitamin or nutritional supplement fad that comes out. You may find your cupboard stacked deep with little bottles and vials of vitamins, minerals, pills, potions, supplements, elixirs and what have you. Others will be going from one 'miracle doctor' to another – in search for the perfect cure, the magic potion, perfect health. No avenue will be ignored. There will be visits to shamans, spiritual healers, metaphysical practitioners, polarity therapists and other alternative healers too numerous to mention. Others among you will explore the high-tech side of orthodox medicine – the newer and more untried these techniques are, the more they attract you. At the root of all this is your basic feeling that health care and health practices need to be radically changed. The old does not work and you feel you must search for the new. But out of all this will come, in time, a totally new attitude towards health and healing. This is the positive side. Sometimes one method will work and sometimes not. This will force you to think and meditate, leading you to personal answers. However, just to save you a lot of time, energy and money as you experiment, keep this guiding principle in mind: Therapies that increase, enhance or unblock the life-force are safe to experiment with; therapies that diminish or weaken it should be avoided. Learn the mysteries of the life-force and you automatically learn the mysteries of health.

The health of a sibling (and your spouse or partner) will also improve dramatically in 1996 – especially after April.

Home and Domestic Life

The home, family, and domestic situation overall was very important last year and continues to be important this year. Many of you either moved, enlarged your present home, or bought additional homes in 1995. Many of you saw your family circle expand, either through marriages or new births. And though further moves or house sales are likely in 1996, the focus is a bit different. Rather than seeking to enlarge the family circle you are intent on reducing it – keeping contact with clan members who really count in your life and letting go of others. There is an emotional distance from certain family members – most likely your parents. Many of you feel that you need to break through the feeling of control that the family has over you and stand on your own two feet. Undesirable family connections are breaking down this year. The feeling of being in bondage to your family is intensified. There is a tremendous focus on psychological purity and transformation this year and for many years to come. You want to transform totally your psychological roots and home base. You give – and need to get – total psychological support for your activities, and those who cannot or will not supply this must go. You are loyal to family members who are loyal to you, but vindictive to those who are not 100 per cent on your side. Those of you undergoing some psychological-type therapies will make great progress and gain much new insight in 1996.

On a more mundane level you are seeking to transform your present home – to renovate and redo it in a very deep way. Cosmetic changes in the home do not satisfy you. You will not be satisfied with moving some furniture from one room to another or shifting the paintings from one wall to another. No, you want to rip out the walls entirely and reshape the whole structure of the house. You want to rip out the pipes and the wires – and especially the plumbing – and create something totally new and improved. Those of you who own your home will probably be involved in these kinds of activities. Those of you who rent will find that your landlord will be engaging in these kinds of things.

One of your parents is in the process of redefining his or her personality this year. His or her personal image is being redefined, and do not be surprised if your parent considers cosmetic surgery this year. Relations with a sibling will improve after April.

You Virgos who are married and of childbearing age are

likely to have a child or to become pregnant this year. Those of you who already have children are enjoying them more and they are the source of much good news.

Love and Social Life

Over the past two years your love and social life was more restricted and limited than usual. For some of you it was restricted because of a marriage – there was no longer a need to go gallivanting around. You felt a sense of duty towards your beloved. For others, the restriction came because of a desire to test prospective lovers and to weed out the good from the bad. You may not have married but you were more choosy and quality conscious. This trend is just about over and by April your love life will become freer and less burdensome.

If your marriage has survived the past two years it will probably survive over the long term now. You are unlikely to face the trials and tests of the past two years for some time to come.

For singles – those who have never been married – a marriage or serious relationship is very much on the cards in 1996 – probably later in the year. Those who are already married will find more romance within their marriage and make new long-term friends. Romantic opportunities come at parties, family gatherings, introductions that come through the family, at resorts, nightclubs and places of entertainment. That special someone is highly educated, cultured, refined and perhaps a bit mystical. There is a high spiritual tone to this new relationship and there will be a feeling that you have known this person for a long time. In some cases you will indeed have known him or her in the past, as it seems that this person is a former lover, or someone you knew in childhood. In other cases you have been in actual telepathic contact for a long time before actually meeting. In all cases there will be a strong past-life connection and a feeling of truly having met a 'soul-mate'. Enjoy.

Singles who have been married once before also have an expanded social life this year, but marriage is not especially on the cards. It does not seem that important to you, for one thing. For another, you enjoy playing the field as romantic opportunities are plentiful.

The social life of a sibling is more restricted this year. This could happen as a result of a marriage – which curtails his or her social life – or because of excessive discrimination. Your sibling wants nothing short of long-term, enduring and committed love.

The marriage of your parents (or one of your parents) is stormy and undergoes radical change – even to the point where survival of the relationship becomes questionable.

Though the self-esteem of children is very high this year, for those of you who have children of marriageable age, marriage is not yet on the cards. There is much personal pleasure and self-indulgence but no special cosmic push one way or another. Romance is most likely to bloom in the summer of 1996.

Career and Finance

There is no question that the search for emotional harmony and tranquillity – though tough to come by – is more important in 1996 than career or money matters. This is not to say that you will not earn money or that you will not advance in your career – you will. But it is not your big focus now.

Jupiter is now in beautiful aspect to you throughout 1996. Your wealth, self-esteem and recognition will increase very naturally and with very little effort on your part. You catch the lucky breaks. You are in the right place at the right time and you prosper while having fun. Speculations are favourable for you this year – but much better before April than afterwards. You will travel this year, for pleasure not for business. The sale of your home (or one of your homes) brings unexpected profits. Other real estate speculations are favourable as well. Though by nature you are not really a speculator – nothing like a Leo or Sagittarius – this year you are more so. Yet you know how to control your risks. Investment in real estate or in mutual funds that invest in real estate may be a source of profit this year.

Venus is your Money Planet, Virgo. Since this planet moves through the Zodiac quite rapidly you tend to have a multi-faceted, adaptable approach to money-making – at one time making it from one area and at another time from another. This year Venus makes an unusually long station in the Sign of Gemini for four months – from 3rd April to 7th August. This calls attention to the fact that sales, marketing and media activities will be very import- ant to your 'bottom line' during these months. Those of you who are investors will probably invest in media, com- munications or transport companies. Your investment philosophy will be that of the 'trader' rather than the long- term investor.

The income of your spouse or partner seems more restricted this year and there is a need for budgeting, cost- cutting and general control of expenses and spending. There is, in actuality, enough for every need, but not enough to waste. Your partner needs better financial management and a more long-term view of finances this year.

Monies due to you from an estate or insurance claim are delayed – you will get what you should but not straight away. Be careful of debt. The credit line is tighter this year. Potential investors in your projects or plans are very cau- tious and unusually suspicious. You can win them over but it takes a lot of work and research. The problem is that while you are seeing the best-case scenario they are con- cerned with the worst-case scenario.

Self-improvement

Your health will improve quite naturally this year – though you attribute the improvement to one miracle cure or another. As mentioned earlier the real cure is the extra life-force available to you. The real place to focus your energies is on the psychological level. This is a year – especially after April – during which you need to focus on emotional and physical habit-patterns that keep you from being who you are and who you want to be. It is a year for looking at your thoughts and feelings as if you were a businessperson, determining which of these habits is profitable and which unprofitable. Once this is discerned you can foster the patterns that bring you happiness and eliminate the ones that cause pain or self-deprecation. This is not an easy task – and you might need the help of a therapist – but it is called for now. You can re-invent yourself and you will be given the tools to do it.

Month-by-month Forecasts

January

Best Days Overall: 1st, 10th, 11th, 19th, 20th, 27th, 28th

Most Stressful Days Overall: 2nd, 3rd, 16th, 17th, 18th, 23rd, 24th, 29th, 30th, 31st

Best Days for Love: 1st, 2nd, 3rd, 10th, 11th, 12th, 13th, 14th, 15th, 19th, 20th, 23rd, 24th, 27th, 28th

Best Days for Money: 2nd, 3rd, 10th, 11th,
12th, 13th, 14th, 19th, 20th, 23rd, 24th,
27th, 28th

This is a fabulously happy and healthy month, Virgo –
enjoy. Your health and vitality are super all month – but
especially until the 20th. You have got all the energy you
need – and some to spare – to achieve any goal you go after.

With 90 to 100 per cent of the planets in your western
hemisphere you are 'other-orientated', putting your social
life and other people's needs ahead of your own personal
interests. Your love life, which has been bittersweet and
perhaps restricted of late, sweetens after the 15th. The 15th
is a good date to remember, especially if you are single. A
special someone is about to come into your life, someone
tender and sensitive. Over-criticalness could definitely nip
this in the bud, so be careful. The New Moon of the 20th
occurs pretty close to Neptune (your Love Planet) and will
thus clarify a current relationship and your love life in general. You are idealistic and altruistic in love now. You want
love that comes from a higher, spiritual source – sanctioned
by the Divine. This is coming.

Early in the month let yourself have some fun. Do not
worry overmuch about work and responsibilities. You have
plenty of time to handle these things after the 20th.

People all around you – especially at the beginning of the
month – are probably pessimistic and sombre – but not you.
You play the unusual role of cheering them up.

Mercury (your Ruling Planet) goes retrograde from the
9th to the 30th, but this has less effect on you than usual.
True you have less power to assert yourself, but you have
no need to either. And your health is so good that not even
a Mercury retrograde can reduce your spirits.

Early in the month money comes through your work and
your service. Later on it comes through social connections

and partners. You are a very lucky speculator this month. The 5th, 6th and 7th bring happy financial surprises – either through a speculation or a creative project. Wealth in general increases by the end of the month.

February

> Best Days Overall: 6th, 7th, 15th, 16th, 23rd, 24th, 25th
>
> Most Stressful Days Overall: 13th, 14th, 19th, 20th, 26th, 27th
>
> Best Days for Love: 1st, 2nd, 6th, 7th, 13th, 14th, 16th, 19th, 20th, 21st, 22nd, 24th, 25th
>
> Best Days for Money: 1st, 2nd, 6th, 7th, 8th, 9th, 10th, 13th, 14th, 15th, 16th, 21st, 22nd, 23rd, 24th, 25th

With the planets still overwhelmingly in the western half of your horoscope you are still very much a social creature, adapting to events rather than creating them and attaining your goals through the good graces of others. This is a month to train, refine and hone your social graces.

Generally a person who pays attention to health issues, this month you are overly so. Though your vitality is not what it should be – or will be – you need not have any fears about health matters. Rest and relax more and in general maximize your physical energy. Wear the colours, gems and scents of your Sign. Visits to a chiropractor or masseuse will help as well. Meditating on the Divine Body – created in the image and likeness of the Divine – will strengthen you mentally and affect your body in an indirect way. The New Moon of the 18th will clarify health issues for you and show you more precisely what is needed.

Your love life is active and happy. Someone you just met and perhaps passed over might be worth a second look from the 10th to the 13th. Part of the reason you want to get your body and health in order is to enhance your romantic and social prospects. Singles are ardently seeking romance. It comes at parties and places of entertainment. Serious, long-term romantic prospects are coming into your life. Be careful of coming on too strong or jumping into something prematurely. Rebellious Virgos could even elope this month.

Married couples are doing more socializing this month and generally having more fun. There is more romance in your marriage than there has been of late.

Your earning power is stronger before the 9th than afterwards. Until the 9th there is a long-term conservative approach to investments. Your financial intuition is keen – almost mystical. You have a knack for picking investments that are profitable over the long haul. You are speculative but in a very conservative and calculated way. After the 9th you are more rash and reckless. Your outlook changes from long-term good to short-term profits. You want to make money quickly. You are a greater risk-taker. This is safe if you indulge these urges with a small percentage of your money. Your financial judgement will stabilize again next month.

March

Best Days Overall: 4th, 5th, 13th, 14th, 22nd, 23rd

Most Stressful Days Overall: 11th, 12th, 17th, 18th, 24th, 25th

VIRGO

Best Days for Love: 1st, 2nd, 3rd, 4th, 5th, 13th, 14th, 17th, 18th, 22nd, 23rd

Best Days for Money: 1st, 2nd, 3rd, 4th, 5th, 6th, 7th, 8th, 13th, 14th, 22nd, 23rd

The planetary concentration is still very much westward this month, thus your focus continues to be on your social life, obtaining the good graces of other people and refining your social skills. With Mercury (your Ruling Planet) in your 7th House of Love and Marriage for most of the month, your view of life is even more social than mentioned above. You see life, history, world events, politics and economics in terms of love and relationships. You see the way that romance can actually shape world events, creating or destroying fortunes and empires, making or breaking kings. It is vital that other people like you and see you in a sympathetic perspective. Yes, you are very Libra-like this month. Unsurprisingly, your love life is good now and very active. A current relationship improves because you are willing to go out of your way to please your partner. You put his or her interests above your own. Singles are likely to meet marriageable prospects now – quality prospects.

Venus (your Money Planet) moves into her own Sign of Taurus on the 6th, increasing your earning abilities and enhancing your 'bottom line'. Real estate investment or divestment opportunities come to you. Your financial judgement is conservative, stable and sound. You are more interested in physical, tangible wealth than in symbols of wealth – such as options to buy or sell futures, or the purchase of other people's debt. Complex, esoteric investment vehicles leave you cold. You want wealth that you can feel and touch – cash, jewellery, land, possessions. Your investment philosophy is more of the 'having-and-holding' sort rather than the 'trading-speculating' sort. You look for high-quality investments and are willing to pay a fair price for them. What you buy now is likely to maintain – or even increase – its value over time. In spite of your 'down to earthness', do not ignore global investments.

Your health is still delicate until the 20th. Rest and relax more and pace yourself. Vitality improves after the 20th.

April

Best Days Overall: 1st, 2nd, 9th, 10th, 18th, 19th, 28th, 29th

Most Stressful Days Overall: 7th, 8th, 13th, 14th, 20th, 21st

Best Days for Love: 1st, 2nd, 3rd, 9th, 10th, 11th, 12th, 13th, 14th, 19th, 20th, 21st, 29th, 30th

Best Days for Money: 1st, 2nd, 3rd, 4th, 9th, 10th, 11th, 12th, 18th, 19th, 20th, 21st, 29th, 30th

The two eclipses this month do not affect you as deeply or radically as they do others. They do affect your financial life and investments – both your own and those of your spouse. Financial weaknesses and vulnerabilities are revealed so you can do something about them. Flaws in present investments or in your investment philosophy are starkly revealed and you must confront it. These will bring about long-term changes in both philosophy and investments – good changes.

Earnings come from work, from your career status, superiors and parents. Government bonds or government-backed securities are attractive now. Your overall earning power – in spite of the two eclipses – remains good. Discuss financial problems with superiors or parents – they have ideas and solutions for you. For most of the month investors can do well by trading on short-term market fluctuations. Having and holding for the long term is not interesting right now. Your ability to track short-term trends is particularly good now.

Your career, which you have been neglecting of late, improves this month. Superiors and women further your career aspirations.

Your partner's finances seem confused – but very active. Your partner works hard to achieve financial goals, but wavers between conflicting financial influences. On the one hand your partner needs to be more conservative and take a long-range perspective on purchases and investments. Yet, because the Sun and Mars move through his or her Money House, there are undue urges to speculate and make quick profits. Let your partner speculate with a small percentage of his or her money. The bulk should be invested with minimum risk. You are very much involved in enhancing the income of your spouse or partner.

After the 8th accept the travel and education opportunities that come to you. Only do not make long trips during the period of the eclipses – the 4th, 5th, 16th and 17th.

Your love life continues to be good – active and happy. Physical intimacy is more important to you than courtship now.

Though your health and vitality are improving this month a hidden health problem could reveal itself in order that you may deal with it. It does not seem long term. A job change is likely – either within the same company or with another one.

May

Best Days Overall: 7th, 8th, 15th, 16th, 17th, 25th, 26th

Most Stressful Days Overall: 5th, 6th, 11th, 12th, 18th, 19th

Best Days for Love: 1st, 2nd, 8th, 9th, 10th,
11th, 12th, 16th, 17th, 18th, 19th, 25th,
26th, 27th, 28th, 29th

Best Days for Money: 1st, 2nd, 7th, 8th, 9th,
10th, 15th, 16th, 17th, 18th, 19th, 25th,
26th, 27th, 28th, 29th

Though you are in an excellent health period early in the month, try to avoid over-assertion and power struggles as Mercury (your Ruler) – along with 40 to 50 per cent of the other planets – goes retrograde now. Be patient with yourself. Those of you who have health problems *are* getting better though you seem to go backwards – healing is happening behind the scenes. Those of you without health problems are not getting sick this month, though your anxiety level is high. It is only the retrograde motion of the planets that are causing these feelings. After the 20th you should rest and relax more as your vitality is temporarily low. Focus on priorities and plan personal goals. More inner activity, less outer activity is called for.

Having said all of the above, this is still a prosperous period – especially before the 20th. Try to make financial moves, commitments and purchases before then and be prepared for fluctuations and temporary setbacks with them after the 20th. If you have chosen wisely – and it looks like you have – your investments will ride out the temporary slowdown. Set aside some of your extra earnings from before the 20th for afterwards. After the 20th Venus (your Money Planet) goes retrograde (quite a rare occurrence) and your financial judgement becomes unrealistic. This is the time to evaluate and review investments, financial strategies, spending and budgetary concerns – not a time to execute financial plans. You need to collect as much data as possible now so as to be ready to make moves in the future.

Your love life is bittersweet. On the one hand your social

charisma is good, on the other both you and your beloved are not sure about what you want in love and where your relationship is going. Neither marriages nor divorces should not be scheduled now. When in doubt, do nothing – make no changes.

After the 20th you are career-focused and there is much career progress going on, but behind the scenes. You will see the results later on – perhaps in a few months. Re-evaluate career goals now. Push forward gently and allow superiors time to think. An astrologer or psychic reader has important information for you.

June

Best Days Overall: 3rd, 4th, 12th, 13th, 22nd, 23rd

Most Stressful Days Overall: 1st, 2nd, 7th, 8th, 14th, 15th, 29th, 30th

Best Days for Love: 3rd, 4th, 5th, 6th, 7th, 8th, 12th, 13th, 14th, 15th, 22nd, 23rd, 24th, 25th

Best Days for Money: 3rd, 4th, 5th, 6th, 12th, 13th, 14th, 15th, 22nd, 23rd, 24th, 25th, 26th, 27th

The long-term, slow-moving planets are mostly below the horizon of your chart, while the short-term, fast-moving ones are above it. Thus, over the long term your main goal is the achievement of emotional harmony and psychological ease; for now, in the short term – for the next few months – you are more ambitious and getting your 'outer-career' life in order. With Mercury now moving fast forward and entering your Career House on the 15th, great progress is made.

You get your way in your career. Go ahead and ask for that pay-rise or promotion. Promote yourself now. A power struggle goes in your favour. Hard work is rewarded. The New Moon of the 15th is also helping your ambitions by bringing clarity and illumination to your situation. As the Moon goes through the Zodiac this month it will be giving you career advice – through her human and non-human channels – on very specific issues such as which friends can help your career (16th, 17th and 18th), how to work spiritually to improve your career (19th and 20th), how to dress and present yourself to further your ambitions (22nd and 23rd), how to spend, and on what to spend in order to further your career (24th and 25th). By the time the Moon has made its complete cycle you will have guidance on every aspect of your career. (When it starts to wane it will show you what you need to get rid of in order to further your ambitions – this is just as important as the positive actions you are called to take.)

One of the dangers this month is in identifying yourself with your public persona. True, you will only do this briefly, but you are more than your public persona or status within the workplace.

Though your self-esteem is much higher now than it was last month and your self-confidence is stronger, you still need to rest and relax more until the 21st. Do what you need to do for your career, but know when to rest as well. Never allow yourself to get over-tired.

Love is very much on hold now. Forcing issues with a current love or with someone new will probably make matters worse. Time and patience will resolve all difficulties.

July

Best Days Overall: 1st, 9th, 10th, 19th, 20th, 28th, 29th

VIRGO

Though many of the people around you – most notably family members, parents and your spouse or partner – are experiencing delays and frustrations, you are moving forward this month. Every day that goes by brings increased personal power, confidence and independence. You are more and more in charge of your life, more in a position to create conditions and circumstances and to please yourself in general.

Your career moves forward now. And, if you can find that delicate balance between family obligations and career duties, even greater progress will be made. You cannot completely ignore your home base, but neither can you let your career opportunities pass you by. Alternate between one and the other. This is the month to ask for that pay-rise or to join your company's stock purchase plan. Elders and superiors are supporting your financial goals and creating financial opportunities. One parent prospers this month while the other is experiencing financial difficulties (temporarily).

There is great power in your 11th House this month. Thus you are involved in group activities and friendships rather than romance. The friends you make now are related to your career and are supportive of your career. Again you need to assuage the negative feelings of family members towards some of your friends. Family members are not too keen on some of your political activities, either.

The 11th House is where 'fondest hopes and wishes' come true. In other words, it is the House of Happiness. Not just fun, games and pleasure, but true and lasting happiness. Thus opportunities for lasting happiness are coming to you now. And this is a good month in which to think about the things that would bring true happiness to you. You need a mental image before things can happen for you.

Though your health is excellent all month there is still a need to study and evaluate any and all 'miracle' diets or pills very carefully. Do not embark on any of these programmes until you have a thorough understanding of them.

August

Best Days Overall: 5th, 6th, 15th, 16th, 24th, 25th

Most Stressful Days Overall: 1st, 2nd, 7th, 8th, 9th, 22nd, 23rd, 28th, 29th

Best Days for Love: 1st, 2nd, 6th, 10th, 11th, 15th, 16th, 20th, 21st, 24th, 25th, 28th, 29th

Best Days for Money: 5th, 6th, 10th, 11th, 15th, 16th, 17th, 18th, 19th, 20th, 21st, 24th, 25th, 28th, 29th

Though there are still many planets in retrograde this month your life continues to move forward in most areas. The short-term planets are moving ever more eastward, making you more independent, self-assertive and powerful in creating conditions for happiness.

Your 12th House of Spiritual Wisdom and Philanthropic Activities is powerful now. This is the month to see gurus, to attend meditation classes and to consult with astrologers and psychics. You shine in spiritual activities this month. Your worth is recognized in religious organizations to which you belong and in the invisible realms. The inner kingdoms are very near, the doorways to heaven are wide open (they are always open but especially so now), and spiritual illumination is yours if you want it.

Your health, vitality and self-esteem are strong this month. You get your way in life – in spite of the fact that many others around you are experiencing delays and frustrations. You excel at sports and exercise regimes. You are fulfilling your sensual and sexual fantasies. Personal pleasures are abundant and, if you were not a Virgo, you might have to be warned about taking things to extremes.

Though you are unusually attractive to the opposite sex now your love life is still not what it should be, has been or will be. Your Love Planet (Neptune) is still retrograde and serious love – committed love – needs careful thought. What you think you want (or do not want) now may not be realistic and is sure to change when Neptune starts moving forward in a month or so. Proceed cautiously in love, but have fun. Take a light-hearted approach to it. Schedule neither a marriage nor a divorce right now. Take your pleasure where you find it. Work on making yourself the lovable person that you want to be and were meant to be.

After the 23rd, people in general become more health- and diet-conscious and thus your knowledge of and skills in these matters are more in demand. You are more appreciated by others now.

Overspending on your home or family can put a dent in your 'bottom line' after the 7th. Spend, but in moderation. Intuition is showing you how to make fondest your financial hopes and wishes come true. Friends are supporting your financial goals and creating opportunities.

September

Best Days Overall: 1st, 2nd, 3rd, 11th, 12th, 20th, 21st, 29th, 30th

Most Stressful Days Overall: 4th, 5th, 18th, 19th, 25th, 26th

Best Days for Love: 2nd, 3rd, 8th, 9th, 12th, 18th, 19th, 20th, 21st, 25th, 26th, 27th, 28th, 30th

Best Days for Money: 1st, 2nd, 8th, 9th, 11th, 12th, 14th, 15th, 18th, 19th, 20th, 21st, 27th, 28th, 29th, 30th

The short-term planets are all in the eastern sector of your horoscope, making you strong, self-assertive and independent. You have all the power to create conditions as you like them. Under normal circumstances you could carry on as you wished – but the retrograde of Mercury (your Ruling Planet) counsels caution. Spend more time thinking about the conditions you want to create before you go about creating them. Your personal judgement on these things might not be realistic, and when Mercury goes direct you might have to undo what you have done. Create but do so cautiously and with much forethought. Let the New Moon of the 12th bring you guidance.

The retrograde of Mercury also signals caution in career matters. Avoid making major career changes one way or the other right now – especially from the 4th to the 26th. Study all proposals thoroughly. Things are not what they seem. When in doubt, do nothing.

Your personal energy and charisma are unusually strong. Personal pleasures and fantasies are fulfilled. Your financial judgement is sound and, by the end of the month, there is a net increase in wealth. A short-term medical or health expense (perhaps for some pills or paraphernalia) causes some concern, but by the end of the month this has no effect on your overall wealth. Until the 7th build wealth through networking and through the help of friends. Some of your fondest financial dreams are coming true this month and – when they do – you will immediately formulate a set of 'new fondest hopes and wishes'. This is in the nature of things. After the 7th your financial judgement becomes more intuitive and – if you can overcome your inherently down-to-earth nature and follow your intuition – you will prosper. Astrologers and psychics can provide you with good financial guidance after the 7th. You increase your charitable giving and find that you prosper more than before. For those of you who are still unclear about the Divine Financial Plan of their lives, this is a good month to find out about it.

The lunar eclipse of the 26th is basically kind to you. It brings with it a move or domestic reorganization. Flaws in your current home are revealed and you are forced to correct them. A parent is likely to move or change his or her residence. Your partner's income suffers a temporary setback. A child changes his or her lifestyle and starts redefining his or her personality. Character flaws (we all have them) and habits that are holding you back come to the surface for purgation.

October

Best Days Overall: 9th, 10th, 18th, 19th, 26th, 27th

Most Stressful Days Overall: 1st, 2nd, 16th, 17th, 22nd, 23rd, 29th, 30th

Best Days for Love: 8th, 9th, 10th, 18th, 19th, 22nd, 23rd, 27th, 28th

Best Days for Money: 8th, 9th, 10th, 11th,
12th, 18th, 19th, 26th, 27th, 28th

This is an active, tumultuous month, but ultimately success-ful. Ninety per cent of the planets are moving forward by the end of the month, signifying action, achievement and progress. Mercury (your Ruler) moves forward speedily, showing that you have confidence and get things done quickly. The planets are still congregated in the eastern sec-tor of your chart, giving you energy, initiative and indepen-dence. You are very much in charge now and have things your way. Push ahead boldly. Disruptions caused by the solar eclipse of the 12th create opportunities for you. Satisfy yourself now and you find that others are also satisfied. They want for you what you want for yourself.

The eclipse of the 12th occurs in your 2nd House of Money, showing long-term changes in your financial life and in your investment strategy and philosophy. Flaws in spending habits or with a cherished possession (perhaps an investment) are revealed now so that they can be corrected. Do not look at these flaws as problems or punishments or bad luck – they are only aids to improvement – they were always there only you did not recognize them. Your financial intuition should be scrutinized this month – make sure you are getting the right message. Finances are your top priority this month. In spite of the temporary upheavals there is a net increase in wealth. The eclipse makes you re-evaluate contributions to a certain charity. Perhaps you now start giving to different ones.

Your love life is changing and for the better. Your Love Planet (Neptune) starts moving forward after many months of backward motion. Moreover, it is affected by the eclipse. Thus you are forced to make hard choices in your social life. You can no longer sit on the fence. Either you commit to a current love or you break it off. Your social life must go forward now. Marrieds re-evaluate their relationship because of a temporary disruption – a needed wake-up call. Your marriage partner starts to redefine his or her personality and goals – putting some tension and suspense into your relationship. Will his or her 'new personality' be as lovable as the one you fell in love with?

November

> Best Days Overall: 5th, 6th, 14th, 15th, 23rd, 24th
>
> Most Stressful Days Overall: 12th, 13th, 18th, 19th, 25th, 26th
>
> Best Days for Love: 5th, 6th, 7th, 8th, 14th, 15th, 16th, 17th, 18th, 19th, 23rd, 24th, 27th, 28th
>
> Best Days for Money: 5th, 6th, 7th, 8th, 14th, 15th, 16th, 17th, 23rd, 24th, 27th, 28th

Towards the end of the month the planets are starting to energize the western half of your chart after many months in the east. Continue to build your personal dream and then help others to build theirs. By the end of the month you should have things the way you want and will be more free to think of other people.

Right now the planets are still mostly at the bottom half of your chart, so the need remains to find or create emotional harmony and inner tranquillity. Home and family issues are gaining in importance day by day.

Financially, Venus in Libra is strong in its own Sign and House – which means that earnings are strong. Financial obstacles are overcome through charm, grace and compromise, not by force. You easily magnetize what you want in life this month.

Yet Venus (your Money Planet) is not as well aspected as it could be. It does make your financial life more interesting, though. You need to tread the fine line between expansion and contraction, between spending and saving, between investing and profit-taking, between spending on your home and family members and spending for pleasure, between aggressive investing and conservative investing. You cannot go too far in either direction.

Until the 23rd you are a 'have-and-hold' kind of investor. You buy quality things in order to hold on to them for a long time. You buy things that please you knowing that value is derived, ultimately, from what you love. But after the 23rd you become more of a 'trader', capitalizing on short-term fluctuations in the market place. Until the 23rd you are more of a spender (though you cannot overdo this) but afterwards you are more of a cost-cutter. Until the 23rd you tend to gain wealth by relying on your own resources and social charm. After the 23rd you rely more on other people's money – and perhaps earn money through leveraging strategies.

Your love life is improving day by day. Marrieds are more in synch with their partners. Singles know how to combine intellectual interests with love. Rest and relax more after the 23rd.

December

Best Days Overall: 2nd, 3rd, 11th, 12th, 20th, 21st, 30th, 31st

Most Stressful Days Overall: 9th, 10th, 15th, 16th, 22nd, 23rd

Best Days for Love: 3rd, 7th, 8th, 11th, 12th, 15th, 16th, 17th, 20th, 27th, 28th

VIRGO

Best Days for Money: 2nd, 3rd, 5th, 6th, 7th, 8th, 11th, 12th, 15th, 16th, 17th, 20th, 21st, 27th, 28th, 30th, 31st

Mars in your own Sign all month shows that you are personally active, aggressive and hard-working. The danger here is of overwork – especially until the 21st. Do what you need to do and then relax. Handle what is necessary and let the unnecessary go. Your health and vitality are going to improve after the 21st. At this time you will get anything you go after – by sheer force of will and energy.

On a personal level, your self-esteem is high. You are sexy, magnetic, forceful, wilful and independent, and tend to want (and get) your way. You excel in sports and exercise regimes this month. Athletes break personal performance records now. Your muscle tone (ruled by Mars) is firmer and stronger now. You are shedding pounds.

Your personal aggressiveness and self-will need to be balanced with the family obligations and what they perceive as their rights. Until the 21st family members feel you are too selfish, but this is short term.

Your personal dynamism is very attractive to the opposite sex. Your partner, spouse or lover is turned on by it. You exude sex appeal. Love blooms, and it is physical and passionate. You tend to be blunt about your needs and wants. Most of you are already involved in some relationship, but if you are not there is something major happening at the end of this month and/or next month. Singles are not single for long.

Most of the planets are still below the horizon of your chart – continue to give priority to family and domestic issues. Support other people's career goals now. Create your stable home base.

Though most people are partying this month your festive period begins in earnest after the 21st – and will go on well into the new year. A financial offer from the family or a family connection – and/or a real estate offer – needs to be studied very carefully after the 23rd. It might very well be good but you need to nail down all the details. Postpone decision-making until after the new year.

Libra

♎

THE SCALES

Birthdays from
23rd September
to 22nd October

Personality Profile

LIBRA AT A GLANCE

Element – Air

Ruling Planet – Venus
   Career Planet – Moon
   Health Planet – Neptune
   Love Planet – Mars
   Money Planet – Pluto
   Planet of Home and Family Life – Saturn

Colours – blue, jade green

Colours that promote love, romance and social harmony – carmine, red, scarlet

Colours that promote earning power – burgundy, red-violet, violet

Gems – carnelian, chrysolite, coral, emerald, jade, opal, quartz, white marble

Metal – copper

Scents – almond, rose, vanilla, violet

Quality – cardinal (= activity)

Qualities most needed for balance – a sense of self, self-reliance, independence

Strongest virtues – social grace, charm, tact, diplomacy

Deepest needs – love, romance, social harmony

Characteristic to avoid – violating what is right in order to be socially accepted

Signs of greatest overall compatibility – Gemini, Aquarius

Signs of greatest overall incompatibility – Aries, Cancer, Capricorn

Sign most helpful to career – Cancer

Sign most helpful for emotional support – Capricorn

Sign most helpful financially – Scorpio

Sign best for marriage and/or partnerships – Aries

Sign most helpful for creative projects – Aquarius

Best Sign to have fun with – Aquarius

Signs most helpful in spiritual matters – Gemini, Virgo

Best day of the week – Friday

Understanding the Libra Personality

In the Sign of Libra the universal mind – the soul – expresses its genius of relationship, that is, its power to harmonize diverse elements in a unified, organic way. Libra is the soul's power to express beauty in all of its forms. And where is beauty if not within relationships? Beauty does not exist in isolation. Beauty arises out of comparison – out of the just relationship of different parts. Without a fair and harmonious relationship there is no beauty, whether it be in art, manners, ideas or your social or political forum.

There are two faculties humans have that exalt them above the animal kingdom. The first is their rational faculty, as expressed in the Signs of Gemini and Aquarius. The second is their aesthetic faculty, exemplified by Libra. Without an aesthetic sense we would be little more than intelligent barbarians. Libra is the civilizing instinct or urge of the soul.

Beauty is the essence of what Librans are all about. They are here to beautify the world. One could discuss Librans' social grace, their sense of balance and fair play, their ability to see and love another person's point of view – but this would be to miss their central asset: their desire for beauty.

No one – no matter how alone he or she seems to be – exists in isolation. The universe is one vast collaboration of beings. Librans, more than most, understand this and understand the spiritual laws that make relationships bearable and enjoyable.

A Libra is always the unconscious (and in some cases conscious) civilizer, harmonizer and artist. This is a Libra's deepest urge and greatest genius. Librans love instinctively to bring people together, and they are uniquely qualified to do so. They have a knack for seeing what unites people – the things that attract and bind rather than separate individuals.

Finance

In financial matters Librans can seem frivolous and illogical to others. This is because Librans appear to be more concerned with earning money for others than for themselves. But there is a logic to this financial attitude. Librans know that everything and everyone is connected and that it is impossible to help another to prosper without also prospering yourself. Since enhancing their partner's income and position tends to strengthen their relationship, Librans choose to do so. What could be more fun than building a relationship? You will rarely find a Libra enriching him- or herself at someone else's expense.

Scorpio is the Ruler of Libra's Solar 2nd House of Money, giving Libra unusual insight into financial matters and the power to focus on these matters in a way that disguises a seeming indifference. In fact, many other Signs come to Librans for financial advice and guidance.

Given their social graces, Librans often spend great sums of money on entertaining and organizing social events. They also like to help others when they are in need. Librans would go out of their way to help a friend in dire straits, even if they have to borrow from others to do so. However, Librans are also very careful to pay back any debts they owe and like to make sure they never have to be reminded to do so.

Career and Public Image

Publicly, Librans like to appear as nurturers. Their friends and acquaintances are their family and they wield political power in parental ways. They also like bosses who are paternal or maternal.

The Sign of Cancer is on Libra's 10th House (of Career) cusp; the Moon is Libra's Career Planet. The Moon is by far the speediest, most changeable planet in the horoscope. It alone among all the planets travels through the entire Zodiac – all 12 Signs and Houses – every month. This is an important key to the way in which Librans approach their careers and also to some of the things they need to do to maximize their career potential. The Moon is the planet of moods and feelings – and Librans need a career in which they have free expression for their emotions. This is why so many Librans are involved in the creative arts. Libra's ambitions wax and wane like the Moon. They tend to wield power according to their mood.

The Moon 'rules' the masses – and that is why Libra's highest goal is to achieve a mass kind of acclaim and popularity. Librans who achieve fame cultivate the public as other people cultivate a lover or friend. Librans can be very flexible – and often fickle – in their career and ambitions. On the other hand, they can achieve their ends in a great variety of ways. They are not stuck in one attitude or one way of doing things.

Love and Relationships

Librans express their true genius in love. In love you could not find a partner more romantic, more seductive or more fair. If there is one thing that is sure to destroy a relationship – sure to block your love force from flowing – it is injustice or imbalance between your lover and the beloved. If one party is giving too much or taking too much, resentment is sure to surface at some time or other. Librans are careful about this. If anything, Librans might err on the side of giving more, but never of giving less.

If you are in love with a Libra make sure you keep the aura of romance alive. Do all the little things. Have candlelit dinners, travel to exotic places. Bring flowers and little gifts. Give things that are beautiful although not necessarily expensive. Send cards. Ring regularly even if you have nothing particular to say. The niceties are very important.

Your relationship is a work of art: make it beautiful and your Libra lover will appreciate it. If you are creative about it, he or she will appreciate it even more; for this is how your Libra will behave towards you.

Librans like their partners to be aggressive and even a bit self-willed. They know that these are qualities they sometimes lack and so they like their partners to have them. In relationships, however, Librans can be very aggressive – but always in a subtle and charming way! Former Soviet leader Mikhail Gorbachev's 'charm offensive' and openness of the late 1980s (which revolutionized the then-Soviet Union) is typical of a Libra.

Librans are determined in their efforts to charm the object of their desire – and this determination can be very pleasant if you are on the receiving end.

Home and Domestic Life

Since Librans are such social creatures, they do not particularly like mundane domestic duties. They like a well-organized home – clean and neat with everything needful present – but housework is a chore and a burden, one of the unpleasant tasks in life that must be done, the quicker the better. If a Libra has enough money – and sometimes even if not – he or she will prefer to pay someone else to take care of the daily household chores. However, Librans like to do some gardening and they love to have flowers and plants in the home.

A Libra's home is modern and furnished in excellent taste. You will find many paintings and sculptures there. Since Librans like to be with friends and family, they enjoy entertaining at home and they make great hosts.

Capricorn is on the cusp of Libra's 4th Solar House of Home and Family. Saturn, the planet of law, order, limits and discipline, rules Libra's domestic affairs. If Librans want their home life to be supportive and happy, they need to develop some of the virtues of Saturn – order, organization and discipline. Librans, being so creative and so intensely in need of harmony, can tend to be too lax in the home and too permissive with their children. Too much of this is not always good; children do need freedom, but they also need limits.

Horoscope for 1996

Major Trends

Last year was an intellectual and communication year for you, Libra. Intellectual pursuits and activities were expanded and successful. This year is shaping up to be more emotional – a year for fulfilling home and domestic goals and for getting the workplace, your health and your love life in order. And though you are still involved in work in 1996 there is much more fun as well. Uranus moves into Aquarius on 12th January – your 5th Solar House – and remains there for many years to come. You are not only having more fun this year but you are becoming, in general – as a long-term trend – more interested in the fun aspect of life. Uranus' move into its own domain has many other important implications for you, which will be discussed later on.

The four eclipses of 1996 occur on the angles of your chart, showing that they are more powerful and significant than usual for you. All of these eclipses occur in either your 1st or 7th House, showing major changes in your personal image and your love life respectively. You will be redefining your personality along healthier lines as weaknesses and vulnerabilities are pushed to the surface. Your marriage and social life in general changes dramatically as well, and the new patterns that emerge will be more to your liking. These marital changes may occur through short-term crises.

Health

Last year was a reasonable health year. This year is also going to be reasonable. Uranus, moving into Aquarius, has moved away from a long-term stressful aspect into a long-term benevolent aspect. This is going to increase your general vitality, making you less erratic, more self-assured and confident, and less prone to pursue every health fad that comes along. True, you will still be attracted to the spiritual, metaphysical side of health, but you will be more stable about it and more likely to stay the course with one programme or regime. The general feeling of restlessness that has been with you for so many years finally leaves – you are calm.

On the other hand, Saturn (the Cosmic Tester) moves into Aries on 7th April and stays there for the next two or two and a half years. This is not considered the greatest health signal. Domestic and social duties tend to pull you away from your own centre, leaving you feeling depleted. You need to continue to do the balancing act which you have been pursuing for some years now – that of harmonizing your own interests and energy levels with the demands of your partner and family. By all means fulfil your responsibilities, but do not leave yourself out of the picture. Give to each what is demanded but never allow yourself to give beyond your energy levels. Give to yourself as well. But there is no need to give you, Libra, lectures on balance! You do it very naturally. It is your genius.

Neptune (your Health Planet) remains in your 4th Solar House, so like last year the key to good health lies in maintaining emotional and family equanimity, in having a secure and supportive home base.

Neptune in your 4th House also shows that you are just

as concerned with the health of family members as you are with your own personal health. One is identified with the other. When family members are healthy you feel healthy. When family members are below par you feel below par.

Two of the four eclipses of 1996 occur in your 1st House. This often produces what seems like health crises – actually they are more like healing crises, in that deep residues are often forced out of the body for cleansing. The process is not usually pleasant but has long-range benefits. Those who are basically healthy to begin with – who watch what they eat and in general take care of themselves – need not concern themselves about these purgations. In your case the eclipses will produce changes in dress style and accessories, and a redefinition of your self-image.

Jupiter (the Planet of Expansion and Benevolence) will come very close to Neptune towards the end of the year. Thus those of you who have been having health problems of late will find them gone or relieved at that time. The health of family members will also improve.

The health of one of your parents (or parental figures) is delicate this year. Surgery and other radical treatments are perhaps too loosely prescribed. Get second opinions. Your parent will benefit from cleansing and purifying regimes.

Home and Domestic Life

Your home and family situation have been important and volatile for many years now. Some of you have moved from house to house many times. You have been searching all these years for your dream house, your ideal domestic situation, your ideal family. This trend continues this year, but the changes you make are more pleasant. And you can certainly feel that you have got as close to your ideal as you are going to get. There are more moves in store for you, Libra – happy moves to larger and more spacious quarters. Happy in spite of the fact that your spouse may object. Those of you who do not physically move will purchase or inherit other homes. Your family circle expands by birth or marriage. Renovations to expand your residence may so recreate your home that functionally it is as if a move has taken place. Women of childbearing age are likely to get pregnant this year. Men are likely to become fathers. By year's end your domestic wanderlust seems over and you are well established in your dream home for years to come. Much of your restlessness was caused by the presence of Uranus in your 4th House for seven years. This year's move is being caused by Jupiter. By next year your domestic situation will be calmer.

The two eclipses in your 1st Solar House also confirm this move. But these eclipses show more of a change in your personal living quarters – like the room where you spend most of your time in – rather than your entire home.

On a psychological level things are well with you. Your general mood is happy and upbeat – not wildly rapturous or uncontrollably ecstatic – merely quiet, happy and optimistic. Moods are much more stable than they have been for many years now. You now feel much more emotional security and equilibrium, sorely lacking for the past seven years. Family relations and family issues bring much joy. You are content to let your spouse or partner focus on your career – you are happy creating a stable home base and attaining emotional harmony. Things would even be happier if one of your parents (or parental figures) did not feel that it was his or her duty to meddle in your social life. He or she feels 'duty bound' to do so, however.

One of your parents (or parental figures) feels cramped in his or her present quarters and could move as a result – but later on in the year. A sibling is totally transforming his or her personal image. A move here is likely as well.

Love and Social Life

Love, romance and social activities are always important to you, Libra. You are by nature a social creature. Only by interacting with others do you get a chance to express your social genius and attain self-knowledge. You see others as aspects of yourself, and your understanding of others heightens your understanding of yourself. This year, however, your social attitudes are somewhat different. You are forced to cut back a little, to organize and structure your social life, to put some semblance of order into it. You cannot attend every party or give to every friend the time that he or she wants from you. Your family and psychological support system need your time. You need some time for yourself to pursue your personal interests. Budget your social time in the same way that you would budget your finances. Allow 'X' amount of time per week or month for social activities and try your best to stick to it. Social addictions can be just as destructive as physical or emotional ones. Focus on the quality of your friendships rather than their quantity. This is difficult for a Libra, but over the next two years the lesson will be learned.

But there is much more here. Saturn (Lord of your 4th House of Home and Family Life) spends the next two years in your 7th House of Marriage and Social Activities. This is going to produce all kinds of interesting phenomena and learning experiences, both positive and negative. First off, it changes your needs in love. You want nurturing and emotional support from your lover or spouse – and this is what you give in return. You attend and host more parties in the home and with family members. You tend to confuse – if you are not careful – friendship with family relationships. Thus you tend to treat friends as if they were your family, and family as if they were your friends. You extend your notions of family to your friendships as well.

Single Librans (who have never been married) will go

through a brief period of isolation and then perhaps marry. This is one way that the 'social restriction' of 1996 is likely to manifest. Your love urges will be focused on one person to the exclusion of others. The person who appeals to you over the next two years is older, settled, frugal, serious, stable, ambitious, perhaps pessimistic and highly organized, with all the virtues of a corporate manager. This person is likely to be involved in real estate or the corporate world – or both. He or she will be family-orientated and a source of emotional support. It is very likely that you already know this person or have been involved with this person in the distant past. You could also meet him or her at a family gathering, party or real estate seminar, or someone in your family could introduce you.

Those of you who are already married will see a transformation occur in your marriage. Your partner becomes more serious and pessimistic, tending to see the dark side of every problem and being more controlling. Moreover, he or she is super-ambitious this year, focusing almost exclusively on your career and outward goals. Your partner seems colder towards you and it will be up to you to create more romance and warmth in the relationship. If you do not handle things correctly your partner will take this as interference with his or her career. So, in your romantic overtures make sure that you are supportive of your partner's career.

Librans who are working towards a second or third marriage have a 'status quo' type of year. Marrieds will tend to stay married and singles will tend to stay single. There is no special cosmic push one way or the other. Love affairs, however, are abundant and very exciting.

Career and Finance

Career and financial issues are less important to you this year than usual, Libra. Your home, family and social life are much more important and take up much more of your time and energy. On the financial and career front you have more freedom to shape these areas as you will – more freedom on the one hand, but less interest on the other.

Your speculative urges are becoming stronger year by year. While it is doubtful that you will be able to repress them completely, you can and should manage them. speculate with a small percentage of your holdings and go with your intuition. If you are in the stock-market, new technology companies, or larger ones that are launching new ventures, seem appealing. Be prepared to stay in for over a year and to ride the fluctuations. Big profits could come in 1997.

Pluto (your Money Planet) has moved in 1995 into your 3rd House of Communication. Thus earnings come through communication, transport, public relations, advertising, sales or the media. Those of you involved in the stock- or bond-markets would do well to research these industries and invest in good, solid companies. You have a 'strong feel' for these industries over the long term.

By nature your investment philosophy is 'buying and holding' – back-and-forth trading is generally not Libra's style. But for now and for some years to come you are more of a trader than an investor. You have a good ability to earn money playing the short-term fluctuations in stocks, bonds, goods and services.

If you have your own business or have a product to sell, advertising and communication become vital now. You prosper by getting the word out about your product or service. Your attitudes to selling and advertising are undergoing radical change, and by the time Pluto leaves your 3rd House you will be master in this area.

Self-improvement

Your home is going to improve, expand and become happier almost by itself this year. Of course you will make an effort, but the money, the opportunities and the circumstances will all be there for you. Improving your love and social life is going to be a more difficult process because you are going against your own natural inclinations. You find it hard to 'cut friends off' or limit your time with them. You like to do the things that make for popularity. Yet you will need to strive to be popular with the people who count in your life and who are really in your corner. You need to learn to let go with unconditional love and with minimum pain and resentment.

Forgiveness of yourself and others will be important this year. There are also important developments taking place in your creative life. Always creative, you are much more so now and over the long term. You express yourself with great originality and it is more important that you express your uniqueness than to be popular. Those of you in the creative or performing arts will have to balance out these urges. When you are too avant-garde the public misunderstands you. If you cater to the public too much you feel repressed and unfulfilled. As always, the answer lies in the middle way.

Month-by-month Forecasts

January

Best Days Overall: 2nd, 3rd, 12th, 13th, 21st, 22nd, 29th, 30th, 31st

Most Stressful Days Overall: 5th, 6th, 19th, 20th, 25th, 26th

Best Days for Love: 1st, 2nd, 3rd, 12th, 13th, 14th, 21st, 22nd, 23rd, 24th, 25th, 26th, 29th, 30th, 31st

LIBRA

With 90 to 100 per cent of the planets below the horizon of your chart all month it is not surprising that you are focused on the home, family and domestic issues. Big changes are going on here. A move or major renovation is brewing – but try to schedule it before the 9th when Mercury starts to go retrograde in your 4th House. Happy financial surprises come from family members or from people in your past as well. This financial bonanza could also take the form of some 'big-ticket' (expensive, long-lasting) item for the home. Enjoy.

With so much action going on in the home it is not surprising that you are having doubts or that some issues remain unresolved – especially if you are moving or renovating. Allow the New Moon of the 20th to clarify things. When in doubt, do nothing. Information and clarity are coming. Do not feel too guilty about ignoring your career this month, this is normal and natural. However, the Full Moon of the 5th is a good day to achieve career goals that must be wrapped up.

If you are a writer or communicator, extra income comes to you from these activities now. Writers sell manuscripts. Media people reap the rewards of added sales. The sale of a home, home furnishings or other residential real estate goes well – but make sure to nail down details during Mercury's retrograde from the 9th to the 30th.

Though family responsibilities and obligations take up most of your time right now, you can still manage to have a good time. Parties and romantic opportunities abound after the 9th. Before that, socializing seems to be with the family or in the home. Accept invitations to parties and outings. Creativity is very strong and original this month. Those of you who have children should be more patient with them as they seem unduly rebellious and restless. Where freedom does not conflict with safety, allow them it.

Rest and relax more until the 20th. Health and vitality improve dramatically afterwards. Venus' move into Pisces on the 15th starts to make you more health- and diet-conscious. Health professionals have greater healing ability.

February

>Best Days Overall: 8th, 9th, 10th, 17th, 18th, 26th, 27th

>Most Stressful Days Overall: 1st, 2nd, 15th, 16th, 21st, 22nd, 28th, 29th

>Best Days for Love: 1st, 2nd, 8th, 9th, 10th, 13th, 14th, 19th, 20th, 21st, 22nd, 28th, 29th

>Best Days for Money: 3rd, 4th, 6th, 7th, 11th, 12th, 13th, 14th, 15th, 16th, 21st, 22nd, 23rd, 24th, 25th

Happily for you the planets are still overwhelmingly congregated in the western half of your horoscope. Thus the Cosmos is pushing you into being what you most love to be – a purely social creature. And since you are coming from strength you can expect much success and achievement this month. (All the planets are moving forward now as well, showing much forward momentum and achievement.)

There is still great focus on the home, family and the attainment of emotional harmony. Home improvement projects go well – successfully – from the 1st to the 9th – though they are tiresome. Those looking to sell their homes or sell real estate in general have good prospects this month as well. Friends, business partners, health professionals and co-workers are good sales prospects.

Children are still rebellious, edgy and nervous until the 15th. Be patient and try not to make matters worse. Your personal creativity continues to be strong, whether of the intellectual or physical sort. Creativity that involves groups or team effort is especially favourable. Your creative juices get further stimulated when you are part of a team. Speculations are favourable though your income from them might have to be shared. The month is fun-orientated until the 19th.

Singles are looking for romance but not commitment. The emphasis is on having a good time and on physical intimacy. Those who want to win the heart of a Libra this month should entertain them – especially until the 15th. After that serve them. Your Libra will more than repay this, going out of his or her way to please you. Romantic opportunities are plentiful for singles.

Finances are strong until the 19th; after that reduce unnecessary expenses for a while. Investment opportunities continue to be in the communications, transport and media industries – this is a long-term trend. An apparent loss around the 15th is short term and will not affect your ultimate 'bottom line'.

Your health is excellent all month, but vitality is probably greater before the 19th.

March

> Best Days Overall: 6th, 7th, 8th, 15th, 16th, 24th, 25th
>
> Most Stressful Days Overall: 13th, 14th, 19th, 20th, 26th, 27th, 28th

Best Days for Love: 1st, 2nd, 3rd, 9th, 10th,
13th, 14th, 17th, 18th, 19th, 20th, 22nd,
23rd, 29th, 30th

Best Days for Money: 1st, 2nd, 4th, 5th, 9th,
10th, 11th, 12th, 13th, 14th, 19th, 22nd,
23rd, 29th

The westward march of planetary power is peaking this month, continuing the focus on social and romantic matters. This is basically a happy and successful month as you are exercising your genius – making new friends, gaining the co-operation of others in your goals and projects, attaining your ends through other people. Not only are others co-operating, they enjoy it.

Your social life is really the headline of the month. Always a social creature, this month you are more so. Your whole perspective on life revolves around relationships. You see history and world events as the effect of love and romance. After the 6th your perspective on life becomes somewhat darker. You are forced to confront some of the seamier aspects of life – perhaps not physically but intellectually. You see life in stark terms – as a struggle for survival. Only the beautiful, socially connected people with the right friends survive – others fall by the wayside. But though this perspective seems gloomy, as you work through it you are led to deeper truths.

Your love life is active and perhaps hectic – overactive. Singles are likely to marry this month or meet someone special – especially later on in the month. You have many options to choose from – the athletic type, the brainy type and the 'show business' entertainer. The best of all possible worlds would be to choose the person who best combines all of these qualities. Again you need to balance between your social urges, family responsibilities and your own needs. All these urges are at present pulling you in different directions. The job here is to make them all support each other – to integrate them. Perhaps you are going too far to please your lover or spouse. It is OK to put his or her interests above your own – at least temporarily – but that does not mean that you totally ignore your own desires.

There are various scenarios for meeting that special someone – the workplace is a strong possibility. The doctor's surgery or hospital is another; family introductions yet another. Fun dates include parties, sporting events, hiking, sightseeing, lectures, and of course the typical night-spots.

Finances improve dramatically around the 20th as Pluto (your Money Planet) receives positive stimulation. Your 'bottom line' is boosted by friends, your partner or spouse, teachers and gurus. Start reducing debts after the 6th.

April

Best Days Overall: 3rd, 4th, 11th, 12th, 20th, 21st, 30th

Most Stressful Days Overall: 9th, 10th, 16th, 17th, 23rd, 24th

Best Days for Love: 1st, 2nd, 3rd, 7th, 8th, 11th, 12th, 16th, 17th, 20th, 21st, 25th, 26th, 27th, 30th

Best Days for Money: 1st, 2nd, 5th, 6th, 7th, 9th, 10th, 16th, 18th, 19th, 20th, 25th, 26th, 29th

A highly tumultuous and active month, Libra. Stay cool, it will all work out in the end. The two eclipses of the month occur at the angles of your chart, denoting more power and greater impact. The angles affected are the 1st and 7th

Houses – the Houses that deal with the Body and Self-image (1st) and Marriage and Social Life (7th).

If your marriage and partnerships are basically sound they will become even better as hidden flaws and repressed resentments come to the fore to be dealt with and corrected. Singles involved in a good relationship might actually marry because of the eclipse. It will goad you Librans into taking the next step in your growth. If the marriage and/or relationship is deeply flawed to begin with, the eclipse marks the beginning of a break-up – and the creation of a new marital and social pattern. Changes are also happening with your friends, lovers or business partners – some of them are moving away from you and out of your sphere for a while. Your parents and/or parental figures are changing their residence and making career changes as well. Those of you who are healthy and watchful in health matters will change your mode of dress, self-image and the way you present yourself to others. Those who are neglectful in health matters will find that deep pockets of toxins reveal themselves in order to be eliminated. Hidden physical flaws rise to the surface to be corrected.

Your social life and ability to adapt to social and marital changes are the main headlines and challenges of the month. The feeling of being cut off from friends and from your social norm is perhaps hardest for you to bear.

Rest and relax more this month, Libra, as this is not one of your best health months. Be sure especially to take a reduced schedule during the two eclipse periods (from the 1st to the 4th and from the 15th to the 18th). Avoid arduous travel, potentially dangerous surgery (that is elective) and hazardous activities. Schedule these things for another time if at all possible. Stay close to home and do not do things that you do not need to do.

May

Best Days Overall: 1st, 2nd, 9th, 10th, 18th, 19th, 27th, 28th, 29th

Most Stressful Days Overall: 7th, 8th, 13th, 14th, 20th, 21st, 22nd

Best Days for Love: 1st, 2nd, 7th, 8th, 9th, 10th, 13th, 14th, 15th, 16th, 18th, 19th, 25th, 26th, 27th, 28th, 29th

Best Days for Money: 3rd, 4th, 5th, 6th, 7th, 8th, 13th, 15th, 16th, 17th, 23rd, 25th, 26th, 30th, 31st

The short-term planets are now moving through the upper portion of your horoscope, Libra, making you much more career-conscious and ambitious than you have been of late. Your partner, too, is unusually wrapped up with financial and career issues, perhaps much more than you – yet it seems to work out between you in spite of some under-standable tension.

Fifty to 60 per cent of the planets are retrograde this month, including Venus (your Ruling Planet). Thus you need to be more patient with yourself and others. You are rethinking personal goals and formulating a new philosophy of life. Much spiritual illumination is coming and you prefer this to asserting you personal will and the pursuits of sen-sual pleasure. A new friend is made in church, or at univer-sity. Higher education, foreign travel and religion are important for the next few months.

Though you find it more difficult to assert yourself, your health is good nevertheless. Healthy Librans will continue in good health. Those of you with health problems will find that progress is being made behind the scenes, in ways that you are not aware of at present. Current treatments are being rethought and re-evaluated and will either be scrapped or replaced with something better. Current diagnoses are likely to change for the better as well.

Romance is physical and passionate this month. There is less nurturing and hand-holding, more passion and physical intimacy. Your partner is thriving financially and goes after what he or she wants with great energy. He or she exhibits a kind of dogged determination to succeed. Your partner's career is on hold for a while, but earnings are not. Sales and marketing are unusually important for your partner's 'bottom line', but with Mercury retrograde he or she might be better off planning sales campaigns rather than actually putting them into action. Your partner deals with financial delays by working harder. He or she overcomes through sheer energy and industry.

Pluto (your Money Planet) is also retrograde this month, but you seem content about it as earnings are not a big priority. You are more interested in travel, physical intimacy and getting more educated. Nevertheless financial caution is indicated for you. Current investments should be reviewed both for performance and as to their suitability to your goals.

June

Best Days Overall: 5th, 6th, 14th, 15th, 24th, 25th

Most Stressful Days Overall: 3rd, 4th, 9th, 10th, 16th, 17th, 18th, 24th, 25th

Best Days for Love: 3rd, 4th, 5th, 6th, 9th, 10th, 12th, 13th, 14th, 15th, 24th, 25th

Best Days for Money: 1st, 3rd, 4th, 9th, 12th, 13th, 19th, 22nd, 23rd, 26th, 27th, 29th

Venus (your Ruling Planet), along with four other planets, is retrograde this month – making this a month of introspection, review, analysis and inaction. Of course inaction does not mean that there will be *no* action, but that less activity is called for. When in doubt, do nothing.

Venus' retrograde occurs in your 9th House, which suggests that there is some confusion regarding your higher education and religious outlook. For those of you of university age, or who are attending university, there is doubt about what to study, or how far to go or what university to attend, etc. You feel – temporarily – that you are going backwards in your educational goals. You find it more difficult to deal with teachers, academics and the institutional hierarchy. The good news is that the New Moon of the 15th is going to clarify all these matters – and you will be shown very specifically what you should (and should not) do.

Those of you involved in the publishing business are also in doubt this month. Should you publish such-and-such a title? If so, how should it be done?, and so on. These issues too will be clarified by the New Moon of the 15th.

Overall your health is good but your self-esteem and self-confidence could be stronger. You find it difficult to assert yourself or get your way because you feel unsure about who you are, where you stand and what you want. Avoid power struggles now. After the 21st, rest and relax more.

Though on a long-term basis your career takes a back seat to home and domestic issues, the short-term planets are now temporarily energizing the upper half of your horoscope, stimulating your ambitions and need for outward achievement. You have got quite a balancing act to accomplish in the next month or so, juggling your personal inclinations with your ambitions, domestic duties and social life. Each of these areas pulls you in a different direction and seems to conflict with the others. Your job is to make them all support each other.

July

> Best Days Overall: 2nd, 3rd, 11th, 12th, 21st,
> 22nd, 30th, 31st
>
> Most Stressful Days Overall: 1st, 6th, 7th,
> 8th, 14th, 15th, 28th, 29th
>
> Best Days for Love: 2nd, 3rd, 6th, 7th, 8th,
> 11th, 12th, 21st, 22nd, 30th, 31st
>
> Best Days for Money: 1st, 6th, 9th, 10th,
> 16th, 19th, 20th, 24th, 25th, 26th, 27th,
> 28th, 29th

Though most people would consider this to be a stressful month, for you there are secret joys and much growth. No one enjoys balancing things – whether it be people, projects or situations – more than you do, Libra. And how can we call something stressful when the Cosmos gives us what we enjoy?

This month – as was the case last month – the balancing act involves your social interests, pressing career matters and family obligations. Each pulls you in a different direction. It is up to you to make them work together and support each other. This is done through diplomacy and compromise. If anyone can make a work of art out of this delicate life situation, it is you. The balancing act is something dynamic rather than rigid. You will not balance these different interests by creating some 'artificial' rule, plan or formula. Rather, you must think of the tightrope walker who now leans one way and then another (and never too far either way) but always moves forward. Be flexible.

Though you are stronger this month than last month – and have more confidence and self-esteem – you nevertheless cannot afford to waste energy. Rest and relax more and refuse to let yourself get overtired. This is not one of your best health periods. Your vitality improves somewhat after the 22nd, but you still need to be careful.

Singles still find romantic opportunities in academia, in foreign lands and at religious functions. Foreigners and highly educated types – teachers and professors – are very appealing. You want someone you can learn from – someone who is capable of guiding you. Intellectual communion and philosophical harmony are unusually important in love right now. If you are not in synch philosophically, chances are you will not be in synch physically or sexually either.

There is a sudden – and probably unexpected – boost in your career around the 15th. The New Moon of the 15th is going to do much to clarify your career situation and show you what to do next. Your career prospers most strongly from the 15th to the 30th. Before the 15th work on eliminating obstructions to your plans.

Be patient in finances and with investments. Progress is happening behind the scenes.

August

Best Days Overall: 7th, 8th, 9th, 17th, 18th, 19th, 26th, 27th

Most Stressful Days Overall: 3rd, 4th, 10th, 11th, 24th, 25th, 30th, 31st

Best Days for Love: 1st, 2nd, 6th, 10th, 11th, 16th, 20th, 21st, 24th, 25th, 28th, 29th

Best Days for Money: 3rd, 5th, 6th, 12th, 15th, 16th, 20th, 21st, 22nd, 23rd, 24th, 25th

Though four planets are still retrograde this month you seem unaffected as your important planets – your Ruler, Money Planet, Love Planet and Career Planet – are all moving forward now. People around you are experiencing difficulties, delays and reverses, but you sail forward on a calm sea. Moreover, since the short-term planets are now energizing the eastern half of your chart you have more initiative, independence and drive than normal. You are getting your way now and others are not in a position to oppose you. They have got their own problems to deal with.

This is a month for pleasing yourself, for doing the things that you really enjoy doing and which make you happy, for creating your own conditions of happiness. Further your goals by self-reliance this month – and for the next few months.

The short-term planets are also – temporarily – energizing your career sector (upper half) of your chart. This was the case last month as well. Continue to promote your career activities and execute plans for career advancement. After the 7th you have opportunities to achieve new career highs and to ingratiate yourself with investors. Your personal charm, style and elegance are appreciated by superiors and by the public at large. Those of you who deal with the public at large will enjoy great success now – but you must not let it go to your head. The demands of your family and spouse or lover will bring you back to earth pretty quickly if you ignore them.

Curiously, your new self-assertion and 'me-first' attitude does not harm your love life – perhaps it even enhances it. For your spouse, partner or lover seems just as ambitious as you are – for the moment anyway – and thus you are both in synch as far as career issues go. Your career success and general popularity enhance the income of your partner either directly or indirectly. Your partner prospers this month, though there are a few difficulties (just to keep things interesting). Your personal earning power is also moving forward now as Pluto (your Money Planet) at long last starts moving forward on the 10th. If you have used the past few months correctly – to review your finances and investment strategy – you are now ready to move. You know what you are going to do with spare cash. You have evolved a new financial strategy and are ready to implement it. It would be recommended, however, that until your birthday your major thrust should be to reduce debt and expenses rather than build wealth outwardly.

September

> Best Days Overall: 4th, 5th, 14th, 15th, 23rd, 24th
>
> Most Stressful Days Overall: 6th, 7th, 8th, 20th, 21st, 27th, 28th
>
> Best Days for Love: 6th, 7th, 8th, 9th, 18th, 19th, 27th, 28th
>
> Best Days for Money: 1st, 2nd, 9th, 11th, 12th, 16th, 17th, 18th, 20th, 21st, 27th, 29th, 30th

This is an active, tumultuous month for you, Libra – never a dull moment. The plans of the One Power in the universe seem hazy and inexplicable – contradictory and chaotic. Those of you on the spiritual path feel confused. Your spiritual progress seems slowed and your faith is tested now. Your ability to tap into your spiritual depths – though you desire it – is hampered by other forces. You must persist through the difficulties.

Moreover, the lunar eclipse of the 26th is creating more confusion – and temporary upheaval. Your marital status is changing. Your partner redefines his or her personality and goals. Flaws in your present living conditions and present marriage are revealed so that they can be corrected one way or another. Flaws in current business partnerships are also revealed. A move or home renovation is likely. Family relations are disquieting. Your moods are erratic and strange; feelings come up that you never knew you had. You must look at all these things with the Single Eye of the Spirit, and know that you are more than your feelings and more than the events happening around you. It is more difficult to do this month, but when you do it you gain strength.

Your personal health is getting better every day, but the health of your partner seems delicate. A lot of your strange feelings and moods are coming not from yourself but from psychic rapport with your family and your spouse or lover.

Your finances are improving this month. Until your birthday channel excess cash into debt-reduction and reducing your expenses. After your birthday you can start focusing on building new wealth and on investments. By the 10th you should have achieved the career goals you set out for last month and are beginning to focus on true and lasting happiness. Your career goals were simply a stepping stone to a larger goal – happiness. Opportunities to manifest your fondest financial dreams come around the 7th. Your partner adds to your 'bottom line' around the 10th.

October

Best Days Overall: 1st, 2nd, 11th, 12th, 20th, 21st, 29th, 30th

Most Stressful Days Overall: 4th, 5th, 18th, 19th, 24th, 25th, 31st

Best Days for Love: 6th, 7th, 8th, 9th, 16th, 17th, 18th, 19th, 24th, 25th, 27th, 28th

LIBRA

With 90 per cent of the planets moving forward this month, there is going to be a lot of action and progress made. Much energy will be demanded of you, and happily you have it to give.

The focus of the planets in the east usually shows that you have an opportunity to create conditions as you like them. But with an important solar eclipse occurring in your 1st House you have little choice – you *must* create your own conditions now. The Cosmos forces you to redefine your personality and your goals, and to get off the fence on projects that affect your personal happiness. You must take action now one way or another. Those of you in good health will probably make changes in the way you dress and accessorize yourself. Those of you whose health is more delicate will begin to cleanse the body as hidden toxins are forced up and out of the body. Many of you will want to redecorate or otherwise alter your personal room – the room where you spend most of your time.

Take a reduced schedule on the 11th, 12th and 13th.

The eclipse is also affecting the workplace and relations with neighbours, siblings and friends. A temporary disruption – caused by hidden festering flaws – leads to greater long-term harmony. A job change is likely.

Your health is basically good. Your self-esteem is strong and this gives you the confidence to make the changes in your image that you want to make. Finances are getting stronger and stronger day by day and your increased self-esteem and confidence boost earnings. Your personal appearance is important in creating financial opportunities right now.

Your love life is basically harmonious. You seem in synch with your spouse, lover or partner. Your partner's ambition appeals to you. Singles and the uninvolved are turned on by ambitious go-getters now. Romantic opportunities come through the pursuit of ambitions and with people involved in shaping your career. Romantic opportunities come in government offices and at corporate parties and/or gatherings. Romantic opportunities are abundant.

November

>Best Days Overall: 7th, 8th, 16th, 17th, 25th, 26th

>Most Stressful Days Overall: 1st, 14th, 15th, 20th, 21st, 27th, 28th

>Best Days for Love: 5th, 6th, 7th, 8th, 14th, 15th, 16th, 17th, 20th, 21st, 23rd, 24th, 27th, 28th

>Best Days for Money: 2nd, 5th, 6th, 10th, 11th, 12th, 13th, 14th, 15th, 20th, 23rd, 24th, 30th

Now that the dust is settling from the eclipses of the past two months you can more or less enjoy yourself. Do not look too much to the world of appearances but rather focus on building the conditions that you desire. Present appearances are merely the result of past mental patterns; start creating happier mental patterns and you will start the ball rolling for a happier future.

Your love life is happier this month than it has been in the past few months. You are more radiant, glamorous and magnetic. You have no problem attracting members of the opposite sex. Your normally excellent style and aesthetic sense is even more enhanced now. This is the month to shop for clothes, jewellery and accessories, and to redecorate your favourite room. Sensual fantasies are fulfilled this month – only beware of too much of a good thing.

You still need to balance your sensual desires with the needs of your family and partner or spouse. Your spouse or lover is supporting you behind the scenes. Singles are likely to be involved in a clandestine affair or to take a low profile in a current affair. Your dream life is filled with images of love and romance. Singles and the uninvolved will profit from meditation on their 'ideal' or 'dream' lover. Focus on the ideal this month. If you have no idea of what that is, formulate an ideal for yourself in your present conditions. Astrologers and psychics have important information to convey to you about love. Romantic opportunities come from spiritual meetings, seminars and gatherings, and from charitable and philanthropic activities. You are looking for an altruistic lover these days; someone who has a rich inner life.

Finances are excellent all month. Not only is your Money House active now but the New Moon of the 11th occurs there. Thus you will be receiving very specific financial guidance and illumination all month. Your financial judgement is sound. You have an eye for investments and products which have intrinsic, core value. Gold, electric utilities and entertainment stocks allure you.

Your health is excellent all month.

December

Best Days Overall: 5th, 6th, 13th, 14th, 22nd, 23rd

Most Stressful Days Overall: 11th, 12th, 18th, 19th, 25th, 26th

Best Days for Love: 2nd, 3rd, 7th, 8th, 11th, 12th, 15th, 16th, 17th, 18th, 19th, 20th, 21st, 27th, 28th

Best Days for Money: 1st, 2nd, 3rd, 7th, 8th, 9th, 11th, 12th, 18th, 20th, 21st, 27th, 30th, 31st

A happy and active month, Libra – enjoy. With 80 to 90 per cent of the planets moving forward there is progress and achievement ahead. Most of the planets are below the horizon, showing interest in emotional harmony and domestic tranquillity. Your career takes a back seat to domestic and family issues right now.

Your 3rd House of Communication is unusually powerful this month, showing a need to pursue intellectual interests – schooling, teaching and reading. Sales and communication projects are important but these should be done before Mercury's retrograde on the 23rd. Short excursions – local and domestic travel – are happy and enjoyable this month – though again, make them before the 23rd. Foreign travel might be better next month than now.

Your health is excellent until the 21st, after that rest and relax more. Family demands are stressing your energies. Remember that you cannot be of service to your family if you have no energy for yourself. Even the best of cars cannot perform when there is no petrol in the tank – refill the tank when it is empty.

Finances are also a top priority this month – especially until the 17th. Your personal appearance and style are major factors both in earnings and in the creation of earnings opportunities. Dress for success; create an image of wealth. Behave as if you were successful and success will come. Until the 17th be careful of over-identifying with your possessions and your earning ability. You are, in essence, much more than your bank account or stock portfolio. Possessions are merely ornaments to what you truly are; treat them that way.

Earnings increase through the elimination of waste and

needless (unnecessary) expenses. Debts are easily made but just as easily paid off. This is a good month to attract investors to your projects – though do not commit to anything long term after the 23rd. You attain financial goals through grace and charm rather than aggression. You give fair value for fair return. Your financial judgement is balanced. As an investor, you are more the 'haver and holder' than the 'trader' – though this changes after the 17th. Your personal likes and dislikes – your personal tastes in things – are good investment guides during this period. If you personally enjoy a given product this is the universe's way of showing you that the company that make it might represent a good investment opportunity. Explore it.

Scorpio

♏

THE SCORPION
Birthdays from
23rd October
to 22nd November

Personality Profile

SCORPIO AT A GLANCE

Element – Water

Ruling Planet – Pluto
   Co-ruling Planet – Mars
   Career Planet – Sun
   Health Planet – Mercury
   Love Planet – Venus
   Money Planet – Jupiter
   Planet of Home and Family Life – Uranus

Colour – red-violet

Colour that promotes love, romance and social harmony – green

Colour that promotes earning power – blue

SCORPIO

Gems – bloodstone, malachite, topaz

Metals – iron, radium, steel

Scents – cherry blossom, coconut, sandal-wood, watermelon

Quality – fixed (= stability)

Quality most needed for balance – a wider view of things

Strongest virtues – loyalty, concentration, determination, courage, depth

Deepest needs – to penetrate and transform

Characteristics to avoid – jealousy, vindictiveness, fanaticism

Signs of greatest overall compatibility – Cancer, Pisces

Signs of greatest overall incompatibility – Taurus, Leo, Aquarius

Sign most helpful to career – Leo

Sign most helpful for emotional support – Aquarius

Sign most helpful financially – Sagittarius

Sign best for marriage and/or partnerships – Taurus

Sign most helpful for creative projects – Pisces

Best Sign to have fun with – Pisces

Signs most helpful in spiritual matters – Cancer, Libra

Best day of the week – Tuesday

Understanding the Scorpio Personality

One symbol of the Sign of Scorpio is the phoenix. If you meditate upon the legend of the phoenix you will begin to understand the Scorpio character, his or her powers and abilities, interests and deepest urges.

The phoenix of mythology was a bird that could recreate and reproduce itself. It did so in a most intriguing way: it would seek a fire – usually in a religious temple – fly into it, consume itself in the flames and then emerge as a new bird. If this is not the ultimate, most profound transformation, then what is?

Transformation is what Scorpios are all about – in their minds, bodies, affairs and relationships (Scorpios are also society's transformers). To change something in a natural and not an artificial way involves a transformation from within. This type of change is a radical change as opposed to a mere cosmetic make-over. Some people think that change means changing just their appearance, but this is not the kind of change that interests a Scorpio. Scorpios seek deep, fundamental change. Since real change always proceeds from within, a Scorpio is very interested in – and usually accustomed to – the inner, intimate and philosophical side of life.

Scorpios are people of depth and intellect. If you want to interest them you must present them with more than just a superficial image. You and your interests, projects or business deals must have real substance to them in order to stimulate a Scorpio. If they have not, he or she will find you out – and that will be the end of the story.

If we observe life, the processes of growth and decay, we see the transformative powers of Scorpio at work all the time. The caterpillar changes itself into a butterfly, the infant grows into a child and then an adult. To Scorpios this definite and perpetual transformation is not something to be feared. They see this as a normal part of life. This acceptance of transformation gives Scorpios the key to understanding the true meaning of life.

Scorpios' understanding of life (including life's weaknesses) makes them powerful warriors – in all senses of the word. Add to this their depth and penetration, their patience and endurance and you have a powerful personality. Scorpios have good, long memories and can be at times quite vindictive – they can wait years to get their revenge. As a friend, though, there is no one more loyal and true than a Scorpio. Few are willing to make the sacrifices that a Scorpio will make for a true friend.

The results of a transformation are quite obvious, although the process of transformation is invisible and secret. This is why Scorpios are considered secretive in nature. A seed will not grow properly if you keep digging it up and exposing it to the light of day. It must stay buried – invisible – until it starts to grow. In the same manner, Scorpios fear revealing too much about themselves or their hopes to other people. However, they will be more than happy to let you see the finished product – but only when it is finished. On the other hand, Scorpios like knowing everyone else's secrets as much as they dislike anyone knowing theirs.

Finance

Love, birth, life as well as death are Nature's most potent transformations and Scorpios are interested in all of these. In our society money is a transforming power, too, and a Scorpio is interested in money for that reason. To a Scorpio money is power, money causes change and money rules. It is the power of money that fascinates them. But Scorpios can be too materialistic if they are not careful. They can be overly awed by the power of money, to a point where they think that money rules the world.

Even the term *plutocrat* comes from Pluto, the Ruler of

the Sign of Scorpio. Scorpios will – in one way or another – achieve the financial status they strive for. When they do so they are careful in the way they handle their wealth. Part of this financial carefulness is really a kind of honesty, for Scorpios are usually involved with other people's money – as accountants, lawyers, stockbrokers or corporate managers – and when you handle other people's money you have to be more cautious than when you handle your own.

In order to fulfil their financial goals, Scorpios have important lessons to learn. They need to develop qualities that are not naturally in their natures, such as breadth of vision, optimism, faith, trust and, above all, generosity. They need to see the wealth in Nature and in life as well as in the more obvious forms of money and power. When they develop this generosity their financial potential reaches great heights, for Jupiter, the Lord of opulence and good fortune, is Scorpio's Money Planet.

Career and Public Image

Scorpio's greatest aspiration in life is to be considered by society as a source of light and life. They want to be leaders, to be stars. But they follow a very different road than do Leos, the other stars of the Zodiac. A Scorpio arrives at the goal secretly, without ostentation; a Leo pursues it openly. Scorpios seek the glamour and fun of the rich and famous in a secretive, undisclosed manner.

Scorpios are by nature introverted and tend to avoid the limelight. But if they want to attain their highest career goals they need to open up a bit and to express themselves more. They need to stop hiding their light under a bushel and let it shine. Above all, they need to let go of any vindictiveness and small-mindedness. All their gifts and insights were given to them for one important reason – to serve life and to increase the joy of living for others.

Love and Relationships

Scorpio is another Zodiac Sign that likes committed, clearly defined, structured relationships. They are cautious about marriage, but when they do commit to a relationship they tend to be faithful – and heaven help the mate caught or even suspected of infidelity! The jealousy of the Scorpio is legendary. They can be so intense in their jealousy that even the thought or intention of infidelity will be detected and is likely to cause as much of a storm as if the act had actually occurred.

Scorpios tend to settle down with those who are wealthier than they are. They usually have enough intensity for two, so in their partners they seek someone pleasant, hard-working, amiable, stable and easy-going. They want someone they can lean on, someone loyal behind them as they fight the battles of life. To a Scorpio a partner, be it a lover or a friend, is a real partner – not an adversary. Most of all a Scorpio is looking for an ally, not a competitor.

If you are in love with a Scorpio you will need a lot of patience. It takes a long time to get to know Scorpios, because they do not reveal themselves readily. But if you persist and your motives are honourable, you will gradually be allowed into a Scorpio's inner chambers of the mind and heart.

Home and Domestic Life

Uranus is Ruler of Scorpio's 4th Solar House of Home and Domestic Affairs. Uranus is the planet of science, technology, changes and democracy. This tells us a lot about a Scorpio's conduct in the home and what he or she needs in order to have a happy, harmonious home life.

Scorpios can sometimes bring their passion, intensity and wilfulness into the home and family, which is not always the place for these qualities. These virtues are good for the warrior and the transformer, but not so good for the nurturer and family person. Because of this (and also because of their need for change and transformation) the Scorpio may be prone to sudden changes of residence. If not carefully constrained, the sometimes inflexible Scorpio can produce turmoil and sudden upheavals within the family.

Scorpios need to develop some of the virtues of Aquarius in order to cope better with domestic matters. There is a need to build a team spirit at home, to treat family activities as truly group activities – family members should all have a say in what does and does not get done. For at times a Scorpio can be most dictatorial. When a Scorpio gets dictatorial it is much worse than if a Leo or Capricorn (the two other power Signs in the Zodiac) does. For the dictatorship of a Scorpio is applied with more zeal, passion, intensity and concentration than is true of either a Leo or Capricorn. Obviously this can be unbearable to his or her family members – especially if they are sensitive types.

In order for a Scorpio to get the full benefit of the emotional support that a family can give, he or she needs to release conservatism and be a bit more experimental, to explore new techniques in child-rearing, be more democratic with family members and to try to manage more things by consensus than by autocratic edict.

Horoscope for 1996

Major Trends

Many of the major trends that were important in 1995 are still important in 1996, Scorpio, with a few minor differences. Your interest in finance – and the expansion of your financial life – though a bit scaled-down this year continues nevertheless. The pursuit of intellectual interests also continues and you are still working to improve your communication abilities. You are a bit more conservative in financial matters and have a longer-range perspective this year than last. There is greater interest in the home and family and a possible move. Sexual expression, which was somewhat limited in 1995, will now expand more. And you are reorganizing your work space and in general becoming more efficient at work.

As in previous years the main thrust of your energy is aimed at attaining emotional and psychological harmony rather than outward career success.

The four eclipses of 1996 happen in your 6th (Health and Work) and 12th (Spiritual Wisdom) Houses. Though these eclipses do not affect you as much as they do some of the other Signs, they nevertheless signal long-term changes in your spiritual life, charitable activities and work. Job changes – not necessarily career changes – are likely this year.

Health

Your overall vitality and life-force are perhaps lessened in 1996 but are still considerable. You have plenty of energy with which to achieve whatever you desire.

Uranus' move into Aquarius makes stressful aspects to you, but of itself this is not enough to cause any major health problem. Many of you – especially those born early in the Sign of Scorpio – will feel a sense of restlessness, wanderlust and emotional nervousness. Mood swings become more pronounced and more volatile. You want change but are not exactly sure of what kind of change. You feel more jumpy, edgy, nervous. There is a fear of the unknown. Learning the art of relaxation will help with these anxieties.

Saturn moves into your 6th House of Health on 7th April and stays there for over two years. Two of the four eclipses of 1996, as mentioned, also occur in this House. Thus you are forced to get this area of your life in order. If you have been neglecting health matters, diet and or exercise, deep-seated, hidden impurities will get flushed to the surface for elimination. They have collected themselves to a point where they can no longer be tolerated by your body. Short-term 'expurgations' – though not always pleasant – lead to long-term health benefits. Sometimes these expurgations are mistakenly diagnosed as this or that 'sickness' – but they really should be seen as signs of self-healing and cleansing.

Saturn in this House shows a need for you to take control of your health, to study more about it and to get on some regular regime. Though your present state of health is likely to be excellent you are now thinking of the long term – how your health will be when you are older. The way you act now will determine your health in old age. So you are entering into regimes that are designed to bring long-term well-being rather than an immediate cure of a particular problem.

Those of you who do have health problems should also think of long-range solutions. It might be tempting to pursue one 'quickie' cure-all or another, but this will not do the trick. You need to change the underlying cause of the problem, which tends to take longer – and is a more gradual process – than quickie solutions which only relieve symptoms. Happily, you are more open to these approaches this year.

The good of all this is that you are more serious about your health and intend to take long-term correctives for improvement. You are likely to stick to your health programme faithfully.

The two eclipses in your 12th House also show that your partner or spouse might face temporary body-cleansings and purifications – best if he or she co-operates with the process rather than trying to thwart it. If a parent (or parental figure) has been having health problems these are resolved very harmoniously this year. Not only are his or her self-healing abilities increased, but so is his or her capacity to heal others.

The health of your children is basically stable – though they seem more serious, pessimistic and of lower self-esteem. The health of your siblings (especially the eldest) also seems stable, though he or she needs to be careful not to over-indulge – too much of the good life is not always healthy.

Home and Domestic Life

You have been restless and experimental on the domestic front for some time, but now that Uranus makes a major move into the Sign of Aquarius this restlessness and experimentation becomes even more pronounced. Over the next few years you will have a series of moves, changes of residences and changes in your living conditions and habits. The domestic routine seems unsettled now. Those of you with children are finding them more rebellious. Many of you are trying to conduct home life as if it were a kind of 'democracy' where everyone has equal say as to what goes on. While there is nothing wrong with this *per se*, if you go overboard and abdicate any kind of authority you will be faced with chaos and anarchy.

Yes, like some of the other Signs you are searching for your dream house, dream family and ideal domestic situation. You want to rewrite the book on these things – casting out tradition and exploring this area in a whole new way. You will experiment with different ways of getting domestic chores done – making domestic chores a 'group project' or alternating chore assignments to different family members. Through trial and error you will evolve something workable – but probably not straight away. Your best bet – according to your horoscope – is to invest in labour-saving technology. Always a lover of 'high-tech' in the home, this year you are even more so.

Perhaps the most important development that comes of this Uranus transit will be the way you extend your notion of family to other people – to friends, groups that you belong to and, for some of you, to the world at large. 'My friends are also my family; the world is one big family and we should treat people like that' – these are your attitudes now. You are also more involved in helping friends find their dream home and ideal domestic situation.

Love and Social Life

Though you will certainly have an adequate social life this year, the fact is that romance and marriage are not your main priorities now. The Cosmos is not impelling you one way or the other. You have freedom to shape your social life as you will. This kind of configuration usually fosters the status quo – singles tend to remain single, marrieds tend to remain married.

Singles are likely to get involved in a hot, passionate affair from 3rd April to 7th August, when Venus (your Love Planet) makes an unusual four-month station in the Sign of Gemini. It is a transforming kind of affair, where both you and the beloved are working to turn some negative or undesirable condition around. This could be a business, an investment or the re-invention of your personality. It is a partnership of transformation – a mutual spiritual mid-wifery, with much physical and psychological intimacy involved. The person could be a stock-broker, money-manager, psychotherapist or occultist.

Love opportunities become more abundant from 6th March to 7th August, with again the period between 3rd April and 7th August most significant.

The married life of one of your parents (or parental figures) goes through wild changes this year and for many years to come. If the relationship is fundamentally sound it will survive, but if it is unsound it will probably break up.

This parent wants freedom and space. If he or she is single (widowed or divorced), a marriage or serious relationship is likely. Things are not the way they appear on the surface.

If you have children, this year their love lives are stable, with the Cosmos pushing neither in one direction nor another. The status quo is fostered.

An unmarried sibling who is prospering greatly this year still needs to be patient in love. The problem is not his or her ability to attract love but in finding the right person. Lovers come and go but nothing seems to last.

Career and Finance

In 1995 your Ruling Planet (Pluto) made a major move from your 1st to your 2nd Solar House. This started a long trend (it will last 20 or so years) of focus on finance and earnings. In 1995 your Money Planet (Jupiter) also moved through your Money House (2nd House), bringing great financial expansion to you. It was a banner money year. You made more and spent more – perhaps even a bit recklessly. Though your financial outlook is very positive you cannot be as reckless a spender as you were last year. You need to cut costs and avoid too much debt. The problem here is that your gift is for making money with other people's cash, and this by definition often means debt. Do not let anything cause you to over-borrow. As you learn how to cut costs in your personal finances you will see how this prudence can be applied to other people's finances and to the finances of companies and corporations. You become a more effective manager.

For now and for many years to come you have the ability to find financial opportunities from dead, defunct or bankrupt companies. You either buy them for a song or get employment with someone who does. Then you proceed to turn it into a profitable concern. Those of you who are investors will find opportunities in these areas as well. You are gifted with both the stock- and the bond-markets, but perhaps a bit stronger with bonds than with stocks.

Your perception into the world of finances is unusually keen now and for many years to come. You see deeply into things and are a difficult person to fool. You see money as a tool and a power now, and often make war or get revenge with your chequebook rather than your fists or material weapons.

With your Money Planet now moving through your 3rd Solar House of Communication it is very important that you grasp the use of media, sales, advertising and communication to enhance your 'bottom line'. Invest in the communication equipment you need now – this is not wasteful spending but a wise investment. Buy computers, fax machines, modems and good telephone equipment. Invest in mailing lists and advertising. Get the word out on your product and/or service whatever it is. A newsletter or frequent mail-shots will enhance your 'bottom line'.

Investment opportunities will come in telecommunications and transport. They seem profitable. Other investment opportunities will come from neighbours or from within your neighbourhood – perhaps a neighbourhood business? This too seems profitable – of course you must research each thing before getting into it.

Your partner's interest in finances seems erratic, and not a major priority for him or her this year. You are probably carrying the can for both of you. The income of a parent, which has been tight of late, begins improving in February and really starts flourishing after 7th April.

Self-improvement

Earlier some of your short-term profit opportunities were mentioned. You can also improve your long-term opportunities by studying and following the publishing, travel and banking industries. You have an affinity for making money in these areas and if you follow the industry you will be aware of when to invest and when to get out. You will understand when a given company is a good investment and when a poor one. You will be in tune with the general trends of the industry and thus in a position to profit. Begin slowly, reading the financial pages, picking a few major companies in each of these industries and following their price fluctuations. After a while you will get a feel for this speculation, so that when extra money comes you will know where to invest it.

The workplace is another area that needs improvement this year. If you are an employer you need to make more effective use of the space you have available. You do not really need new space, just better management of existing space. If you are an employee there is a need to become more efficient, to achieve greater productivity with less time and effort. Planning and common sense will guide you. Eliminate repetitious motions and procedures. You will become a more valuable employee and will be noticed by your employer. The way things will work out is that you either take the initiative and do this voluntarily or your employer will force efficiencies on you. Better that you create your own efficiency – an efficiency that is more in tune with your nature.

Month-by-month Forecasts

January

Best Days Overall: 5th, 6th, 14th, 15th, 23rd, 24th

Most Stressful Days Overall: 1st, 7th, 8th, 21st, 22nd, 27th, 28th

Best Days for Love: 1st, 2nd, 3rd, 12th, 13th, 14th, 23rd, 24th, 27th, 28th

Best Days for Money: 10th, 11th, 16th, 17th, 18th, 19th, 20th, 27th, 28th

With 90 to 100 per cent of the planets below the horizon of your chart you are focusing on building a solid home base and on attaining emotional harmony. It is not that you want to ignore your career completely but want it to be emotionally comfortable for you. Those of you involved in psychological therapies make great progress this month. Your moods are very erratic later on in the month and your emotional stability depends upon not identifying with them. You have moods but you are *not* your moods. The domestic restlessness mentioned in the yearly report above is accentuated this month. You are itching to move – and an opportunity could come suddenly and unexpectedly around the 20th.

The Sun (your Career Planet) moves through your 3rd and 4th Houses this month. This shows that you can, and should, further career goals through networking, marketing and advertising until the 20th. After that you can pursue ways of doing more of your work at home and at your own pace. This is a growing trend these days. Working from home is more comfortable and makes you more productive.

A happy financial surprise – and a substantial one at that – comes through siblings, neighbours or correspondents. This could also manifest as an expensive piece of communication equipment – or a car – that comes your way. Profitable writing or advertising ideas come around the 5th.

Investors should seek investments with high yields this month. Interest and dividend income increase from existing investments. A real estate sale could come out of the blue – suddenly and unexpectedly – around the 20th.

Love is tender and nurturing all month. Those involved

romantically with a Scorpio should be maternal/paternal until the 15th. Afterwards focus on showing him or her a good time. Love feelings are much more sensitive this month than usual, so watch your chance remarks, tone of voice and unconscious gestures. Little things are likely to be blown out of proportion. Singles meet romantic opportunities through the family and at parties and places of entertainment.

Your health is good all month, but rest and relax more after the 20th.

February

> Best Days Overall: 1st, 2nd, 11th, 12th, 19th, 20th, 28th, 29th
>
> Most Stressful Days Overall: 3rd, 4th, 5th, 17th, 18th, 23rd, 24th, 25th
>
> Best Days for Love: 1st, 2nd, 13th, 14th, 21st, 22nd, 23rd, 24th, 25th
>
> Best Days for Money: 6th, 7th, 13th, 14th, 15th, 16th, 23rd, 24th, 25th

The planets have now shifted into the western half of your horoscope, signalling a greater focus on your social life and the need to achieve goals through the good graces of others. With the planets still mostly below the horizon your career takes a back seat to home and family issues. If you are going to move, remodel or modernize your home, this is a great time to do it. Start honing and refining your social skills; become more adaptable and flexible towards conditions and circumstances; and keep working on building your psychological support system. Family relations are bittersweet now and tempers flare. Family members –

especially parents or parental figures – are more edgy, nervous and rebellious now. Be patient with them. The New Moon of the 18th is going to clear up any family or domestic confusion.

The Cosmos is still helping you financially, and your wealth increases this month. The need to focus on advertising and marketing is still paramount. Investments in communication, transport and journalistic companies are still attractive. With Pluto (your Ruling Planet) now in your Money House over the long term you look at the world from an economic perspective. You tend to see everything in terms of pounds and pence – history, politics and everyday relationships are seen in terms of their economic underpinnings, in terms of profit and loss. This is the thread that weaves through all your thoughts and perceptions. There is nothing wrong with this *per se* – but it is not the whole picture. On the positive side it does strengthen your business abilities. A businessperson must see things this way. But lovers, children and other creative types might attack you for this after the 19th.

Love is happy-go-lucky and uncommitted for singles, though romantic opportunities are plentiful. An affair with a neighbour who is older is brief and not especially happy – the person seems too controlling – though it does have some potential.

Singles want fun and entertainment in love until the 9th. After that they want to serve and be served.

March

Best Days Overall: 9th, 10th, 17th, 18th, 26th, 27th, 28th

Most Stressful Days Overall: 1st, 2nd, 3rd, 15th, 16th, 22nd, 23rd, 29th, 30th

SCORPIO

Best Days for Love: 1st, 2nd, 3rd, 13th, 14th, 22nd, 23rd

Best Days for Money: 4th, 5th, 11th, 12th, 13th, 14th, 22nd, 23rd

With the planets now marching westward in your horoscope you are less self-absorbed than you have been of late. You have the opportunity to get out of yourself and involved in other people. There are many parties and entertainments this month and in general it is a 'personal pleasure period'.

After the 20th you become more serious and start to focus on work goals. You have amazing energy now and achieve goals easily and effortlessly. Those of you who work for others are probably pleasing their employers at this time. Health too becomes an important focus after the 20th. Sports and exercise – physical activity in general – will enhance your vitality.

Money is earned easily until the 20th. You earn it in ways that are pleasurable and creative. Speculations are favourable. Writers sell manuscripts, artists sell their work, performers get breaks. The sale of a home – or of household items – goes well. Your parent/s and family as a whole prosper.

After the 20th money is more difficult to earn. You will probably do well but will have to work harder – go the extra mile – to maintain earnings. Investments in steel, sporting goods or military contractors may sound fine on paper but they create financial problems for you – best to have a rethink about these things. With your investment philosophy being basically conservative this year (this will change next year) beware of offers of quick money after the 20th. And with Pluto (your Ruling Planet) going retrograde on the 5th you need to exercise more caution about finances in general. When in doubt, do nothing.

Career opportunities are opening up after the 20th but you seem hesitant – perhaps wisely so. There is no rush.

Your love life is interesting and exciting this month. Singles meet someone new suddenly and unexpectedly. This is a serious love month and you and your beloved are thinking commitment. Those already involved in relationships could experience a sudden break-up and the meeting of someone new. If the relationship is sound it changes dramatically – for the better – around the 6th.

There is some conflict or tension between your lover/spouse and your family (perhaps one of your parents) early in the month but it is short term.

April

Best Days Overall: 5th, 6th, 13th, 14th, 23rd, 24th

Most Stressful Days Overall: 11th, 12th, 18th, 19th, 25th, 26th, 27th

Best Days for Love: 1st, 2nd, 3rd, 11th, 12th, 18th, 19th, 20th, 21st, 30th

Best Days for Money: 1st, 2nd, 7th, 8th, 9th, 10th, 18th, 19th, 20th, 29th

This is an active and tumultuous month, Scorpio, but you are not as affected as others are. Still, the lunar eclipse of the 3rd brings some short-term financial upheaval which forces you to take corrective measures. Perhaps an unexpected expense reveals that your financial planning has been amiss. Or hidden flaws are revealed in certain investments you have made – flaws you knew nothing about. Use these short-term negatives as opportunities to create long-term positives.

This lunar eclipse also brings changes in a professional or social organization to which you belong. These changes – shake-ups in management or new rules that affect you – or changes in the way you are treated – cause you to re-evaluate your membership. Acquaintances leave your sphere through moves or involvements in other areas. You re-evaluate your notions of happiness this month – perhaps by getting the things that you thought would make you happy and finding out that they do not.

The solar eclipse of the 17th seems to cause a shake-up in your workplace and career. If you are an employee, job changes are happening. If you are an employer, there is a reshuffling of employees – some are leaving. Temporary demotions lead to long-term promotions. Hidden flaws at the workplace and in your career now come to the fore so that you can take corrective measures. What makes eclipses so scary is that 'worst-case scenarios' tend to dominate your mind (and other people's minds) with regard to a specific subject – in this case your work and career. All of us must confront our own personal 'underworld' during these periods. Focus this month on achieving work objectives.

Your love life is becoming more active now. Singles are meeting significant others – people who can assist them in transforming their image and character traits – breaking addictions and habits and the like – and who can help them renew themselves. Romance is physical and passionate. Both you and your lover have this unspoken agreement that each will co-operate in the 'making over' of the other.

Take a reduced schedule during the eclipse periods.

May

Best Days Overall: 3rd, 4th, 11th, 12th, 20th, 21st, 22nd, 30th, 31st

Most Stressful Days Overall: 9th, 10th, 15th, 16th, 17th, 23rd, 24th

Best Days for Love: 1st, 2nd, 9th, 10th, 15th, 16th, 17th, 18th, 19th, 27th, 28th, 29th

Best Days for Money: 5th, 6th, 7th, 8th, 15th, 16th, 17th, 25th, 26th

Two things are making you more extroverted and socially conscious, and less introspective. First, Pluto (your Ruling Planet) is retrograde, making you less self-assertive, more cautious and less sure of yourself. Second, the short-term planets have now moved into the western sector of your horoscope. Thus, this is a month for getting your way with the co-operation of others. This is a period for balancing your own interests with those of others. This is the month to develop adaptability and social grace – not a month for power struggles.

Singles are dating more now and meeting significant others. Co-workers, bosses and intellectuals are coming into your social sphere. There are more parties and social gatherings. Feelings of love are expressed ardently, passionately and physically. Beware of jealousy and possessiveness. In spite of all this romance it would not be wise to schedule a wedding just yet. Give a current relationship time. Wait a few months before committing.

Fifty to 60 per cent of the planets are retrograde this month. Be patient with yourself and others. The universe itself is pausing and reviewing, so it is not surprising that people are more confused and tending to look backwards rather than forwards. Allow yourself more time to get things done. Do not over-schedule. This is especially true with your finances. It is best to review past investments and to plan future investment strategies and purchases than actually to engage in them. Be patient when payments due to you are late or not as grand as you had thought. They will come in eventually. Getting angry and annoyed does not help matters. Rather than waste energy you are better off visualizing your highest financial ideals.

Your health is not what it should be right now. Rest and relax more until the 20th.

Your spouse or partner needs to be more cautious in financial matters as well. Overall he or she is prospering, but purchases, investments and financial commitments should be avoided until after the 27th. When in doubt, let him or her do nothing.

June

> Best Days Overall: 7th, 8th, 16th, 17th, 18th, 26th, 27th
>
> Most Stressful Days Overall: 5th, 6th, 12th, 13th, 19th, 20th
>
> Best Days for Love: 5th, 6th, 12th, 13th, 14th, 15th, 24th, 25th
>
> Best Days for Money: 1st, 2nd, 3rd, 4th, 12th, 13th, 22nd, 23rd, 29th, 30th

All your important planets – your Ruler, Money Planet and Love Planet – are retrograde this month, Scorpio, making this a period of introspection, introversion, review and inaction. If you try to force issues now you run the risk of making things worse. Achieve things by not doing, by letting the cosmic forces take over. Yes, there are times when we can achieve more by inaction than by action – by inner work rather than by outer labour. This is one of those times.

Continue to study all financial propositions, purchases and spending patterns carefully. Do not make moves unless you are absolutely clear in your mind about them. Nagging questions are signals to delay action and long-term commitments. Work to get to a place of inner certainty.

It may seem to you that you are going backwards in life these days – that you are moving away from your financial and love goals – that your life is a mess. But nothing could be further from the truth. Great progress is being made behind the scenes, in the invisible realms of life. Your job is to be patient and have faith in the cosmic law.

Inaction on the outer, objective level often means terrific action within the inner, subjective realms. When there is nothing you can do about financial delays or love relationships it is still possible to visualize your goals as you would like them to be. Thus you should dwell in fulfilment on a psychological level though objective fulfilment seems far away. The more you live in psychological fulfilment the quicker the objective world changes in ways that are pleasing to you. These kinds of actions – and they are powerful – are what is called for these days. If you do this kind of inner work these retrograde periods will be a boon and a blessing to you – and just as fun-filled and successful as when the planets move direct. I know you Scorpios understand what is being said here.

Spend more time this month clearing out psychological obstructions, patterns and addictions – things that keep you from being the person you are and want to be. Great progress is being made in this area.

July

Best Days Overall: 4th, 5th, 14th, 15th, 24th, 25th

Most Stressful Days Overall: 2nd, 3rd, 9th, 10th, 16th, 17th, 30th, 31st

SCORPIO

Best Days for Love: 2nd, 3rd, 9th, 10th, 11th, 12th, 21st, 22nd, 30th, 31st

Best Days for Money: 1st, 9th, 10th, 19th, 20th, 26th, 27th, 28th, 29th

Fifty per cent of the planets are retrograde this month, Scorpio – including some of your important ones. As a result, be patient with yourself, with others and with life. Use delays to your advantage. When one door closes look for another to open. When there is nothing to be done 'outwardly' work inwardly with your imagination and intellect. Take some of the focus off yourself and put it on others – expand your social circle. If you cannot please yourself you can at least make others happy and create good karma.

Happily, your social life is starting to move forward again – after a few months of delay and frustration. Romance is stormy and passionate – very physical – just the way you like it. Singles are intrigued by partners who can help them transform a present condition or character trait. And these kind of people present themselves to you as well. You like the feeling of being needed, of being able to help someone break an addiction or bad habit, of being able to reform someone. This is the kind of month where patients fall in love with their therapists and social workers and/or probation officers with their charges. The flaws in your beloved are not hindrances to love but rather attractions – giving Scorpio the opportunity to exercise its genius.

Be patient on the financial front. For the next few months use spare cash to reduce your debts and expenses rather than to build wealth. Sales and marketing projects need more planning and thought before being executed. Your sales judgement tends to be unrealistic this month. Avoid major purchases or long-term financial commitments for a while. Delays in monies due to you are just part of the game right now – the money will come in due course.

Your health is excellent until the 22nd, but self-esteem is the problem. You feel unable to assert yourself and your will fully this period. So do not. You need to do more research on what your real will is.

August

> Best Days Overall: 1st, 2nd, 10th, 11th, 20th, 21st, 28th, 29th
>
> Most Stressful Days Overall: 5th, 6th, 12th, 13th, 14th, 26th, 27th
>
> Best Days for Love: 5th, 6th, 10th, 11th, 20th, 21st, 28th, 29th
>
> Best Days for Money: 5th, 6th, 15th, 16th, 22nd, 23rd, 24th, 25th

Though your social life is still good and your social charisma still strong, the short-term planets are now beginning – ever so gradually – to leave your western sector and to rejoin their long-term brethren in the east. Social affairs are becoming ever less important. Your dependency on others is decreasing day by day. Your need to adapt to others is diminishing – not completely just yet – but very soon now.

The Cosmic Solar Cycle and your personal Solar Cycle are both in their waning phase until your birthday. Thus your major financial thrust should be to cut expenses and reduce long-term debt. After your birthday – and preferably after 22nd December – you can shift your priorities to wealth-building and positive investing.

The retrograde of your Money Planet – which has been going on for a few months now – continues. Thus you still need to be patient and prudent in financial matters. Your financial judgement is not as realistic now as it normally is. What you think looks good now will undoubtedly change when your Money Planet (Jupiter) starts moving forward again. Thus, study investments carefully, formulate financial plans and goals, but hold off on executing on them until later. Expenses caused by your spouse or lover (perhaps friends as well) are causing you some concern and feeling of financial pressure, but this is temporary. Moderate your expenditures but do not necessarily cut them off. The health of a sibling or neighbour is also causing you some financial concern – this too is temporary. Unexpected expenses come up with your car or phone equipment. You can handle all of this but you feel some anxiety about it. Remember that you can never out-spend your Spirit – the true source of your supply – but also sharply differentiate between necessary and unnecessary expenses. Your Spirit can supply for your true needs but not for the false ones.

Love is stormy but exciting. Your educational interests and those of your partner conflict and you are forced to compromise. Singles are still attracted to intellectual/mentor types – though they still want emotion and nurturing. Foreign travel this month may promote romance but may be a strain on your wallet.

Your health is good all month but will improve even further after the 23rd.

September

Best Days Overall: 6th, 7th, 8th, 16th, 17th, 25th, 26th

Most Stressful Days Overall: 1st, 2nd, 3rd, 9th, 10th, 23rd, 24th, 29th, 30th

Best Days for Love: 1st, 2nd, 3rd, 8th, 9th, 18th, 19th, 27th, 28th, 29th, 30th

Best Days for Money: 1st, 2nd, 11th, 12th,
18th, 19th, 20th, 21st, 29th, 30th

By the 10th all the short-term planets will be in the eastern
sector of your horoscope and you will feel yourself becoming more wilful, assertive and courageous. You begin to see
that fear is the great enemy and that fear is what has
blocked you from your goals. You are in a better position to
vanquish fear now – and to have things your own way.

The short-term planets are still above the horizon of your
chart, fuelling and empowering your ambitions and need
for outer achievement. Good career progress is being made.
Networking is still a powerful tool to further your career.
Joining professional and social organizations is also a help.
A partnership or alliance – formal or informal – furthers
your career now. Your partner and friends are boosting you;
you are making powerful friends now and socializing with
the 'high and mighty'. You rise as much because of who you
know as who you are.

Though you are more into pleasing yourself these days,
your social life is still very much a priority – perhaps a top
priority. Singles find love in the pursuit of their careers or
with people involved with their careers. Corporate types
and government employees are more alluring now. The
power and prestige of a lover or partner make him or her
very sexy to you. Prospects who are of lowly professional or
social status – and who lack ambition – are not likely to turn
you on this period. Beware, though, of becoming overly
enamoured with outer trappings. It is OK to admire ambition, but look at the inner person as well.

The lunar eclipse of the 26th creates a job change and
temporary financial upheaval. Flaws in your present job
or workplace are revealed and something must be done
one way or another to correct them. Some of you may
change jobs within the same company. Others will change

companies. Employers will lose employees this period and otherwise be forced to realign the workplace. Larger employers may face threats of a strike or work stoppage. All of this is temporary – merely one of the ways that the universe uses to change patterns.

October

Best Days Overall: 4th, 5th, 13th, 14th, 22nd, 23rd, 31st

Most Stressful Days Overall: 6th, 7th, 20th, 21st, 26th, 27th

Best Days for Love: 8th, 9th, 18th, 19th, 26th, 27th, 28th

Best Days for Money: 9th, 10th, 16th, 17th, 18th, 19th, 26th, 27th

Though the solar eclipse of the 12th causes some temporary disruption in your career and financial life, it is kinder to you than to most of the other Signs, and the changes that it brings are pleasant.

This solar eclipse occurs in your 12th House of 'behind the scenes happenings'. This not only stimulates your dream life and fosters amazing ESP experiences, but brings about secret changes in your career and corporate hierarchy. Unresolved scandals – both personal and with corporate superiors – can come to the fore during this period. Best to confess, recognize past mistakes, and resolve never to repeat them.

Your Money Planet (Jupiter) is very much affected by the eclipse. Flaws in your investment philosophy or strategy will be revealed so that you can take corrective measures. Investments that you thought were sound may not be as sound as you think – at least temporarily. But things do work out in the end. A temporary financial scare leads to greater financial wisdom.

Your love life is very favourable. Love is pursuing you ardently – coming ever closer. Until the 4th you are playful in love and are attracted to party-going, light-hearted people. Though these people are deadly serious about their careers they seem light-hearted about love. After the 4th you seek friendship and ideal love – perfect love with perfect freedom, committed but unconfined. By the end of the month you seek idealistic, spiritual love. The person who can best combine all these attributes is the one you should choose. Marrieds find that their partners are more ambitious this month and perhaps put ambitions ahead of all else – for a while. There is a need to balance your personal interests with those of your partner as they seem to be at odds. But this is temporary and both you and your spouse get into better synch towards the end of the month. Those working towards a third marriage meet a special someone after the 4th.

Your health is good all month.

November

Best Days Overall: 1st, 10th, 11th, 18th, 19th, 27th, 28th

Most Stressful Days Overall: 2nd, 3rd, 4th, 16th, 17th, 23rd, 24th, 30th

Best Days for Love: 7th, 8th, 16th, 17th, 23rd, 24th, 27th, 28th

Best Days for Money: 5th, 6th, 12th, 13th, 14th, 15th, 23rd, 24th

SCORPIO

With your 1st House very active and with many planets in the eastern part of your horoscope, you basically have things your way this month. The world agrees that fulfilment is to be yours and assents to your assertiveness and independence. Create your personal kingdom this month. Please yourself (without violating other people's rights) and others will be pleased. You are in one of your peak 'personal pleasure periods' of the year. Your sensual and physical desires are fulfilled now.

Your health and self-esteem are good now as well. Maintaining harmony with friends will further enhance things.

Your love life is fabulous, too. If you are married or involved your lover is going out of his or her way to please you – especially after the 23rd. If you are not yet involved rest assured that love is pursuing you ardently and relentlessly. It is on its way. A live-in (or quasi live-in) relationship is happening for singles. Love is altruistic and spiritual early in the month but becomes very physical and sensual later on.

Increased self-esteem always increases earnings, but you have other things going for you as well. Your Money House becomes strong after the 15th. Stocks or other investments increase in value. Windfalls come from partners, insurance companies, the government or from royalties. Your overall net worth is increased. After the 22nd money is earned through your public status and professional standing. The public image you have created boosts your 'bottom line'. Your professional standing becomes as much of an asset as money in the bank or an investment portfolio. Elders, bosses and parental figures are supporting your financial goals. With Mercury going through your Money House this month you have a greater appreciation for 'intellectual property'. Intellectual wealth is seen as paramount now. This is a good month for profit-taking from your investments – and a good time to reduce debts. Later on – after 21st December – you can start building more positive wealth and planting your future investment seeds.

December

> Best Days Overall: 7th, 8th, 15th, 16th, 25th, 26th
>
> Most Stressful Days Overall: 1st, 13th, 14th, 20th, 21st, 27th, 28th
>
> Best Days for Love: 7th, 8th, 15th, 16th, 17th, 20th, 21st, 27th, 28th
>
> Best Days for Money: 2nd, 3rd, 9th, 10th, 11th, 12th, 20th, 21st, 30th, 31st

The planets are still in the east and below the horizon of your chart; thus you are creating conditions of personal happiness according to your own terms. Personal fulfilment – sensual fulfilment – is very important to you now. Emotional harmony and domestic tranquillity take precedence over fame, honour and glory. You would rather be happy now than famous. Yet honours come to you and career success pursues you.

With Venus in your 1st House until the 17th, your self-esteem is high and sensual pleasures are fulfilled. After the 21st, though, you might want to start feeding your mind and intellect – intellectual pleasures are, after all, also satisfying.

Venus (your Love Planet) now in your own Sign shows happiness in love and great attractiveness and magnetic power. You are irresistible to the opposite sex right now. Your lover, partner or spouse goes far out of his or her way to please you. Your interests and desires come ahead of his or her own. You get your way in love right now. Singles are most certainly involved with someone now and it looks very happy. After the 17th your lover becomes more financially supportive and either gives you 'big-ticket' (expensive, long-lasting) gifts or creates earning opportunities for you. You are turned on by presents and by practical, material things in love. You feel more possessive of your lover or partner during this time (you are always possessive but after the 17th even more so) and you need to be careful not to treat him or her as another 'material object' – a 'thing' that you own and can do with however you please.

Your aesthetic sense is still very sharp and refined this month – so buy clothing, accessories or art now. This is the month to engage in artistic projects, have your hair done, or otherwise beautify your image.

Finances are going very well this month as well. Many planets are energizing your Money House, indicating that money comes to you from many and varied sources – your partner, social connections, a parent or parental figure, elders, superiors and bosses, the government, and from investments. A pleasurable financial bonanza or possession comes to you around the 17th – it could be money or some piece of jewellery or clothing – something artistic – a gift of some kind (your horoscope seems to indicate that your partner or lover has a very nice Christmas present in store for you!)

Sagittarius

↗

THE ARCHER
Birthdays from
23rd November
to 20th December

Personality Profile

SAGITTARIUS AT A GLANCE

Element – Fire

Ruling Planet – Jupiter
  Career Planet – Mercury
  Love Planet – Mercury
  Money Planet – Saturn
  Planet of Health and Work – Venus
  Planet of Home and Family Life – Neptune
  Planet of Wealth and Good Fortune – Jupiter

Colours – blue, dark blue

Colours that promote love, romance and social harmony – yellow, yellow-orange

Colours that promote earning power – black, indigo

SAGITTARIUS

Gems – carbuncle, turquoise

Metal – tin

Scents – carnation, jasmine, myrrh

Quality – mutable (= flexibility)

Qualities most needed for balance – attention to detail, administration and organization

Strongest virtues – generosity, honesty, broad-mindedness, tremendous vision

Deepest need – to expand mentally

Characteristics to avoid – over-optimism, exaggeration, being too generous with other people's money

Signs of greatest overall compatibility – Aries, Leo

Signs of greatest overall incompatibility – Gemini, Virgo, Pisces

Sign most helpful to career – Virgo

Sign most helpful for emotional support – Pisces

Sign most helpful financially – Capricorn

Sign best for marriage and/or partnerships – Gemini

Sign most helpful for creative projects – Aries

Best Sign to have fun with – Aries

Signs most helpful in spiritual matters – Leo, Scorpio

Best day of the week – Thursday

Understanding the Sagittarius Personality

If you look at the symbol of the archer you will gain a good, intuitive understanding of the people born under this astrological Sign. The development of archery was humanity's first refinement of the power to hunt and wage war. The ability to shoot an arrow far beyond the ordinary range of a spear extended humanity's horizons, wealth, personal will and power.

Today, instead of using bows and arrows we project our power with fuels and mighty engines, but the essential reason for using these new powers remains the same. These powers represent our ability to extend our personal sphere of influence – and this is what Sagittarius is all about. Sagittarians are always seeking to expand their horizons, to cover more territory and increase their range and scope. This applies to all aspects of their lives: economic, social and intellectual.

Sagittarians are noted for the development of the mind – the higher intellect – which understands philosophical, metaphysical and spiritual concepts. This mind represents the higher part of the psychic nature and is motivated not by self-centred considerations but by the light and grace of a higher power. Thus, Sagittarians love higher education of all kinds. They might be bored with formal schooling but they love to study on their own and in their own way. A love of foreign travel and interest in places far away from home are also noteworthy characteristics of the Sagittarian type.

If you give some thought to all these Sagittarian attributes you will see that they spring from the inner Sagittarian desire to develop. To travel more is to know more, to know more is to be more, to cultivate the higher mind is to grow and to reach more. All these traits tend to broaden the intellectual – and indirectly, the economic and material – horizons of the Sagittarian.

The generosity of the Sagittarian is legendary. There are

many reasons for this. One is that Sagittarians seem to have an inborn consciousness of wealth. They feel that they are rich, that they are lucky, that they can attain any financial goal – and so they feel that they can afford to be generous. Sagittarians do not carry the burdens of want and limitation – which stop most other people from giving generously. Another reason for their generosity is their religious and philosophical idealism, derived from the higher mind. This higher mind is by nature generous because it is unaffected by material circumstances. Still another reason is that the act of giving tends to enhance their emotional nature. Every act of giving seems to be enriching, and this is reward enough for the Sagittarian.

Finance

Sagittarians generally entice wealth. They either attract it or create it. They have the ideas, energy and talent to make their vision of paradise on Earth a reality. However, mere wealth is not enough. Sagittarians want luxury – earning a comfortable living seems small and insignificant to them.

In order for Sagittarians to attain their true earning potential they must develop better managerial and organizational skills. They must learn to set limits, to arrive at their goals through a series of attainable sub-goals or objectives. It is very rare that a person goes from rags to riches overnight. But a long, drawn-out process is difficult for Sagittarians. Like Leos, they want to achieve wealth and success quickly and impressively. They must be aware, however, that this over-optimism can lead to unrealistic financial ventures and disappointing losses. Of course, no Zodiac Sign can bounce back as quickly as Sagittarius, but only needless heartache will be caused by this attitude. Sagittarians need to maintain their vision – never letting go of it – but must also work towards it in practical and efficient ways.

Career and Public Image

Sagittarians are big thinkers. They want it all: money, name, fame, glamour, prestige, public acclaim and a place in history. They often go after all these goals. Some attain them, some do not – much depends on each individual's personal horoscope. But if Sagittarians want to attain public and professional status they must understand that these things are not conferred to enhance one's ego but as rewards for the amount of service that one does for the whole of humanity. If and when they figure out ways to serve more, Sagittarians can rise to the top.

The ego of the Sagittarian is gigantic – and perhaps rightly so. They have much to be proud of. If they want public acclaim, however, they will have to learn to tone the ego down a bit, to become more humble and self-effacing, without falling into the trap of self-denial and self-abasement. They must also learn to master the details of life, which can sometimes elude them.

At their jobs Sagittarians are hard workers who like to please their bosses and co-workers. They are dependable, trustworthy and enjoy challenging work assignments and situations. Sagittarians are friendly to work with and helpful to their colleagues. They usually contribute intelligent new ideas or new methods that improve the work environment for everyone. Sagittarians always look for challenging positions and careers that develop their intellect, even if they have to work very hard in order to succeed. They also work well under the supervision of others, although by nature they would rather be the supervisors and increase their sphere of influence. Sagittarians excel at professions that allow them to be in contact with many different people and to travel to new and exciting locations.

Love and Relationships

Sagittarians love freedom for themselves and will readily grant it to their partners. They like their relationships to be fluid, loose and ever-changing. Sagittarians tend to be fickle in love and to change their minds about their partners quite frequently.

Sagittarians feel threatened by a clearly defined, well-structured relationship, as it tends to limit their freedom. The Sagittarian tends to marry more than once in life.

Sagittarians in love are passionate, generous, open, benevolent and very active. They demonstrate their affections very openly. However, just like an Aries they tend to be egocentric in the way they relate to their partners. Sagittarians should develop the ability to see another's point of view, not just their own. They need to develop some objectivity and cool intellectual clarity in their relationships so that they can develop better two-way communications with their partners. Sagittarians tend to be overly idealistic about their partners and about love in general. A cool and rational attitude will help them to perceive reality more clearly and help them to avoid disappointment.

Home and Domestic Life

Sagittarians tend to grant a lot of freedom to their family. They like big homes and many children and are one of the most fertile Signs of the Zodiac. However, when it comes to their children Sagittarians generally err on the side of allowing them too much freedom. Sometimes their children get the idea that there are no limits. However, allowing freedom in the home is basically a positive thing – so long as some measure of balance is maintained – for it enables all family members to develop as they should.

Horoscope for 1996

Major Trends

Last year – especially for those of you born early in the Sign – was a year of re-invention and redefinition. Your efforts were greatly rewarded in terms of increased self-esteem, self-worth and recognition by the world. It was a year of great personal expansion and happiness – though this could have come a bit easier than the way it did. You were being yourself and basically doing what you love to do. This happy trend continues in 1996 but more in the financial realm. The process of transforming your body, personality and image is a continuing one that goes on for many years to come. You are becoming, year by year, a deeper, keener and more perceptive person.

Though 1996 continues to be a fun year you will have to put some limits on these activities when Saturn starts to move through your 5th House of Fun and Creativity from 7th April onwards. Of course you should continue to enjoy life, but structure the fun and get it under your control. Focus on quality fun – fun that is creative and growth-producing rather than that which depletes and drains you.

Major changes are going on in your education and intellectual interests as well. Modern devices or methods are enabling you to learn and communicate much more quickly than you ever dreamed. All kinds of new communication equipment is coming to you this year and next.

Health

Your health was basically good last year; this year it should be even better. Saturn, which was making stressful aspects to you last year (especially those of you born later in the

286

Sign) is, by 7th April, moving away from this stressful location. Thus your already superabundant vitality is increased even further. You have all the energy you need to achieve whatever you desire. It is up to you to invest it wisely.

A further reinforcement of the good health prognosis is the fact that your 6th House of Health is relatively inactive this year. You are not paying too much attention to this area, which astrologers consider to a be a fortunate signal.

Pluto in your 1st House for many years to come shows – unlike last year – a tendency to slim down, to be more careful of diet and in general to be focused on eliminating impurities from your body. Herbs and foods that cleanse and purify are very healthy for you this year.

Pluto in the 1st also makes for great physical drive and single-minded concentration on the physical world. Pluto's transit through a person's 1st House is considered by astrologers to be the opportunity of a lifetime – for most people never get to experience this. (Pluto's motion is so slow that in a normal lifetime it only transits three or four Signs). Great achievements are possible now.

Many of you, because of your drive to transform your image, are contemplating some cosmetic-type surgery now. Others will transform their image through metaphysical techniques; still others through diet, exercise and vitamins. The main lesson this year is that you can renew your body not by adding new things to it but by ridding it of blockages and undesirable elements. When these are gone renewal happens almost by itself.

Changes in your personality are going to become evident this year. Normally you are 'wide' person in that you like to see the big picture, the broad scope of things. But now you are becoming deeper, more psychic, more penetrating into others and yourself. Your normal optimism, which up to now has been instinctive and probably unconscious, now becomes based on a knowledge of deeper realities. It is a stronger optimism – less likely to be shaken by outer events – because of this.

Home and Domestic Life

Your home and family situation were very important last year, but as 1996 progresses they become less and less important to you. Burdens and responsibilities from the family or with your home are lifted off you. And even if you are still carrying them they seem easier to bear – you have mastered their lessons. The feeling of being cramped in the home – of lack of space – also disappears. This could come from a move or a reorganization of your current living space. The lesson of last year was not that you needed more space – though you felt that you did – but that you needed to maximize and put to better use the space that you have.

Last year you seemed to be spending more on the home – perhaps on a burdensome rent or mortgage – and on family members. This spending decreases this year.

Pluto in your 1st House shows that you still have a desire to completely renovate and redo your personal room or personal space within the home. You do not want to change it cosmetically – just rearrange furniture or move a few pictures about – but to change it in deep, fundamental ways: tearing down the walls and changing the shape of the room, or ripping out the wires or plumbing and replacing them with newer and better alternatives.

On a psychological level you become more free in the expression of your feelings after April. There is less of a need to repress or manage them. You feel emotionally free.

Neptune, your Home Planet, has been stimulated by Uranus for many years now. This made you feel restless about your living quarters – restless and at the same time idealistic. You probably moved around a lot over the past few years. But this trend is just about over. There is yet one more major move (or acquisition of a new home) this year, and this seems to be *it*. The opportunity will come late in 1996 as Jupiter contacts Neptune in Capricorn. This is a very happy move. Those of you who are looking to sell property will probably find a buyer at that time as well – and at a good price. Both men and women are more fertile during this period. Marriages and births occur in the family circle, and so your family circle expands. Last year your family circle probably diminished.

A sibling is unusually restless and is about to go through a series of moves and changes of residences as well.

Love and Social Life

Your 7th House of Love and Marriage is not particularly active this year, showing that it is a status quo kind of year. Singles will tend to remain single and marrieds will tend to remain married. The Cosmos grants you freedom to make of your social life what you will. Those who truly want to get married can probably do so if they work hard at it. But most of you are wisely focusing on yourselves. Singles are better advised to manifest and create in themselves the lovable personality that they desire rather than run around looking for love in all the wrong places. If you become your own ideal self – a very strong possibility this year – or even come closer to your ideal of yourself – you will not have to go running in the pursuit of love. Love will find you – and quite quickly at that.

This is most definitely a year for ridding yourself of the 'unlovable' aspects of yourself – character traits, habits, mannerisms, etc. that you dislike. It is a year for the caterpillar to become the butterfly.

Having said all this, there is a serious relationship brewing this year. But will it last? Is it a fling or something more? The Cosmos neither pushes nor obstructs. You can afford to be patient. This relationship is most likely to occur from 3rd April to 7th August as Venus makes an unusually long station in your 7th House of Marriage. Venus goes through all kinds of gyrations during this transit. It goes fast forward for a while, then slows down, then actually moves backwards and then fast forward again. This describes the relationship: never a dull moment.

The marriage and/or social life of a parent or parental figure starts to improve dramatically after April. If the parent is single (widowed or divorced) a marriage or serious romantic involvement is likely towards the end of 1996. This relationship is with someone prominent, cultured, spiritual and refined whom your parent meets at a party in the neighbourhood. Or it could happen through a neighbour 'playing Cupid'.

A sibling, like yourself, needs to focus more on his or her own self – to become the person he or she wants to be – rather than running after romance this year.

The marriage of a friend goes through a crisis this year as the friend's partner lacks self-esteem because of financial worries. If love exists here it will prevail, but there will be many changes and tests in the next two years.

Career and Finance

Finances have been important in your life for many years now and this trend continues this year. For seven years now you have been experimenting financially – either changing jobs or exploring all kinds of investments, different ways to manage your money and various techniques to attain wealth. Some of these alternatives worked, some did not. You learned big lessons – especially what to avoid – but you also developed your own distinctive method for investing and managing your money. The Cosmos is now going to provide opportunities and lucky breaks. Your wealth expands this year, but conservatively and in gradual stages.

By nature you are a speculative type of person. A risk-taker. Risks that you take as a matter of course, without batting an eyelash, would absolutely terrify more conservative types. This trait is further reinforced in 1996. Some of your likely speculative investments will be in sports and sporting goods, the steel industry, and perhaps military contractors. Though these industries as a whole are having a rough time of it in 1996 – especially later on in the year – given companies could still do well. As the well-known maxim goes, 'the time to buy is at the point of maximum pessimism.' Invest with a small percentage of your holdings and be prepared to hang in there for the long haul. Pay more attention to these industries – or to given companies in these fields – so that you are in a position to know when to buy and when to sell. Your instincts are outstanding, but do your homework.

Your creativity is also a source of financial expansion. Those of you involved in the creative or performing arts are likely to see your 'bottom line' enhanced. You have a good instinct for creating things that sell – that bring profits to you. On the other hand, you need to be careful not to let financial considerations have too much weight in your creativity lest you stunt it. Pursuing your natural creative instincts will, in general, bring earning opportunities to you.

Your personal appearance and personal presentation play unusually important roles in the way you earn money this year. Those of you who are in the fashion industry or in sales will do well. Those involved in manual work will also fare well. But no matter what your line of work, dress for success and project an image of wealth and success. Do not confuse image with substance, but remember that though the goal is actually to be wealthy, it will not hurt to have others perceive you as already affluent and 'upscale'.

Other, more conservative investments that could turn into profits would be in real estate – either commercial or residential – government bonds and securities, publishing, travel, and for-profit higher education institutions.

Your partner or spouse seems much less concerned about

earnings than you. This is not a priority in his or her life. The income of a sibling improves dramatically after 7th April. The income of one of your parents (or parental figures) is tight this year and there is need for more budgeting, cost-control and effective financial management. He or she needs to make the most of the present income and present resources.

Self-improvement

Your financial life is going to improve almost regardless of what you do. The opportunities will come and you must merely make the motions to carry them out. The pursuit of intellectual interests will be more important this year and gives you a chance to express some of your uniqueness and creativity. Take up journalism or creative writing as a hobby. Take a course in either of these fields – it should be a lot of fun.

Creativity becomes important to your 'bottom line' this year. But you need to be more controlled with it, to structure your creations better and to pay more attention to details. Your problem is not with the creative ideas *per se* – you have plenty of those. The challenge is in the execution of these ideas – in your ability to craft them into something that conforms to their initial conception.

Those of you with children have many learning experiences in 1996 – especially after April. Generally you are a believer in freedom but now you are put into a position where you have to be a disciplinarian. Giving too much freedom to your kids will not work this year. Overly disciplining them will not work either. You have got to find that subtle, wordless point of balance. The horoscope suggests that the purse strings rather than other forms of control are most effective.

Month-by-month Forecasts

January

Best Days Overall: 7th, 8th, 16th, 17th, 18th, 25th, 26th

Most Stressful Days Overall: 2nd, 3rd, 10th, 11th, 23rd, 24th, 30th, 31st

Best Days for Love: 2nd, 3rd, 12th, 13th, 14th, 19th, 20th, 23rd, 24th, 27th, 28th, 29th, 30th

Best Days for Money: 5th, 6th, 10th, 11th, 14th, 15th, 19th, 20th, 23rd, 24th, 27th, 28th

The planets are clustered both below the horizon and in the eastern sector of your chart this month. Thus, you are focused on personal interests, personal desires and your own emotional well-being. This is the month to please yourself; to increase personal earnings, to feel good about yourself and attain personal psychological harmony. The time for people-pleasing will come, but later on in the year. If you feel in emotional harmony within yourself you will be better able to help others – particularly family members. You set the tone and the pace this month. You create conditions and will have to live with your creations. Others have to adapt to you.

Money and investments are the number-one priority for most of the month. Happily this area is very successful. You get your way and achieve your goals. You are financially fearless and you enjoy the financial game. Resist the temptation to be over-speculative, however, and avoid – though this will be difficult – the lure of 'quick cash'. Focus on solid investments. A big financial bonanza – either actual cold cash, a material possession, or even 'intellectual wealth' – comes to you around the 5th, unexpected like a bolt from the blue. A financial seed that was planted last year blooms. Enjoy!

Interest and dividend income increase moderately after the 20th. Investments in property go well. Investments in gold or gold stocks appeal to you, but be prepared to wait a few months for profits.

Mercury (your Career Planet) is retrograde from the 9th to the 30th. Your career is on hold for a while and perhaps a bit confusing. Use the time to plan future career moves. When in doubt, do nothing. Rash action could make things worse. This applies to your love and social life as well – for Mercury rules these areas, too. Maintain the status quo in love for a while and see what you really feel. You are really not sure what it is you want from a lover or a relationship right now; take the time to become clear.

Your health is great until the 20th, after which you should rest and relax more.

February

Best Days Overall: 3rd, 4th, 5th, 13th, 14th, 21st, 22nd

Most Stressful Days Overall: 6th, 7th, 19th, 20th, 26th, 27th

Best Days for Love: 1st, 2nd, 6th, 7th, 13th, 14th, 16th, 17th, 21st, 22nd, 26th, 27th

Best Days for Money: 1st, 2nd, 6th, 7th, 11th, 12th, 15th, 16th, 19th, 20th, 23rd, 24th, 25th

This is a very happy and successful month for you, Sagittarius. You are still calling the shots, getting your way and having tremendous personal drive and initiative. All the planets moving forward this month show that the cosmic momentum is forward-moving – fostering action and achievement. There will be some resistance to your personal will after the 15th and you will be forced to compromise, but before that it is all clear sailing.

Your interest is still focused on the personal level – on personal finance, family relations, personal pleasure and inner emotional harmony. Though this is not your true nature – you like to be involved in world affairs – it is good for now. You can better serve the world from a stable domestic and financial base.

As for Scorpio, your Ruling Planet is in your Money House this year. Thus you tend to view life, art, politics, history and even mundane social relationships in economic terms – in terms of pounds and pence, profit and loss, the struggle for capital and market share. Though this is not a true view of life – only part of the picture – it does enhance your business and earning abilities. It is the perspective of the businessperson, the capitalist, the entrepreneur and not the philosopher and theologian. (You are more comfortable with latter perspective.) A friend or co-worker gives your 'bottom line' a boost early in the month. News from foreign lands – foreign economic developments – provide a financial boost later on in the month and next month as well.

Now that Mercury (your Love Planet) moves fast forward all month you have more confidence in love and social matters. Early in the month you view love in terms of pounds and pence – costs and benefits. Beware of treating the beloved as another financial asset in your portfolio. On the positive side you give and receive financial support – and want this kind of relationship with your beloved. After the 15th your love nature widens and you are more interested in the sharing of ideas and thoughts – intellectual communion and harmony – than in finances. Where early on you were turned on by expensive gifts and material things, now you are turned on by witty conversation and brilliant ideas. Love opportunities increase for singles after the 15th.

March

Best Days Overall: 1st, 2nd, 3rd, 11th, 12th, 19th, 20th

Most Stressful Days Overall: 4th, 5th, 17th, 18th, 24th, 25th

Best Days for Love: 1st, 2nd, 3rd, 9th, 10th, 13th, 14th, 17th, 18th, 22nd, 23rd, 24th, 25th, 29th, 30th

Best Days for Money: 4th, 5th, 9th, 10th, 13th, 14th, 17th, 18th, 22nd, 23rd, 27th, 28th

This is definitely a month for dealing with family, domestic and psychological issues. Not only are 80 to 90 per cent of the planets at the bottom half of your horoscope, but your 4th House (of Home and Family Life) is powerful as well. If you are going to move, renovate, redecorate, buy or sell a home, buy or sell furniture, mend fences with family members and/or embark on psychological therapies, this is the time to do it. Outer achievements can wait for a while as you build and strengthen your home base. The need for emotional harmony right now is not a luxury but a necessity.

Try to rest and relax more until the 20th. Pace yourself. Rest when you feel tired. This dip in vitality is only temporary and after the 20th you are ready to take on the world again. Health is enhanced by feelings of emotional security, creative pursuits and artistic expression.

Your social charisma, though strong, is not fixed on what it wants. You have many different needs in love this month. Until the 7th you want intellectual communion and the sharing of ideas. After the 7th you want nurturing and emotional support. After the 24th you want fun, games and entertainment. The perfect person will be the one who best combines all these qualities. Until the 7th singles find romantic opportunities at schools, computer or science seminars, and perhaps with teachers/students. After the 7th romantic opportunities come through family introductions, family gatherings or through people from your past. After the 24th they come at sporting events, parties, places of entertainment, the sports centre or exercise class and through the pursuit of creative projects. There is a lot of dating.

After 20th March you enter a fun-filled period. Personal pleasures and parties abound. It is an upscale, optimistic period quite in contrast to the tone of the early part of the month. Spring has arrived and you are feeling frisky and happy.

Finances are good all month but you enjoy them more later in the month than earlier on. You need to work harder for earnings early in the month.

April

Best Days Overall: 7th, 8th, 16th, 17th, 25th, 26th, 27th

Most Stressful Days Overall: 1st, 2nd, 13th, 14th, 20th, 21st, 28th, 29th

Best Days for Love: 1st, 2nd, 3rd, 7th, 8th, 9th, 11th, 12th, 18th, 19th, 20th, 21st, 28th, 29th, 30th

Best Days for Money: 1st, 2nd, 6th, 7th, 9th, 10th, 15th, 16th, 18th, 19th, 20th, 25th, 26th, 29th

This is basically a happy, harmonious month, Sagittarius, with two eclipses thrown in to keep things interesting. After all, too much happiness creates boredom.

This is a fun-orientated month. You want to explore the rapturous side of life, and have many opportunities to do so. Personal creativity is at an all-time high. Relations with children, though sometimes stormy, are fundamentally sound – though the solar eclipse of the 17th is signalling long-term changes here. An eclipse in the 5th House of Fun and Creativity can manifest in various ways. If you have older children you are somehow more separated from them – perhaps they go off to university or get married or move to a different town or different country. If the children are younger, repressed resentments in them come out (or you realize mistakes you have made) and you are forced to make changes in the way you are raising them. Often an eclipse in this House shows that the proceeds from a house or an inheritance is not what you planned on and that adjustments need to be made. Income from your parents is not what you thought it would be. Some hidden glitch comes to light.

Creative artists and performers make long-term changes in their careers this month – favourable ones. Though you feel more speculative now, try to avoid it this month. Your abstract judgement could be off.

The lunar eclipse of the 3rd occurs in your 11th House of Friends and Group Activities. There are various scenarios through which this cosmic event can manifest. Friends and acquaintances leave your sphere. Secret flaws in a friendship come to light and you are forced to make adjustments. A shake-up in a social or professional organization is not to your taste. What you thought would bring happiness to you does not and you are forced to re-evaluate your ideals. An 'ism' that was supposed to save the world does not and cannot. The income of a parent is in temporary upheaval. This parent's (or parental figure's) earning abilities change for the long term. Income that you thought would come because of your status in society is not what you imagined. Though these are not major things – your health and love life seem good – they are troublesome and do force you to action.

May

> Best Days Overall: 5th, 6th, 13th, 14th, 23rd, 24th

> Most Stressful Days Overall: 11th, 12th, 18th, 19th, 25th, 26th

> Best Days for Love: 1st, 2nd, 7th, 8th, 9th, 10th, 15th, 16th, 17th, 18th, 19th, 25th, 26th, 27th, 28th, 29th

> Best Days for Money: 7th, 8th, 15th, 16th, 17th, 25th, 26th

A bit of a delicate month for you, Sagittarius. Fire Signs feel comfortable when the pace of events is fast; the fast track is where they love to be – and where they belong. But May is more of a 'stop-stop-stop' month than a 'go-go-go' one. Your strongest virtues, optimism, faith and belief in eternal growth and expansion, are considered unrealistic this month – not in tune with the times. People in general feel unusually cautious, perhaps pessimistic and undecided about things. To you this sounds like unbridled pessimism. To them it is 'realism'. Over the long term your optimism is well founded, but in the short term this is a sticky stretch of road.

Most of your important planets are retrograde this month: Jupiter (your Ruling Planet); Mercury (your Love and Career Planet); and Venus (your Health and Work

Planet). Most of your financial planets (you have more than one this year) are also retrograde. So this is a month during which you learn the wisdom of doing nothing. Many of you Fire types do not realize that constructive inaction can further your goals as much as direct action can. Sometimes time itself is what makes things happen. Just as you cannot rush a pregnancy or a soufflé, you cannot rush success now. Let time do its perfect work.

For most of the month 40 to 60 per cent of the planets are in Earth Signs, which makes people conservative and down to earth. They are less prone to speculations and risk-taking now – especially until the 20th – than is comfortable for you. The general psychology this month is that 'a bird in the hand is worth two in the bush'. Vision is limited to what can be perceived with the five senses. Your higher vision of infinite possibility seems 'pie in the sky' – wonderful if it were true, but probably too good to be true. This is how most people are thinking now. Those of you who are in sales and marketing need to take this into account – stress the practical benefits of whatever you are trying to sell.

Though romance is happy and good this month it would not be wise to send out wedding invitations just yet. Give a current relationship lots of time. Re-evaluate what it is you want and need in a love relationship. Hidden flaws in a current relationship are coming to light in the coming months. Your romantic judgement is probably not realistic after the 20th.

June

Best Days Overall: 1st, 2nd, 9th, 10th, 19th, 20th, 29th, 30th

Most Stressful Days Overall: 7th, 8th, 14th, 15th, 22nd, 23rd

SAGITTARIUS

Best Days for Love: 3rd, 4th, 5th, 6th, 12th, 13th, 14th, 15th, 24th, 25th

Best Days for Money: 1st, 2nd, 3rd, 4th, 9th, 12th, 13th, 19th, 22nd, 23rd, 29th, 30th

Though 50 per cent of the planets are still in retrograde motion this month you are less affected – feel less frustrated and are achieving more – this month than last. Your Financial Planet (Saturn) continues to move forward, while Mercury (your Love Planet) is now moving fast forward. Your life is starting to progress again. Now that you have experienced some delays and frustrations you are better able to sympathize – and be patient – with many others around you who are still under the full impact of the retrogrades.

Earnings are strong until the 21st. The only financial problem is your uncertainty as to what your true financial goals should be. If you clear this up you should have no problem, for the Cosmos is aiding you now. Be careful of rash speculation in gold right now – if you do invest here use only a small percentage of your holdings. Investments in sporting goods, military equipment or military contractors will not pay off straight away, but over time. After the 21st you face some tough financial choices – should you spend on a foreign holiday or on more lasting possessions for yourself? Should you spend on higher education or on personal accessories? You are pulled in different directions. Spend a little on each in a comfortable way. After the 21st you are very active on the financial level but need to work harder than usual to achieve your financial goals. Go the extra mile and you will see a net increase in your wealth; you will convert a stressful financial shortage into plenty.

Your social life is much more active this month than last. Singles are meeting serious romantic possibilities. But hold off on commitment while Venus is still retrograding. Your social charisma is strong and you have great social confidence. The New Moon of the 11th occurs in your House of Marriage; it will clarify your social agenda and a current relationship. Romance is playful, fun and entertaining. There are many evenings out and much physical passion. The workplace, social gatherings, parties and schools are likely meeting grounds for singles. Those of you already involved in a relationship are now seeing progress.

Your health is good but rest and relax more this month.

July

Best Days Overall: 6th, 7th, 8th, 16th, 17th, 26th, 27th

Most Stressful Days Overall: 4th, 5th, 11th, 12th, 19th, 20th

Best Days for Love: 2nd, 3rd, 4th, 5th, 11th, 12th, 14th, 15th, 16th, 21st, 22nd, 26th, 27th, 30th, 31st

Best Days for Money: 1st, 6th, 7th, 8th, 9th, 10th, 16th, 17th, 19th, 20th, 26th, 27th, 28th, 29th

Five planets – including some of your important ones – are retrograde this month Sagittarius, so be patient with yourself and with life in general. Progress is being made in unseen realms. The stage needs to be set and the props need to be shuffled about a bit in order for your expectations to come to pass. Use delays to your advantage. Frustration is the food of the wise, say the sages. Victory over discouragement is one of the great triumphs of life. Prepare the way for your good in the meantime. What cannot be done physically is still very possible to do in imagination. You may not be able physically to get that coveted 'thing' you want this month, but you can certainly envision yourself having it – this is the next best thing and guarantees that what you want will eventually come your way. The problem is knowing what you want – and visualization can help with this.

Though financial issues are much delayed there are two unexpected bonanzas – out of the blue – on the 1st and the 15th (approximately). But these too could take the form of a delayed reaction. Continue to study all financial commitments, purchases or proposed investments very carefully. Do not get involved in anything that you do not fully understand.

Your social life continues to be active and you are wisely putting other people ahead of yourself. Your social confidence and judgement are strong. Your social charisma – your power to attract – is also very strong. Singles have an embarrassment of romantic riches this month. Many of you are forced to choose between someone who is romantic and someone who just wants a good time. Both are appealing. Until the 22nd people in general are hyper-sensitive – and easily hurt. You must take great care in how you talk to people and in your tone of voice.

Your health is excellent all month but especially after the 22nd. Your personal outlook improves after the 22nd. You feel more confident and optimistic then, and more fun-loving. Opportunities for higher education and foreign travel will come and this is the perfect time to take advantage of them.

August

Best Days Overall: 3rd, 4th, 12th, 13th, 14th, 22nd, 23rd, 30th, 31st

Most Stressful Days Overall: 1st, 2nd, 7th, 8th, 9th, 15th, 16th, 28th, 29th

Best Days for Love: 5th, 6th, 7th, 8th, 9th, 10th, 11th, 15th, 16th, 20th, 21st, 25th, 26th, 28th, 29th ·

Best Days for Money: 3rd, 4th, 5th, 6th, 12th, 13th, 15th, 16th, 22nd, 23rd, 24th, 25th, 30th, 31st

Like last month, the short-term planets are all in the upper sector of your chart, fostering your ambitions and your need for outward, career success. Push career goals boldly now. Opportunities for travel and education related to your career should be taken now. Networking, lobbying and campaigning are effective tools for career success this month. Let the powers that be know what you want and what you can do. Work to create – through visualization and meditation – your desired public image. Your partner, spouse or lover is a strong career ally. Friends are also inclined to promote your career goals.

Romance seems uncommitted this month. The physical side is most interesting right now and the fulfilment of sexual fantasies is on the cards, but this has nothing to do with marriage or commitment. You also feel a strong interest in romantic involvements with government figures, superiors, and people of power and prominence. You are temporarily infatuated with power and status. Singles look for people who can help their careers and are dating superiors and/or elders. You are more in love with what the person can do for you than what he or she really is. Your spouse (for those of you who are married) seems more ambitious or involved with the government right now.

The retrograde of your Money Planet continues and you should thus avoid incurring long-term debt or making major purchases and investments. From now until your birthday use spare cash to reduce debts and expenses. Pay off your credit cards, mortgage or bank loans.

Proposed home and domestic projects should likewise be thought through very carefully before you commit to them. Your judgement in these matters seems unrealistic and is likely to change when more facts are available.

Your health is excellent until the 23rd, after which you should rest and relax more. The work you have been doing to transform your personal image can now go forward. This is a good month in which to drop the pounds and detoxify the body.

September

Best Days Overall: 9th, 10th, 18th, 19th, 27th, 28th

Most Stressful Days Overall: 4th, 5th, 11th, 12th, 25th, 26th

Best Days for Love: 4th, 5th, 8th, 9th, 12th, 18th, 19th, 20th, 21st, 27th, 28th, 29th, 30th

Best Days for Money: 1st, 2nd, 9th, 11th, 12th, 18th, 19th, 20th, 21st, 27th, 28th, 29th, 30th

The lunar eclipse of the 26th is basically kind to you. True, you may start to redefine your personality or embark on a change of image, but these changes seem pleasant. The eclipse brings a temporary financial upheaval – perhaps an unexpected expense or the revelation that the investment strategy needs to be changed. But this is nothing you cannot handle. Those of you with children will see a change in your relationship with them. Your children embark on some radical new course or they redefine their own personalities in a new and radical way.

Avoid speculations this month. Rest and relax more until

the 23rd. After that, the Sun's entrance into Libra improves your vitality.

With most of the planets in the upper half of your chart this month, and with the Sun in your Career House, you are in one of the most powerful career periods of your year. Push forward with career goals, but carefully. Let your ambitions be known to those who can help you, but take the time to make sure that they really get the message and not some garbled version of the truth. Mercury's retrograde through your Career House shows that miscommunication with elders and superiors is more likely. You have to take corrective measures. Career progress will come but it is likely to be somewhat delayed. Communication problems are really the main danger to career advancement. Many of you are going to have dealings with the government or large bureaucracies during this period – take nothing for granted and make sure that they get your message and that you get theirs.

Career offers should be studied carefully before you make any decisions. Read the fine print in all contracts.

Your love life, too, requires caution. You are unsure about a current relationship – and rightly so. Give it time. Do not schedule a marriage or a divorce now. You are not sure whether your current love is a friend or a controlling influence. Conversely, you are not sure whether you want power in a lover – someone who can help you attain ambitions – or just friendship.

Channel spare cash into debt-reduction until your birthday. Use this period to plan future investment strategies.

October

> Best Days Overall: 6th, 7th, 16th, 17th, 24th, 25th
>
> Most Stressful Days Overall: 1st, 2nd, 9th, 10th, 22nd, 23rd, 29th, 30th

SAGITTARIUS

Best Days for Love: 1st, 2nd, 8th, 9th, 11th, 12th, 18th, 19th, 20th, 21st, 27th, 28th, 29th, 30th, 31st

Best Days for Money: 6th, 9th, 10th, 16th, 17th, 18th, 19th, 24th, 26th, 27th

You are very much in the fast lane this month Sagittarius, so you should feel basically comfortable. Still, the solar eclipse of the 12th will throw in a few challenges to keep things interesting.

Finances are starting to improve – delayed deals, projects and payments are starting to move forward again – but caution is still called for. Your Money Planet (Saturn) is still retrograde. Long-term investments, purchases and financial commitments need further study. Avoid investment vehicles which you do not completely understand.

Your health is good all month but take a reduced schedule on the 11th, 12th and 13th. The solar eclipse makes an exact aspect to Jupiter (your Ruling Planet). Healthy people will make changes in their mode of dress and daily lifestyle. You are redefining your personality. Your personal image of wealth – which you have been working so hard to create – is also being redefined, ultimately for the better. Perhaps you have been identifying with what you own and with your earning power rather than seeing these things as mere ornaments to your true self. If so, you can expect events to change that. You cannot allow your self-esteem to rise and fall like the stock-market. It must be something steady and secure – based on something permanent and immutable. The solar eclipse also affects Neptune (your Home and Family Planet), causing either a move or changes within your residence and your family situation. Those of you involved in the academic world – either as teachers or students – have big changes coming up. Students change schools or change the subject they are studying; teachers depart; course requirements change; new education either begins or ends. Your personal philosophy and faith get tested. Friends move from your personal sphere and your partner makes major changes in his or her creative life. A parent (or parental figure) has a temporary financial setback. A child marries or gets divorced. Enjoy these changes as much as possible – patterns change for the better in all cases.

Your love and social life are top priorities until the 9th. Romantic opportunities come from people involved with your career, and with bosses. You socialize with people of high social status. Your lover, spouse or partner is unusually ambitious until the 9th. Your own social charisma is strong. Singles are dating more than usual.

November

Best Days Overall: 2nd, 3rd, 4th, 12th, 13th, 20th, 21st, 30th

Most Stressful Days Overall: 5th, 6th, 18th, 19th, 25th, 26th

Best Days for Love: 1st, 7th, 8th, 10th, 11th, 16th, 17th, 20th, 21st, 25th, 26th, 27th, 28th, 30th

Best Days for Money: 2nd, 3rd, 5th, 6th, 12th, 13th, 14th, 15th, 20th, 21st, 23rd, 24th

The need to finish things and wind down your activities and projects has been strong for many months now – especially since the summer. Bringing things to a successful conclusion, tying up loose ends, clearing the decks and the like are just as important as starting new projects. Right now – until your birthday – you are in one of the optimum periods of the year for these kinds of activities. Before you can set the table for the new meal you must clear it. So pay bills, reduce debts and bring old projects to a satisfying close this month. Review the past year and see how close you came to attaining your goals; then set new goals for the coming year. Admit your mistakes and vow never to repeat them. See where improvements can be made. Spend more time in seclusion and self-analysis (though you do not need to overdo this either). Spiritual and psychological illumination is yours this month if you desire it – and what Sagittarius does not?

Your love life is improving day by day. Singles have no need to run after love this month as it is seeking them ardently. Keep a low profile in a current relationship for a while. No one needs to know what is going on except for you and your beloved. Later on the relationship will reveal itself naturally. Love is altruistic early in the month but becomes more physical and sensual later on. You have your way in love this month as your lover is going out of his or her way to please you and to cater to your desires.

Best also to keep a low profile on your career plans and goals. When they are attained the world will know about it naturally without your having to say anything. Present the world with a *fait accompli*. If you speak too prematurely you run the risk of creating unneeded opposition or antagonism. Your career goals would still be met, but with more difficulty at your end.

Your health is excellent all month but you can further enhance it through metaphysical practices – positive affirmations, positive thinking and the like. You seem more concerned with the health of others – especially your partner or friends – than with your own health.

December

Best Days Overall: 1st, 9th, 10th, 18th, 19th, 27th, 28th

Most Stressful Days Overall: 2nd, 3rd, 15th, 16th, 22nd, 23rd, 30th, 31st

Best Days for Love: 1st, 7th, 8th, 11th, 12th, 15th, 16th, 17th, 20th, 21st, 22nd, 23rd, 27th, 28th, 20th, 31st

Best Days for Money: 1st, 2nd, 3rd, 9th, 10th, 11th, 12th, 18th, 19th, 20th, 21st, 27th, 28th, 30th, 31st

Many planets in the east and below the horizon of your chart show that this is a period of personal pleasure, sensual fulfilment, emotional harmony and domestic tranquillity. You are more independent, self-willed and self-assertive now. You create your own conditions in life and others will support you in this. You would rather have personal happiness than name, fame and honour. Family issues come before your career.

With 80 to 90 per cent of the planets moving forward there is great progress being made in your life. Your goals are on the way to being fulfilled. It is an action-orientated month – just the way you like it.

Both Venus and your Love Planet (Mercury) move through your own Sign this month – though at different times. Thus you have things your way in love this month. Your lover or spouse goes out of his or her way to please you. Your desires come ahead of his or her own. Both these planets moving through your own Sign give you a stronger aesthetic sense and more social grace and glamour. You get your way through charm rather than through brute force. You are irresistible to the opposite sex. You have a charming personal style. You dress elegantly and attract what you want into your life. Romance blooms, but do not schedule a wedding just yet. Your Love Planet goes retrograde on the 23rd – so let a current relationship grow and mature for a while. Do not make rash decisions either to marry or break up. Miscommunication and misunderstanding are the probable causes of any love traumas – not lack of love.

Finances are going well – especially after the 21st. Money comes through educators or from foreign lands. Legal rulings go in your favour. Purchases and investments are made with a sense of intrinsic, innate value. You shine in the financial world later in the month.

Your health is excellent all month.

Capricorn

♑

THE GOAT
*Birthdays from
21st December
to 19th January*

Personality Profile

CAPRICORN AT A GLANCE

Element – Earth

Ruling Planet – Saturn
   Career Planet – Venus
   Love Planet – Moon
   Money Planet – Uranus
   Planet of Health and Work – Mercury
   Planet of Home and Family Life – Mars

Colours – black, indigo

*Colours that promote love, romance and social
harmony* – puce, silver

Colour that promotes earning power –
ultramarine blue

CAPRICORN

Gem – black onyx

Metal – lead

Scents – magnolia, pine, sweet pea, wintergreen

Quality – cardinal (= activity)

Qualities most needed for balance – warmth, spontaneity, a sense of fun

Strongest virtues – sense of duty, organization, perseverance, patience, ability to take the long-term view

Deepest needs – to manage, take charge and administrate

Characteristics to avoid – pessimism, depression, undue materialism and undue conservatism

Signs of greatest overall compatibility – Taurus, Virgo

Signs of greatest overall incompatibility – Aries, Cancer, Libra

Sign most helpful to career – Libra

Sign most helpful for emotional support – Aries

Sign most helpful financially – Aquarius

Sign best for marriage and/or partnerships – Cancer

Sign most helpful for creative projects – Taurus

Best Sign to have fun with – Taurus

Signs most helpful in spiritual matters – Virgo, Sagittarius

Best day of the week – Saturday

Understanding the Capricorn Personality

The virtues of Capricorns are such that there will always be people for and against them. Many admire them, many dislike them. Why? It seems to be because of Capricorn's power urges. A well-developed Capricorn has his or her eyes set on the heights of power, prestige and authority. In the Sign of Capricorn, ambition is not a fatal flaw but rather the highest virtue.

Capricorns are not frightened by the resentment their authority may sometimes cause. In Capricorn's cool, calculated, organized mind all the dangers are already factored into the equation – the unpopularity, the animosity, the misunderstandings, even the outright slander – and a plan is always in place for dealing with these things in the most efficient way. To the Capricorn, situations that would terrify an ordinary mind are merely problems to be managed, bumps on the road to ever-growing power, effectiveness and prestige.

Some people attribute pessimism to the Capricorn Sign, but this is a bit deceptive. It is true that Capricorns like to take into account the negative side of things. It is also true that they love to imagine the worst possible scenario in every undertaking. Other people might find such analyses depressing, but Capricorns only do these things so that they can formulate a way out – an escape route or 'golden parachute'.

Capricorns will argue with success. They will show you that you are not doing as well as you think you are. Capricorns do this to themselves as well as to others. They do not mean to discourage you but rather to root out any impediments to your greater success. A Capricorn boss or supervisor feels that no matter how good the performance there is always room for improvement. This explains why Capricorn supervisors are difficult to handle and even infuriating at times. Their actions are, however, quite often effective – they can get their subordinates to improve and become better at their jobs.

Capricorn is a born manager and administrator. Leo is better at being king or queen, but Capricorn is better at being prime minister – the person who administrates the monarchy, government or corporation, the person actually wielding power.

Capricorn is interested in the virtues that last, in the things that will stand the test of time and trials of circumstance. Temporary fads and fashions mean little to a Capricorn – except as things to be used for profit or power. Capricorns apply this attitude to business, love, to their thinking and even to their philosophy and religion.

Finance

Capricorns generally attain wealth and they usually earn it. They are willing to work long and hard for what they want. They are quite amenable to foregoing a short-term gain in favour of a long-term benefit. Financially, they come into their own later on in life.

However, if Capricorns are to attain their financial goals they must shed some of their strong conservatism. Perhaps this is the least desirable trait of the Capricorn. They can resist anything new merely because it *is* new and untried. They are afraid of experimentation. Capricorns need to be willing to take a few risks. They should be more eager to market new products or explore different management techniques. Otherwise, progress will leave them behind. If necessary, Capricorns must be ready to change with the times, to discard old methods that do not work in modern conditions.

Very often this experimentation will mean that Capricorns have to break with existing authority. They might even consider changing their present position or starting their own ventures. If so, they should be willing to accept all the risks and just get on with it. Only then will a Capricorn be on the road to highest financial gain.

Career and Public Image

A Capricorn's ambition and quest for power are evident. It is perhaps the most ambitious Sign of the Zodiac – and usually the most successful in a worldly sense. However, there are lessons Capricorns need to learn in order to fulfil their highest aspirations.

Intelligence, hard work, cool efficiency and organization will take them a certain distance but will not carry them to the very top. Capricorns need to cultivate your social graces, to develop a social style along with charm and an ability to get along with people. They need to bring beauty into their lives as well as efficiency and to cultivate the right social contacts. They must learn to wield power and have people love them for it – a very delicate art. They also need to learn how to bring people together in order to fulfil certain objectives. In short, Capricorns require some of the gifts – your social graces – of the Libra to get to the top.

Once they have learned this, Capricorns will be successful in their careers. They are ambitious, hard workers who are not afraid of putting in the required time and effort. Capricorns take their time in getting the job done – in order to do it well – and they like, slowly but surely, moving up the corporate ladder. Being so driven by success, Capricorns are generally liked by their bosses, who respect and trust them.

Love and Relationships

Like Scorpio and Pisces, Capricorn is a difficult Sign to get to know. They are deep, introverted and like to keep their own counsel. Capricorns do not like to reveal their innermost thoughts. If you are in love with a Capricorn be patient and take your time. Little by little you will get to understand him or her.

Capricorns have a deep romantic nature, but they do not show it straight away. They are cool, matter of fact and not especially emotional. They will often show their love in practical ways.

It takes time for a Capricorn – male or female – to fall in love. They are not your love-at-first-sight kind. If a Capricorn is involved with a Leo or Aries, these Fire types will be totally mystified – to them the Capricorn will seem cold, unfeeling, unaffectionate and unspontaneous. Of course none of this is true, it is just that Capricorn likes to take things slow. They like to be sure of their ground before making any demonstrations of love or commitment.

Even in love affairs Capricorns are deliberate. They need more time to make decisions than is true of the other Signs of the Zodiac, but given this time they get just as passionate. Capricorns like a relationship to be structured, committed, well regulated, well defined, predictable and even routine. They prefer partners who are nurturers and they in turn like to nurture their partners. This is their basic psychology. Whether such a relationship is good for them is another issue altogether. Capricorns have enough routine in their lives as it is. They might be better off in relationships that are a bit more stimulating, changeable and fluctuating.

Home and Domestic Life

The home of a Capricorn – as with a Virgo – is going to be neat, orderly and well organized. Capricorns tend to manage their families in the same way they manage their businesses. Capricorns are often so career-driven that they find little time for the home and family. Capricorns should try to get more actively involved in their family and domestic life. Capricorns do, however, take their children very seriously and are very proud parents, particularly should their children grow up to become respected members of society.

Horoscope for 1996

Major Trends

Last year was a time of great spiritual and metaphysical growth. Your charitable and philanthropic activities cleared out a lot of negative karma. And, as the Cosmic Law states, 'As above, so below; as within, so without.' In 1996 this spiritual expansion starts to manifest on the physical plane – first in terms of your self-esteem, self-worth and self-confidence, then in financial terms, and then in the recognition you get from other people.

This year brings more personal pleasure, self-indulgence, foreign travel, perhaps a move, more money, pay-rises, promotions and a general feeling of optimism. This is a year during which you live the good life. Make sure you show gratitude for it, lest it be taken away. Nothing diminishes prosperity or opportunity more than ingratitude. One can make many mistakes in life, or lack certain talents, but if one has gratitude life will steadily improve.

Do not think that because you are living the good life, materialism is the focus. Not at all. Pluto moving through your 12th House (Spiritual Wisdom and Charity) and Jupiter moving through your own Sign will see to that. You are going to become a 'dweller in two worlds' this year – enjoying both the spiritual and the material aspects of life. By the end of the year you will have a keener understanding of the relationship between the two.

CAPRICORN

Health

Health is a mixed picture this year. One major planet, Jupiter, moves into harmonious alignment with you; another, Saturn, moves into stressful alignment. You alternate between feeling strong and weak, between energy and fatigue. Your overall vitality is not what you are used to. Having said this, there are no major health problems in your chart. Your (6th) House of Health is relatively inactive and thus you have little need or inclination to focus on health matters. As you know, that which does not call attention to itself is usually healthy. Healthy organs do not complain or cause pain. You take them for granted. Too much focus on health is usually a sign of ill-health. So your health prospects look good.

One of the things you need to watch out for is having too much of a good thing – too much of the good life. Beware of overeating or any other excess – you will have plenty of opportunity for this in 1996. Happily, you Capricorns are moderate – if not downright stoic – by nature and will sense when you are overdoing things.

One of the things that saps your vitality and diminishes some of your optimism this year is your relationship with your family – especially a parent (or parental figure). Your feelings in this regard seem totally blocked. Talking to a professional therapist or even writing out your feelings will be a big help. The demands of family and your obligations to them conflict strongly with your personal desires and with what you really want to do for yourself. Somehow or other – and no one can tell you specifically how to do it – you need to fulfil your obligations and fulfil yourself. This balancing point is an ever-changing, dynamic thing beyond rules or words. In some cases you will deny yourself in favour of family duties. In other cases you will ignore the family and fulfil yourself. Day by day and moment by moment you will lean one way and then another, never completely ignoring one nor the other. Think of a see-saw or pendulum. It is never completely on one side or the other but is constantly alternating between the two.

Home and Domestic Life

Family and domestic issues are important in 1996, as mentioned earlier. Family harmony is a factor in the state of your health and vitality. Increased self-esteem and personal confidence make you feel cramped in your present living quarters – especially after 7th April. It is as if your enlarged mental horizons have heightened your need for personal space. Your increasing affluence makes you feel dissatisfied with your present domestic arrangement. You feel that you deserve more and should have more. A move is likely in 1996. There are many astrological signals that point to this: Jupiter moving through your 1st House (of the Body and Personal Image), Saturn moving through your 4th House (of Domestic Life) in April, and the two eclipses that also occur in your 4th House.

At first you will valiantly re-order your present space, getting the most from it and using it more efficiently. You will be re-shuffling furniture and generally rearranging your living situation. But after a while even this will not work and you will most likely move into a bigger place. Moreover, structural flaws in the home will be brought to light by the eclipses, further inclining you to move. Your personal space within the home – the room or place where you spend the most time – will be enlarged.

Though you are always ambitious and status conscious, your main thrust for the next two to two and half years is to build a stable home base. The home base and your family life are to your career what the foundation is to a house. The more stable and secure the foundation, the sturdier the house will be. The more stable and secure your domestic situation, the sturdier and more enduring will be your career.

CAPRICORN

This is a year for reorganizing and re-structuring domestic chores so that they are done most efficiently. Some of you will be taking on more of the domestic burden, some less. Much depends on your situation beforehand. If you were under-doing on the domestic level, 1996 forces you to take on more domestic responsibility. If you were already taking on too much responsibility, 1996 will lessen some of the burden. Saturn does not look to punish, only to bring conditions into a realistic and fair perspective. By the time Saturn finishes transiting your 4th House you will have a stable, secure and enduring home environment.

One of your parents is having a rough time this year. Vitality is not what it should be and self-esteem is low. This person needs to guard against depression, for he or she is tending to see the dark side of everything. This parent will benefit from changes of diet, exercise and purifying regimes. If he or she is obese there is good opportunity to drop the pounds now. If your parents are married to each other, one wants to move while the other wants to stay put. The eclipses will probably cause them to move or renovate.

Relations with siblings and neighbours start improving after April. A sibling becomes less erratic, less restless and in general more stable. Relations with children are stable.

Love and Social Life

Since your 7th House of Love and Marriage is not particularly active this year, your love life and/or marriage is not one of your big priorities. The status quo is fostered by this planetary pattern. Singles tend to stay single and marrieds tend to stay married. Your marital status or lack of same does not bother you too much. Of course, if you want to marry – and are willing to work hard and rather force things – you can do it. But it does not seem likely.

This year many Capricorns are wisely focusing on themselves rather than on being socially popular. You are working on making yourself a better person, increasing your self-esteem, developing spiritual and mental qualities and just enjoying life as it comes. You know that as you become more you will attract more, and that relationships ultimately depend on you. You are more concerned with pleasing yourself than with pleasing your spouse or lover. Your attitude is basically 'me first'. You want others to adapt to you. There are periods in life when this is called for.

Your social magnetism is strong this year and romantic opportunities are plentiful – but these do not seem serious.

Other people view you as more refined, educated, wealthy and prominent this year. Keep working to strengthen this image of yourself.

The Moon is your Love Planet; when it waxes you have more enthusiasm for love and more social magnetism, when it wanes your romantic enthusiasm and social magnetism are reduced. The monthly forecasts (below) can provide more detailed information about the Moon's movements and the resulting fluctuations in how you feel.

The marriage of a parent (or parental figure) is stressful this year. If this parent is single (widowed or divorced), a change in marital status is likely, though there should be no rush or rashness about this. A slow courtship is best. The love and social life of your siblings seems to maintain the status quo this year. The same is true for your children.

Your spouse or business partners are increasing their level of social activity, attracting new and happier friends into their lives. Your spouse wants to socialize more than you do. A business partner is likely to marry. In general your social life shrinks due to disappointments with friends and a desire for more stable and secure friendships.

Career and Finance

You are always interested in finance and career, but this year the financial side is more important to you than your career. Remember that 'career' is defined as something more than mere earnings. A career is a person's life-work and professional status. Generally these are related, but not always. A person can attain much status but not earn very much, and vice versa. Public and professional prestige can take a back seat to financial considerations.

Two of the four eclipses of 1996 occur in your 10th House of Career, so there will be career advancement in spite of your lack of interest. Upheavals and shake-ups in the corporate structure create opportunities for you. Jupiter moving over your Sun is also a signal for career advancement. You get more public recognition.

Earnings are your main focus this year, however, as they have been for many years. By now, financial experimentation has become a way of life. Change has become your friend. You know how to capitalize on quickly shifting market changes and financial developments.

If you are in your own business – whether it be making products or providing services – develop clients and customers in the high-tech fields. If you are an investor focus on high-tech, scientific industries. Follow them and invest in those that are poised for long-term growth. You will be in a strong position to profit in 1997. Other industries that are good for you now are publishing, foreign travel and shipping. With Saturn leaving Pisces, stocks in shipping, oil and other nautical industries become good long-term buys.

There is one more thing that needs to be mentioned: your Money Planet (Uranus) is now in its own House – its own domain. It will be there for the next seven years or so. This is a fabulous financial signal. It shows that you have unusual financial power and exceptional ability to create prosperity. You can start taking the bull by the horns now and shape your financial future more or less as you want it. Next year is going to be even better than 1996.

Self-improvement

Pluto has made a long-term move into your 12th House of Spiritual Wisdom. Your spiritual life is being transformed on very deep levels. Old fears – probably of a collective rather than individual nature – are surfacing so that you can deal with them. Like St George you will be slaying many a (psychic) dragon – do not worry, you will be shown how. Secret enemies are being revealed to you. Some are actual people whom you thought were your friends – others are unconscious character traits and/or inhibitions that have been obstructing you. Of the two, the latter are more dangerous. Once these enemies are revealed – a great blessing, rejoice when this happens – they become de-fanged and no longer a danger. They were dangerous precisely because they were hidden. Once exposed to the light of day you will see various ways of dealing with them.

Pluto in your 12th House increases your ability to meditate and focus – not just on spiritual matters but on anything you choose (a good art to master).

The need to reorganize and re-structure your domestic living situation has already been mentioned. Allocate domestic duties in a way that is both just and efficient. Neither avoid your responsibilities nor try to take on more than you can handle. Keep a diary and write out your feelings. Pour your heart out into the diary and release negative emotion. Keep the diary secret.

Charitable and philanthropic activities are still prominent in your chart, though in a different way than last year. Last year you gave money or contributed time in secret and behind the scenes. This year you give more openly and your good works increase your self-esteem.

Month-by-month Forecasts

January

Best Days Overall: 1st, 10th, 11th, 19th, 20th, 27th, 28th

Most Stressful Days Overall: 5th, 6th, 12th, 13th, 25th, 26th

Best Days for Love: 1st, 2nd, 3rd, 5th, 6th, 10th, 11th, 12th, 13th, 14th, 19th, 20th, 23rd, 24th, 29th, 30th

Best Days for Money: 1st, 10th, 11th, 19th, 20th, 21st, 22nd, 27th, 28th, 29th, 30th, 31st

A happy but tumultuous month, Capricorn – unusually active and filled with major personal and financial changes (happy ones). But first things first: the planets (90 to 100 per cent of them) are clustered in the east and below the horizon of your chart. This indicates a focus on personal things. Career and worldly issues are de-emphasized. Social relationships are de-emphasized. You are focused on yourself and your own needs and desires; the rest of the world can manage itself. You are intent on pleasing yourself, working on yourself and getting your own life in order. You are going to create your own personal conditions and let the world adapt to them. And you are very successful at this sort of thing right now. If others do not co-operate you have all the power, energy and resources to go it alone if need be – a nice position to be in.

January is a month of personal pleasure. There is much good food, romance and passion, shopping for clothes and accessories, massages, and other forms of indulgence. You are into the body and its delights. Your personal magnetism is strong. You are attractive to the opposite sex. You assert yourself with great force and tend to get your way. A big and unexpected financial or material bonanza comes to you around the 5th. Usually sedate and even stoic, this month (and this year) you project an image of the fun-lover and epicure. You are perceived as wealthy – perhaps wealthier than you really are. You live and dress as if you were wealthy. Your mood is optimistic and jovial. Unsurprisingly, your health is just fabulous all month.

The financial picture is changing in wonderful ways as well. Uranus (your Money Planet) moves into your Money House on the 13th, initiating a major cycle of wealth. You are looser, freer, more experimental in both your earnings and your investments. New financial investment vehicles are not intimidating to you, but rather useful in enhancing your 'bottom line'. You have an unusual affinity with high-tech, scientific industries this month (and for many years to come) and choose stocks shrewdly. You seem more interested in capital appreciation than in dividends or interest – though you should choose investments that combine both. Money comes to you either through your own new invention or through investments in a company that markets new inventions.

Love blooms around the 5th.

February

Best Days Overall: 6th, 7th, 15th, 16th, 23rd, 24th, 25th

Most Stressful Days Overall: 1st, 2nd, 8th, 9th, 10th, 21st, 22nd, 28th, 29th

CAPRICORN

Best Days for Love: 1st, 2nd, 8th, 9th, 10th, 13th, 14th, 17th, 18th, 19th, 21st, 22nd, 28th, 29th

Best Days for Money: 6th, 7th, 8th, 9th, 15th, 16th, 17th, 18th, 23rd, 24th, 25th, 26th, 27th

The planets still empower the eastern and bottom halves of your chart, Capricorn, making you unusually focused on personal concerns – personal pleasure, personal finances, personal intellectual interests and the attainment of emotional harmony. This is not like you, Capricorn, as in general you are a world person – a person who wants to have a worldwide impact and who is vitally interested in politics and world affairs. But now you probably feel that you can best serve the world by getting your own house in order, by establishing a solid financial and home base and feeling good about yourself.

The planetary focus in the east and the planets' forward momentum gives you unusual initiative, drive and self-direction. You have all the energy and vigour you need to achieve any personal goal. You get your way and assert yourself strongly. You are bold and courageous, especially in financial matters – not a person to be trifled with or obstructed.

This is still a great financial month in a great financial year. The Sun moving through your Money House makes you a financial star. You become a standard of wealth for others; that is, your peers judge their wealth by comparing it to yours. The Sun in your Money House makes you ethical and upright in your financial dealings and you tend to attract ethical and upright people to you. You have a feel for stable values – regardless of public fads and fancies. There is a healthy optimism about your present and future earning ability. Thus your investment and purchasing judgement is good. Investors might find opportunities in gold, electric utilities, and entertainment stocks – either to buy or sell at a profit.

Mars in your Money House until the 15th is the only fly in the ointment: it makes you a bit rash, speculative and keen for 'quick money'. If you can rein in these tendencies you have got a super financial month ahead.

Your health and energy are great all month. Your love life waxes and wanes with the Moon, and shows no special tendencies. Love and romance are not your priorities right now and the status quo is fostered.

March

Best Days Overall: 4th, 5th, 13th, 14th, 22nd, 23rd

Most Stressful Days Overall: 6th, 7th, 8th, 19th, 20th, 26th, 27th, 28th

Best Days for Love: 1st, 2nd, 3rd, 9th, 10th, 13th, 14th, 18th, 19th, 22nd, 23rd, 26th, 27th, 28th, 29th, 30th

Best Days for Money: 4th, 5th, 6th, 7th, 13th, 14th, 15th, 16th, 22nd, 23rd, 24th, 25th

Planetary power is just beginning to shift this month from the eastern sector of your horoscope to the western sector, making this a month of transition. You are still very much involved in pleasing yourself and pursuing personal goals and desires, but you are starting, later in the month, to reach out to others. Your social desires are getting stronger.

CAPRICORN

The planets are still very much below the horizon of your chart – as they have been for some months now. Home, family, domestic and psychological issues are still your basic focus. It is not that you ignore outer achievement and your place in the world – you are merely getting your house in order to prepare for it.

This is the month – especially after the 20th – to make a move, buy or sell a house, buy or sell furniture, redecorate, renovate, create family harmony and embark on psychological therapies where called for. There is plenty of energy available and you have a yen for these things. Family relations are bittersweet. Family members (especially a parent) are not shy about expressing their feelings. But negative feelings are short term and pass quickly. The air will be cleared and harmony will be restored next month.

Finances are stable all month – perhaps a bit easier after the 20th than before. Earnings come through moderate increases in dividends or interest. Writers and journalists sell manuscripts or articles this month. Advertising and other promotional activities boost your 'bottom line' and seem successful. Ideas that come from employees or co-workers boost your wealth.

Though you are magnetic and attractive to the opposite sex, your love life and marriage still seem unimportant right now. Your social charisma and enthusiasm are strongest from the 1st to the 5th and from the 19th to the end of the month. The Full Moon of the 5th brings romantic opportunities in academia and at churches and other religious institutions. The New Moon of the 19th begins a social cycle that centres on the neighbourhood and people close to home. Your love needs this month involve intellectual communion and the sharing of ideas and thoughts.

Watch your health after the 20th and try to rest and relax more. Try to carve out some personal time for things that you enjoy. Until the 7th you are more concerned about your financial health than your physical health. After the 7th health is enhanced through writing and creative self-expression.

April

> Best Days Overall: 1st, 2nd, 9th, 10th, 18th, 19th, 28th, 29th
>
> Most Stressful Days Overall: 3rd, 4th, 16th, 17th, 23rd, 24th, 30th
>
> Best Days for Love: 1st, 2nd, 3rd, 7th, 8th, 11th, 12th, 16th, 17th, 20th, 21st, 23rd, 24th, 28th, 29th, 30th
>
> Best Days for Money: 1st, 2nd, 3rd, 9th, 10th, 11th, 12th, 18th, 19th, 20th, 29th, 30th

The two eclipses this month affect you more strongly than they do most other people. Stay cool, rest and relax more and avoid unnecessary action until the dust settles.

The two eclipses are powerful because they occur on the angles of your solar horoscope – the 4th and the 10th Houses. (Planetary phenomena on the angles – the 1st, 4th, 7th and 10th Houses – are always more powerful than when they occur in other places.) This shows major long-term changes in the home, your family and your career. They also affect your parents (or parental figures) – probably with reference to their marriage and their personalities. If their marriage has been sound to begin with the relationship will probably change in a positive way. If the marriage is unsound, the eclipse will provoke a crisis.

The solar eclipse of the 17th occurs in your 4th House of Domestic Life, showing a move, a change in family relations or the need to make major – and perhaps expensive – renovations in the home. When the dust clears the domestic pattern will be changed for the better in some way. On the domestic front you are looking for long-term stability. You do not want to be moving from house to house every other year or so. You want one good one and *finis*.

The lunar eclipse of the 3rd occurs in your 10th House of Career, indicating job changes and perhaps a promotion that comes out of a seeming demotion. This eclipse also brings shake-ups and uncertainties in the corporate structure. Management is changing. If you are in your own business, the eclipse leads you to a new business policy or new direction.

Though you are basically optimistic this year, the need to control feelings and emotions can dampen some of your optimism. Best to express repressed feelings in productive ways – with a therapist or through a personal diary – rather than hold them in. Family relations force you to take a lower profile and become less self-centred.

Finances are stable and you are still in a wealth-building period. Spare cash should be channelled towards investments rather than the reduction of debt. Your health will be much improved after the 20th.

May

Best Days Overall: 7th, 8th, 15th, 16th, 17th, 25th, 26th

Most Stressful Days Overall: 1st, 2nd, 13th, 14th, 20th, 21st, 22nd, 27th, 28th, 29th

Best Days for Love: 1st, 2nd, 7th, 8th, 9th, 10th, 15th, 16th, 17th, 18th, 19th, 20th, 21st, 22nd, 27th, 28th, 29th

Best Days for Money: 1st, 2nd, 7th, 8th, 9th, 10th, 15th, 16th, 17th, 18th, 25th, 26th, 27th

Though the universe seems to be standing still, and in certain areas actually going backwards, you are personally happy and content. As a Capricorn you are a veteran at handling delays and snarls. This is your strength. You like things to proceed slowly. You feel comfortable when the general psychology is conservative, down to earth and traditional – as it is this month. You are doing well and people are recognizing – and in tune with – your basic virtues. Your self-esteem is high.

Saturn (your Ruling Planet) is perhaps the only planet moving fast forward this month – another reinforcement of the personal progress you are making. No need to remind you to be cautious about investments and speculations – you are already that way.

Wisely, and perhaps because of knowledge gained from past experience, you are relaxing and enjoying life. Rather than getting upset about the delays and backwardness of events, you turn your attention to the rapture of life – to parties, the theatre, the nightclub and perhaps a jaunt to the casino. When there is nothing to be done, why not use it as an opportunity to have some fun? An eminently practical thing to do.

Your personal creativity is at an all-time high right now. Relations with children also seem good. Those of you who have children enjoy taking them to sporting events or getting involved in the sport-orientated side of their lives.

Earnings are a bit low this month but will improve after the 20th. Income from a speculation or from the sale of one of your creations is probably delayed until next month. The income of children, though strong, is also subject to various delays. Personal investments, investment strategies and investment psychology are being reviewed now – and this is as it should be.

Your health is excellent all month. You are taking a look at recent changes to your image and dress sense. Diet and exercise regimes are being reviewed and re-evaluated. This is not a good month – especially from the 3rd to the 27th – to embark on some new and radical diet. Study it further, as there are hidden things about it of which you may not be aware.

June

Best Days Overall: 3rd, 4th, 12th, 13th, 22nd, 23rd

Most Stressful Days Overall: 9th, 10th, 16th, 17th, 18th, 24th, 25th

Best Days for Love: 5th, 6th, 14th, 15th, 16th, 17th, 18th, 24th, 25th, 26th, 27th

Best Days for Money: 3rd, 4th, 5th, 6th, 12th, 13th, 14th, 22nd, 23rd, 24th

You are in a unique position this month, Capricorn. Your whole psychology and training have prepared you for these kinds of periods when the universe seems to be going backwards instead of forwards, when people around you are facing setbacks, delays and frustrations. You are in your prime and glory now. For you, more than almost any other Sign, knows how to deal with these things constructively.

Your virtues are admired and respected this month. Your coolness, foresight and equanimity help to calm and uplift others. You are a role model for the people around you. For you, the current retrograde motion of 50 per cent of the planets is merely another bump on the road soon to be put behind you. You have already – perhaps months ago – foreseen the worst-case scenarios and have prepared for them. You are already turning your attention to other areas where action is possible. You are making effective use of your time and taking maximum advantage of the situation. You come out of this more prosperous than before.

Your financial life is still in a temporary lull, but – as mentioned earlier – you have foreseen this and are prepared for delays. Earnings are better than last month but not really what they should be or will be. You are still reviewing past investments and spending patterns. Children are earning more now than last month. Income arises from a creative or artistic project.

You are more serious this month than last month – working harder, achieving work goals and quotas and in general getting the workplace in ship-shape order. Health and exercise regimes go well. Dietary issues will be clarified by the New Moon of the 15th.

Your love and social life start becoming more active after the 21st. You try to combine love and business this period. An investor or broker has romantic ideas. Singles meet new prospects now. Love is physical and passionate. Married Capricorns are more romantic in their relationships.

July

Best Days Overall: 1st, 9th, 10th, 19th, 20th, 28th, 29th

Most Stressful Days Overall: 6th, 7th, 8th, 14th, 15th, 21st, 22nd

Best Days for Love: 2nd, 3rd, 4th, 5th, 11th, 12th, 14th, 15th, 21st, 22nd, 26th, 27th, 30th, 31st

Best Days for Money: 1st, 2nd, 3rd, 9th, 10th, 11th, 19th, 20th, 21st, 28th, 29th, 30th, 31st

CAPRICORN

Fifty per cent of the planets – including some of your important ones – are retrograde this month, Capricorn. But for you this is not as stressful as for other Signs. You are good at handling delays and at looking at the long-range view of things. Moreover, since you are naturally cautious you do not need to be told the wisdom of prudence.

The short-term planets are now all in the western sector of your horoscope, making you more social and extroverted. You are not totally social – the long-term planets are still in the east – but more so than you have been recently. Everything is relative. July is one of your more sociable peaks of the year. Singles have many romantic opportunities. Love is serious and committed now. The New Moon of the 15th is going to clarify any social confusion and – as the month progresses – will show you precisely what you need to do to achieve your social and romantic goals.

The major challenge of this month lies in balancing your social interests with your personal desires and family obligations; the needs of your partner with your personal needs; the needs of your spouse with the needs of your family; the needs of the family with your own personal needs. You cannot go too far in any direction and you must make these disparate influences work harmoniously together.

This is not one of your best health months. Accordingly, be sure to rest and relax more and avoid undue self-exertion and unnecessary power struggles. Though you will be very active, see if you cannot just 'coast' while in action – like a high-speed, finely tuned car that effortlessly eats up the miles. Act, but without stress.

Though financial issues are still much delayed this month, you do receive an unusual financial bonanza on the 1st, and perhaps around the 15th. These financial windfalls seem unconnected with your usual earnings and come from your partner, spouse or from insurance companies, or possibly from a tax dispute which works out in your favour.

Maybe someone remembers you in his or her will, or a stock you own splits or pays an extra dividend. You collect an unexpected royalty cheque. Someone invests in your project. In short, money comes from others rather than from your personal efforts. Enjoy, but study well what you do with this windfall.

August

Best Days Overall: 5th, 6th, 15th, 16th, 24th, 25th

Most Stressful Days Overall: 3rd, 4th, 10th, 11th, 17th, 18th, 19th, 30th, 31st

Best Days for Love: 3rd, 4th, 10th, 11th, 12th, 13th, 14th, 20th, 21st, 23rd, 24th, 28th, 29th

Best Days for Money: 5th, 6th, 7th, 15th, 16th, 17th, 24th, 25th, 26th, 27th

In life there are times when we must do for ourselves and times when we must do for others. You are in one of the times when others come before you. Besides, when there is nothing positive that you can do for yourself – when the channels seem blocked – you can at least be useful to your friends and those you love. Besides earning good karma, you get the added satisfaction of knowing that you are useful and needed.

Personal desires, the urge for sensual pleasures, and financial issues all seem on hold for the moment. The greatest things that you can do to further progress in these areas are in the subjective rather than the objective realm. Employ thought, reason and imagination to achieve goals that seem blocked on the physical plane. If you cannot physically and materially meet that financial goal, you can still imagine that you did. Unrealistic? Perhaps, but powerful and workable none the less. On the physical plane your actions are now devoted to others and to social issues.

Romance is very much in the air, and is both passionate and tender. You exhibit a social aggressiveness – which some might find offensive – but along with it a grace and charm. You go after what you want but in a charming way. You are ready either to make love or war with your beloved – and perhaps you are doing a bit of both. Rows end up in passionate reconciliations. Though your charitable activities are good, you might be advised to tone them down where your spouse or lover is concerned. He or she feels these things as an affront or neglect. Intellectual interests also seem to create tension in romance – but tension is not the same as a break-up.

Your health is excellent all month but will improve even further after the 23rd. News from foreign lands boosts your self-esteem. Opportunities to travel come your way.

September

Best Days Overall: 1st, 2nd, 3rd, 11th, 12th, 20th, 21st, 29th, 30th

Most Stressful Days Overall: 6th, 7th, 8th, 14th, 15th, 27th, 28th

Best Days for Love: 1st, 2nd, 3rd, 6th, 7th, 8th, 9th, 11th, 12th, 18th, 19th, 21st, 22nd, 23rd, 27th, 28th

Best Days for Money: 1st, 2nd, 4th, 11th, 12th, 14th, 20th, 21st, 23rd, 24th, 29th, 30th

Take a reduced schedule this month, Capricorn – but especially after the 23rd and around the time of the lunar eclipse (25th to 27th September). Do not worry, you are not going to be able to avoid action – this is a tumultuous month – but you can limit your actions only to what is necessary. Pace yourself.

The lunar eclipse has an unusual impact on you – more so than for most of the Signs. It occurs on the angle of your chart – denoting action and power – and it conjoins Saturn (your Ruling Planet). It brings major long-term changes in the home, with family, with your personal image and perhaps your career. Hidden, secret flaws in these areas are going to be forced up by the eclipse to compel needed corrections. For example, if your wardrobe is inadequate or does not suit you, some accident will happen with it and you will be forced to buy new clothes or amend your old look. If your eating habits have been poor your body is going to reveal this by purging itself of built-up toxins. If there is domestic discord, or flaws in your current home (inadequate wiring, a bad oil burner, faulty tiles, termites and the like) they will reveal themselves. Thus you are compelled either to correct them or move house. Family relationships are also more delicate now.

With Mercury retrograde from the 4th to the 26th you need to be careful in all of your dealings with foreigners or foreign lands. Miscommunication is more likely to happen during this time. Take the time to nail down details and make sure that both you and the other party get the true message. With this configuration there are often delays in communication with foreign lands – the telephone service gets disrupted or the foreign post office or parcel delivery union goes on strike. Be patient. Try to handle these foreign communications either before Mercury goes retrograde or afterwards. Though you have the itch to travel this month it would be best to postpone any foreign trip until next month.

CAPRICORN

Your ambitions are unusually strong this month, but you are also seeing the seamy side of ambition – the machinations, selfishness and hardball politics that go on. Look at the seamy side but realize that you can overcome all of it. This would be a good time to clear out the impurities in your ambitions – character traits or habits that obstruct your success.

October

> Best Days Overall: 9th, 10th, 18th, 19th, 26th, 27th

> Most Stressful Days Overall: 4th, 5th, 11th, 12th, 24th, 25th, 31st

> Best Days for Love: 1st, 2nd, 4th, 5th, 8th, 9th, 11th, 12th, 18th, 19th, 20th, 21st, 27th, 28th, 31st

> Best Days for Money: 1st, 9th, 10th, 11th, 18th, 19th, 20th, 21st, 26th, 27th, 29th

With all the dramatic action going on this month you understandably pull in your horns until the dust settles. Too much action in the world makes you more cautious rather than more active. You need to work out all the different scenarios before taking action.

The solar eclipse of the 12th is especially dramatic for you as it occurs on the angle of your solar horoscope. First off it affects your career. It signals a new shift in your career orientation. If you work for a company there is a shake-up in the corporate hierarchy, leaving your status uncertain for a time. Many of you will even change your career – not just your job but your actual profession. The eclipse forces you to make hard career choices – you can no longer sit on the fence and wait; you must act one way or another. A parent (or parental figure) moves and otherwise changes his or her lifestyle. A business partner moves or makes changes in his or her daily lifestyle. A foreign investment throws a scare your way. Flaws in it are revealed. Charitable activities get re-evaluated. A spiritual or philanthropic organization you belong to is shaken up and you perhaps sever connections with it. Flaws in your spiritual life are revealed so that they can be corrected. And while you undergo a period of uncertainty in these issues, the final result will be an improvement.

Rest and relax more until the 23rd but especially around the 11th, 12th and 13th. Do what you need to do but reschedule the unnecessary for another time. Your vitality improves dramatically after the 23rd.

The heavenly T-square formation this month indicates that you have to work harder to balance personal desires, family obligations, and career demands. It will be testing to make these different areas of life co-operate rather than pull you in different directions.

November

Best Days Overall: 5th, 6th, 14th, 15th, 23rd, 24th

Most Stressful Days Overall: 1st, 7th, 8th, 20th, 21st, 27th, 28th

Best Days for Love: 1st, 7th, 8th, 10th, 11th, 16th, 17th, 18th, 19th, 27th, 28th, 30th

Best Days for Money: 5th, 6th, 7th, 14th, 15th, 16th, 17th, 23rd, 24th, 25th

With 70 to 80 per cent of the planets in the eastern sector of your chart – and moving ever more eastward month by month – your social life and other people in general are becoming less and less important while personal fulfilment is becoming ever more important. Now there are two kinds of personal fulfilment: the first kind is purely sensual – physical pleasure, good food, personal earning power, self-esteem and the like; the second kind is more universal – the longing for happiness in a happy world. This second kind of happiness – which sees personal well-being in the context of the happiness of the friends, acquaintances and the wider world – is what you are after now (in coming months this will change – and you will be more interested in the happiness of the moment). This happiness is more permanent. It is not enough for you now to 'get yours' and to hell with everyone else. You do not feel truly happy when others are suffering. So you are pursuing personal fulfilment through group activities and collective enterprises. The group you belong to will fulfil your fondest hopes and wishes. You are less concerned with one-on-one partnerships and more concerned with group activities. New friends come into the picture this month.

If you can balance your personal inclinations with family obligations and your career, you will make good career progress this month. Superiors are kindly disposed to you. Relations with the government will go well though you must be ready to compromise. Your public popularity is good. Pleasure and fulfilment come from pursuing career goals and objectives now.

Finances are straightening out after the 23rd. Before that you have to work harder – exert more effort – to achieve your financial goals.

Your health is good all month. Romance is on the back-burner most of the month, but romantic ardour is stronger from the 11th to the 25th and less strong from the 1st to the 11th and from the 25th onwards. The New Moon of the 11th guides you to the fulfilment of your fondest hopes and wishes.

December

Best Days Overall: 2nd, 3rd, 11th, 12th,
20th, 21st, 30th, 31st

Most Stressful Days Overall: 5th, 6th, 18th,
19th, 25th, 26th

Best Days for Love: 1st, 7th, 8th, 9th, 10th,
15th, 16th, 17th, 18th, 19th, 25th, 26th,
27th, 28th, 30th, 31st

Best Days for Money: 2nd, 3rd, 5th, 11th,
12th, 13th, 14th, 20th, 21st, 22nd, 30th, 31st

An active, happy and successful month, Capricorn. Enjoy! Until your birthday continue to wind down your affairs and bring old projects to a successful conclusion. You are still in a period of tying up loose ends, paying off debts and cutting costs. But after your birthday you can start building positive wealth and planting financial seeds for the future.

The planets are mostly in the east, indicating much initiative, independence and the urge to personal fulfilment. You get your way in things and if others do not co-operate you go it alone. This is the month to plan and design your future. Make positive mental images now; after your birthday you can start making them reality.

Another change occurs this month: You are (especially after the 21st) more concerned with sensual happiness – the happiness of the physical body – than last month when you were more interested in 'lasting and true happiness' for all.

Your dream life and ESP ability are sharply enhanced this month. Your interest in meditation and the paranormal is on the increase. Those of you on a spiritual path should spend the early part of the month in prayer, meditation and atonement. Spiritual illumination is there if you want it. Others might enjoy a visit to a psychic or astrologer. Charitable deeds go well until the 21st. You shine through these philanthropic activities.

After the 21st you spend money on clothing, jewellery and personal accessories. Buy the best – less but of good quality. Create an appearance of wealth and substance. Look wealthy, behave as if you are already wealthy and you will become wealthy.

Your earning power is strong all month. An opportunity to travel abroad comes after the 21st – and should be happy and successful. Educational opportunities come your way as well.

Your health is good all month but do not embark on any new diet or 'miracle regime' after the 23rd – not unless you have studied it very carefully first. Be careful of how you communicate to co-workers or employees after the 23rd, as (with Mercury retrograde) they are likely to get the wrong end of the stick. Take time to clarify what they are saying to you as well.

After the 21st you excel in sports and physical activities. Passionate fantasies are fulfilled beyond your wildest imaginings. Be careful about putting on the pounds. Rather than over-indulging and then having to diet later on, limit indulgence right from the start. Women who want to have children are much more likely to conceive after the 21st.

Aquarius

≈

THE WATER-BEARER
Birthdays from
20th January
to 18th February

Personality Profile

AQUARIUS AT A GLANCE

Element – Air

Ruling Planet – Uranus
   Career Planet – Pluto
   Health Planet – Moon
   Love Planet – Venus
   Money Planet – Neptune
   Planet of Home and Family Life – Venus

Colours – electric blue, grey, ultramarine blue

Colours that promote love, romance and social harmony – gold, orange

Colour that promotes earning power – aqua

AQUARIUS

Gems – black pearl, obsidian, opal, sapphire

Metal – lead

Scents – azalea, gardenia

Quality – fixed (= stability)

Qualities most needed for balance – warmth, feeling and emotion

Strongest virtues – great intellectual power, the ability to communicate and to form and understand abstract concepts, love for the new and the avant-garde

Deepest needs – to know and to bring in the new

Characteristics to avoid – coldness, rebelliousness for its own sake, fixed ideas

Signs of greatest overall compatibility – Gemini, Libra

Signs of greatest overall incompatibility – Taurus, Leo, Scorpio

Sign most helpful to career – Scorpio

Sign most helpful for emotional support – Taurus

Sign most helpful financially – Pisces

Sign best for marriage and/or partnerships – Leo

Sign most helpful for creative projects – Gemini

Best Sign to have fun with – Gemini

Signs most helpful in spiritual matters – Libra, Capricorn

Best day of the week – Saturday

Understanding the Aquarius Personality

In the Aquarius-born, the intellectual faculties are perhaps the most highly developed of any Sign in the Zodiac. Aquarians are clear, scientific thinkers. They have the ability to think abstractly and to formulate laws, theories and clear concepts from masses of observed facts. Geminis might be very good at gathering information, but Aquarians take this a step further, excelling at interpreting the information gathered.

Practical people – men and women of the world – mistakenly consider abstract thinking as impractical. It is true that the realm of abstract thought takes us out of the physical world, but the discoveries made in this realm generally end up having tremendous practical consequences. All real scientific inventions and breakthroughs come from this abstract realm.

Aquarians, more so than most, are ideally suited to explore these abstract dimensions. Those who have explored these regions know that there is little feeling or emotion there. In fact, emotions are a hindrance to functioning in these dimensions; thus Aquarians seem – at times – cold and emotionless to others. It is not that Aquarians have not got feelings and deep emotions, it is just that too much feeling clouds their ability to think and invent. The concept of 'too much feeling' cannot be tolerated or even understood by some of the other Signs. Nevertheless, this Aquarian objectivity is ideal for science, communication and friendship.

Aquarians are very friendly people, but they do not make a big show about it. They do the right thing by their friends, even if sometimes they do it without passion or excitement.

Aquarians have a deep passion for clear thinking. Second in importance, but related, is their passion for breaking with the establishment and traditional authority. Aquarians delight in this, because for them rebellion is like a great game or challenge. Very often they will rebel strictly for the fun of rebelling, regardless of whether the authority they defy is right or wrong. Right or wrong has little to do with the rebellious actions of an Aquarian because to a true Aquarian authority and power must be challenged as a matter of principle.

Where Capricorn or Taurus will err on the side of tradition and the status quo, an Aquarian will err on the side of the new. Without this virtue it is doubtful whether any progress would be made in the world. The conservative-minded would obstruct progress. Originality and invention imply an ability to break barriers; every new discovery represents the toppling of an impediment to thought. Aquarians are very interested in breaking barriers and making walls tumble – scientifically, socially and politically. Other Zodiac Signs, such as Capricorn, also have scientific talents. But Aquarians are particularly excellent in the social sciences and humanities.

Finance

In financial matters Aquarians tend to be idealistic and humanitarian – to the point of self-sacrifice. They are usually generous contributors to social and political causes. When they contribute it differs from when a Capricorn or Taurus contributes. A Capricorn or Taurus may expect some favour or return for their gift; an Aquarian contributes selflessly.

Aquarians tend to be as cool and rational about money as they are about most things in life. Money is something they need and they set about scientifically to acquire it. No need for fuss; they get on with it in the most rational and scientific ways available.

Money to the Aquarian is especially nice for what it can do, not for the status it may bring (as is the case for other Signs). Aquarians are neither big spenders nor penny-pinchers and use their finances in practical ways, for example to facilitate progress for themselves, their families or even strangers.

However, if Aquarians want to reach their fullest financial potential they will have to explore their intuitive nature. If they follow only their financial theories – or what they believe to be theoretically correct – they may suffer some losses and disappointments. Instead, Aquarians should call on their intuition – which knows without thinking. For Aquarians, intuition is the short-cut to financial success.

Career and Public Image

Aquarians like to be perceived not only as the breakers of barriers but also as the transformers of society and the world. They long to be seen in this light and to play this role. They also look up to and respect other people in this position and even expect their superiors to act this way.

Aquarians prefer jobs that have a bit of idealism attached to them – careers with a philosophical basis. Aquarians need to be creative at work, to have access to new techniques and methods. They like to keep busy and enjoy getting down to business straight away, without wasting any time. They are often the quickest workers and usually have suggestions for improvements that will benefit their employers. Aquarians are also very helpful with their co-workers and welcome responsibility, preferring this to having to take orders from others.

If Aquarians want to reach their highest career goals they have to develop more emotional sensitivity, depth of feeling and passion. They need to learn to narrow their focus on the essentials and concentrate more on their job. Aquarians need 'a fire in the belly' – a consuming passion and desire – in order to rise to the very top. Once this passion exists they will succeed easily in whatever they attempt.

Love and Relationships

Aquarians are good at friendships, but a bit weak when it comes to love. Of course they fall in love, but their lovers always get the impression that they are more best friends than paramours.

Like the Capricorn they are cool customers. They are not prone to displays of passion nor to outward demonstrations of their affections. In fact, they feel uncomfortable when their mate hugs and touches them too much. This does not mean that they do not love their partners. They do, only they show it in other ways. Curiously enough, in relationships they tend to attract the very things that they feel uncomfortable with. They seem to attract hot, passionate, romantic, demonstrative people. Perhaps they know instinctively that these people have qualities they lack and so seek them out. In any event, these relationships do seem to work, Aquarius' coolness calming the more passionate partner while the fires of passion warm the cold-blooded Aquarius.

The qualities Aquarians need to develop in their love life are warmth, generosity, passion and fun. Aquarians love relationships of the mind. Here they excel. If the intellectual factor is missing in a relationship an Aquarian will soon become bored or feel unfulfilled.

Home and Domestic Life

In family and domestic matters Aquarians can have a tendency to be too nonconformist, changeable and unstable. They are as willing to break the barriers of family constraints as they are those of other areas of life.

Even so, Aquarians are very sociable people. They like to have a nice home where they can entertain family and friends. Their house is usually decorated modernly and full of state-of-the-art appliances and gadgets – an environment

Aquarians find absolutely necessary.

If their home life is to be healthy and fulfilling Aquarians need to inject it with a quality of stability – yes, even some conservatism. They need at least one area of life to be enduring and steady; this area is usually their home and family life.

Venus, the planet of love, rules the Aquarian's 4th Solar House of Home and Family as well, which means that when it comes to the family and child-rearing, theories, cool thinking and intellect are not always enough. Aquarians need to bring love into the equation in order to have a great domestic life.

Horoscope for 1996

Major Trends

If you thought you were restless for the past seven years, just watch the next seven years, Aquarius. Your need to experiment, to break barriers and set off on your own is even stronger now than it has been. Your need for total freedom is simply incredible and you have more power to achieve it now you have had in a long time. Enjoy the ride, for it is going to be quite exciting.

Last year was, all in all, a happy year. You were involved in groups and professional organizations and saw some of your fondest hopes and wishes come to pass. This year is still happy but you are growing on a spiritual rather than social level. Your philanthropic activities over the past seven years now bring you increased status in the religious or charitable organizations to which you belong. You make friends with people who are idealistic and charity-orientated. The world cannot understand your courage and seeming self-sufficiency this year, but the horoscope shows where they come from – you enjoy secret support and secret protection in all your endeavours. You are bolstered by invisible protectors and therefore fear no evil.

If 1996 could be summed up in one word it would be 'wanderlust'.

Health

Your health and vitality were strong in 1995, and this trend continues in 1996. Of course there will be periods of greater or lesser vitality during the course of the year, but the over-all trend is good. None of the long-term planets is stressing you any more. And the stresses that come from the short-term planets are of short duration.

Another positive health signal is that your 6th House of Health is relatively inactive this year. Thus you have no need to focus over-much on your health. No news is good news. A healthy body does not call attention to itself.

Since the Moon is your Health Planet, as a general rule you will feel more energetic and have more healing ability (for yourself and others) when the Moon waxes. You will feel less energetic and have lessened healing abilities when it wanes. Try to schedule yourself accordingly.

More good health news: the health of your spouse or business partner is improving greatly this year. If he or she has had health problems you will hear good news about their resolution. A grim prognosis made in 1995 is not as grim as it looked at the time. In general you are more concerned about other people's health than your own.

Siblings and neighbours with whom you are involved need to be more careful this year – they need to conserve energy and to rest and relax more. They are feeling their physical limits this year. The health of your children and grandchildren (where this applies) is stable and will even improve after April of 1996.

The health of a parent (or parental figure) becomes more delicate after April. Two of the four eclipses of 1996 occur in his or her 6th House of Health, showing health progress through temporary upheavals. Concealed problems reveal themselves so that they can be resolved and dealt with. 'Quickie' solutions are not called for now, but rather long-term solutions that involve changes in lifestyle and habits.

Home and Domestic Life

Though your 4th House of Home and Family is relatively inactive this year, multiple moves and changes of residence are foreseen. This has to do with Uranus moving into your 1st House of the Body and Personal Image. You want change for the sake of it. Change itself is seen as good. Psychologically you are like a wandering nomad looking for a domestic situation in which you can find the 'ideal of absolute freedom'.

The absence of activity in your 4th House – traditionally the House that shows moves and family relationships – shows that you are less concerned about relationships within the family, less concerned with family obligations and more concerned with self-fulfilment. It is not that you are anti-family, but you are more pro-freedom and personal fulfilment than pro-family and family considerations. Your spouse is more concerned with maintaining family relationships and family harmony than you are. You feel that if you please yourself, everyone else will also be pleased. Those of you born early in the Sign of Aquarius will experience this from early on 1996; those of you born later in the Sign could experience this over the next few years. Uranus (the planet that is causing this) moves very slowly.

Venus (your Home and Family Planet) makes an unusual four-month station in Gemini 3rd April to 7th August. This would indicate family gatherings, parties, reunions and perhaps a new birth. This is a very happy family period.

A parent (or parental figure) also shares in your wanderlust and is also likely to make multiple moves in the coming years ahead. As soon as he or she settles in one place, another apparently better one beckons. He or she is likely to acquire additional properties or residences as well. Grandchildren are also moving around quite a bit this year.

Love and Social Life

Your 7th House of Love and Marriage is not a particularly active House this year. Thus you have more freedom to shape your social life as you will. Normally this inactivity (or lack of interest) would foster the status quo. Singles would tend to remain single and marrieds would tend to remain married. But with Uranus moving over your Sun, anything but the status quo is fostered. Change is the now the rule. Unless you have a very understanding partner – someone willing to cope with your need for freedom, change and travel – your marriage is in jeopardy. Marriages can survive under this configuration, but not easily. It is trial and travail for your partner or spouse. For you are intent on pleasing yourself, gaining new experiences, experimenting with different lifestyles and new aspects of personal pleasure, and redefining who you are. Your lover, partner or spouse has trouble understanding this.

Those involved romantically with Aquarians this year had better be patient and give them lots of freedom. Your Aquarian is not out of love with you or trying to hurt you, but is simply under the sway of Uranus – always difficult to resist. If the Aquarian in question is young, people will ascribe his or her behaviour to youthful rebellion. If the Aquarian is older they will ascribe it to mid-life crisis or some other label from the pop-psychology lexicon. But the real truth lies in the immensely powerful pull of Uranus.

It is not only romantic involvements that are in trouble this year, but business partnerships as well. Anything that does not conform to the Aquarian's ideal goes by the way-side.

Single Aquarians are likely to have serial love affairs this year, with none lasting too long. Lovers come suddenly and leave just as abruptly. Sexual fantasies are fulfilled this year. A love affair with someone from your past is likely from 3rd April to 7th August, but it does not seem to endure. Thoughts of marriage cross your mind briefly from 22nd July to 22nd August, but the phase passes. The Cosmos is not pushing towards long-term commitment this year.

Those looking to make a third marriage are likely to meet someone prominent – perhaps a superior at work, someone above you in status – with romantic inclinations. Serious involvement is likely. You meet this person through a professional or social organization to which you belong. But will he or she be able to cope with your need for freedom?

Those of you who have children of marriageable age will see their marital and social life completely transformed. If they are already married the relationship goes through a crisis. If it is sound to begin with it can be renewed in a way that makes it almost unrecognizable to what it was. Singles will marry. Loners will become social butterflies. Social butterflies will crave solitude. Your children need to explore the other side of their usual social inclinations.

The marital status of parents (or parental figures) tends towards the status quo.

Your interest in pleasing yourself causes – or helps along – the changes going on in your friendships. Old friends leave the picture and new ones enter it. Friendships die and new friendships are made. It is bittersweet.

Career and Finance

Career and outer achievement are less important to you this year, Aquarius. Your 10th House of Career is not especially active. You seem to be satisfied with the way your career is going now and are not pushing too hard one way or another. This is a 'me-first' year; you are more intent on pleasing yourself than on pleasing the public or superiors. Curiously, superiors and authority figures support your need for freedom and change. They are not obstructing you.

The people involved with your career are friends and they seem – happily – to have your fondest hopes and wishes in mind. Your career is furthered through networking activities, through social and professional organizations and through the pursuit of political causes that you believe in. These bring promotions, pay-rises, approval from superiors and other opportunities for advancement. What is really wonderful about this is that these are the activities that you are good at and love most to do.

You are more concerned about finances earlier in the year than later. As 1996 begins you are still budgeting and managing your resources to get the most for your pound. After April the feeling of lack and constriction leaves you and you will be more optimistic and courageous in this area. The good news here is that after two years of cost-cutting, budgeting and greater efficiency both in your personal and business finances you are now poised for healthy long-term growth.

You are still a cautious investor with an eye for long-term value. And with Saturn leaving the Sign of Pisces in April you might find good long-term investment opportunities in oil, shipping, tobacco and pharmaceutical companies – these stocks are probably selling near their lows early in 1996 and should do much better in future years. Do your homework, though, and research specific companies. Look for companies with potential for capital appreciation rather than high dividends.

Intuition has been important in your financial life for many years now, and this trend continues in 1996. The whole cosmic purpose of your Money Planet's move through your 12th House of Spiritual Wisdom and Charity

– for many years now – has been to train your financial intuition, to make it a useful tool in your life. Intuition continues to be your short-cut to financial success. Your dream-life provides you with financial messages. Intuition has many ways of revealing itself to you – sometimes through a newspaper, sometimes through a chance remark, sometimes through a psychic or astrologer. The point is that something said or seen will 'trigger' something in you, strike a chord deep in your soul or answer a nagging question. This is your intuition calling. This is the universe answering your silent calls.

Self-improvement

Early in the year you will still be working to improve and organize your finances. Not only earnings are involved but the whole way you manage and spend money – the way you keep track of it and the like. It is still good to keep a daily diary of expenses and earnings. Put expenses on one side and earnings on the other. Know how much you need to earn per day to be profitable – whether you are in your own business or just an employee. Watch how often you meet this goal and how often you fall below it. Make it a goal to earn the 'X' amount that insures profitability. It does not matter how much you spend as long as you are meeting targets that exceed your expenses.

After April it is good to organize your intellectual interests. Are there subjects you want to study and learn about? Are you too dispersed in your studies? Are you taking on too much or too little? Give this area some thought. It is better, for the next two years anyway, to study fewer subjects in a deep way than many subjects superficially. This applies especially to your spiritual studies – for Saturn (the Planet of Order and System) is also the Lord of your 12th House. And Saturn is the planet that wants to organize your intellectual pursuits. Rather than study 10 metaphysical subjects, take two or three that are most interesting and master them. Put yourself on a schedule and budget your studying time. You will be amazed at your progress after two years. Those of you still in school will have to earn your grades. Teachers are stern but fair. They will honour only real scholarship. Those of you who have Aquarian children in school should take note of this. Encourage them to study more and to apply system and order to their studies.

Month-by-month Forecasts

January

Best Days Overall: 2nd, 3rd, 12th, 13th, 21st, 22nd, 29th, 30th, 31st

Most Stressful Days Overall: 1st, 7th, 8th, 14th, 15th, 27th, 28th

Best Days for Love: 1st, 2nd, 3rd, 7th, 8th, 10th, 11th, 12th, 13th, 14th, 19th, 20th, 23rd, 24th, 29th, 30th

Best Days for Money: 1st, 10th, 11th, 19th, 20th, 23rd, 24th, 27th, 28th

An unusually happy month, Aquarius, which gets even happier as it progresses. With 90 to 100 per cent of the planets focused in the eastern half of your chart, you have unusual initiative and self-direction and the ability to create conditions as you desire them. You are personally magnetic and dynamic now and will get your way on most issues. You are not shy about letting others know what you want and need, and you fully expect that these requests will be complied with. Others, but especially your lover or spouse, are going out of their way to please you. Your health and vitality are super all month.

This is a spiritual month in a spiritual year. This is not to say that you are ignoring the body and its needs. On the contrary, the body is also seen as something holy and spiritual and the fulfilment of its needs are just as sacred as any other form of worship. But you are also concerned with your spiritual contacts, your alignment with the source of your being and with charitable and philanthropic enterprises. In this process you find that in helping the needy and the unfortunate you are personally fulfilled as well. There is great spiritual growth this month, and your dream-life is unusually active. In your inner realms you discover secret friends and secret protectors. Your spiritual guides will make themselves known to you now. Meditation practices which hitherto might have been a chore now become joyous – a pleasure in their own right – as much a pleasure as going to the disco or nightclub.

The New Moon of the 20th brings financial clarification and wonderful wealth ideas. The Full Moon of the 5th also brings a happy financial surprise – either from co-workers or from some charitable organization to which you belong.

Love is both idealistic and physical this month. Your romantic fantasies are fulfilled – either through your spouse/current relationship or through someone new that you meet. Singles find love suddenly and unexpectedly – but these affairs seem highly unstable. Enjoy them for what they are without projecting into the future.

February

Best Days Overall: 8th, 9th, 10th, 17th, 18th, 26th, 27th

AQUARIUS

The planets are still focused in the east, giving you vim,
vigour, initiative and courage. Mars in your own Sign does
not hurt either. You know what you want and go after it.
You create your own conditions now. You succeed or fail by
your own efforts. Sheer physical drive is as much a part of
your success as intelligence. Intelligence backed up by brute
physical energy is an unbeatable combination. Goals are
achieved this month – and quickly at that.

Most of the month is a 'personal pleasure period'. You
are focused on the body, its needs and its pleasures. Sensual
fantasies are fulfilled. By the time Mars leaves your Sign
on the 15th many of you will have already moved, and
the intense wanderlust that you have been feeling is now
slightly abated.

Those of you involved in sports or athletics do exceptionally well – though perhaps you take too many physical risks.
You are experimental with the body now – ready to test its
limits and go beyond them. Your athletic grace is superb.
Even those of you who are not usually athletic are more so
this month. Exercise regimes are successful and fun – but do
not take unnecessary risks. Your health is outstanding all
month. Over-indulgence in sensual delights or recklessness
when driving or taking part in athletic competitions are the
only dangers here. You can have too much of a good thing.

Many wealth planets are moving through your Money
House this month, signalling an increase in wealth, earnings

and earning opportunities. Venus' move through your Money House is always favourable financially. Here it indicates financial opportunities through real estate – the purchase or sale of same – and financial support from your family. The Sun's move through your Money House from the 19th onwards makes you a financial star – a financial measure for others. It shows that your lover or partner is financially supportive of your goals – both with money and time; that your social contacts in general bring profits to you. Wealth ideas come to you from the 10th to the 14th, as well as the possibility of good news about children and/or a creative project. You earn and spend fearlessly – and perhaps rashly.

You are still a trial to your partner, spouse or beloved this month. You need to work harder to see his or her position. But your partner is adapting to you.

March

Best Days Overall: 6th, 7th, 8th, 15th, 16th, 24th, 25th

Most Stressful Days Overall: 1st, 2nd, 3rd, 9th, 10th, 22nd, 23rd, 29th, 30th

Best Days for Love: 1st, 2nd, 3rd, 9th, 10th, 13th, 14th, 18th, 19th, 22nd, 23rd, 29th, 30th

Best Days for Money: 4th, 5th, 13th, 14th, 17th, 18th, 22nd, 23rd

The planets are still in east and bottom halves of your chart, Aquarius – push ahead with your plans with confidence. This is a month of personal achievement – especially financially – and personal fulfilment. Continue to engineer your life according to your personal specifications. Fulfil your own needs first, then – if you have time, energy and resources left over – you can take care of other people's needs. Remember that when your own energy is potent you are more in a position to help others. When you are low you are of no use to yourself or others. Sounds selfish and 'me-first', does it not? Perhaps – but called for now.

Your health and vitality are excellent all month, but you seem more concerned with your financial health than with your physical health. Have no fear, finances continue to be good. They are your main focus for most of the month. With Mars, the Sun and Saturn all in your Money House you feel conflicting urges in your financial life. The Sun and Mars make you more speculative and rash. They make you keen for quick money, quick profits, quick success. Saturn, on the other hand, slows you down, makes you more conservative – perhaps fearful of risk – and forces you to look long term. How will you resolve these opposites? Well, one way is to take calculated risks and to hedge your speculative bets. Another way is to divide your resources proportionately. Invest one part for the long term and with minimum risk (thus satisfying Saturn, the arch-conservative in you); invest another part in more aggressive speculations – thus satisfying the buccaneer and the gambler in you. You will prosper by either method this month.

This month you are more financially fearless and bold than has been normal of late. You need to go after what you want aggressively – making your own breaks and creating your own opportunities. When this happens you find that others – namely siblings, neighbours, children, and partners – are more co-operative. All of these people are helping you achieve your financial goals – and quite willingly. (You are also probably spending more on these people as well.)

April

Best Days Overall: 3rd, 4th, 11th, 12th, 20th, 21st, 30th

Most Stressful Days Overall: 5th, 6th, 18th, 19th, 25th, 26th, 27th

Best Days for Love: 1st, 2nd, 3rd, 7th, 8th, 11th, 12th, 20th, 21st, 25th, 26th, 27th, 28th, 29th, 30th

Best Days for Money: 1st, 2nd, 9th, 10th, 13th, 14th, 18th, 19th, 20th, 29th

The month begins with a lunar eclipse on the 3rd in your 9th House of Travel, Education, Religion and Philosophy. Any eclipse of the Moon – regardless of House position – creates temporary upheavals at the workplace and with workers. The Moon happens to be Lord of your 6th House of Health and Work. Thus, if you are an employee there are changes in the workplace – perhaps even a change of job. Some co-workers leave and you are shifted about, or you change companies. If you are an employer, employees are leaving and you are forced to hire new ones. Flaws in working conditions – the physical plan of the workplace – are revealed so that they can be corrected. This eclipse in the 9th indicates that a foreign trip may need to be postponed or re-arranged, or that a glitch occurs in your higher education – perhaps a course you enrolled in is cancelled, or the teacher leaves – there are various scenarios for how this occurs. What you thought you would get from an institution of higher learning is not what comes to pass – you must alter your course and strategy. Your partner's interest, dividend income or sales activities are not what he or she thought they would be – your partner needs to take corrective measures. And though you should take a reduced schedule on the 2nd, 3rd and 4th, your health is basically sound.

The solar eclipse of the 17th is still relatively kind to you. It occurs in your 3rd House – not on an angle – and affects relations with siblings, sales and marketing activities, interest and dividend income (personal) and your marriage and social life. The eclipsed planet here is the Sun – your Marriage Planet. So there are going to be changes in your marriage or marital status over the long term – the next six months. Singles involved in healthy relationships might decide to tie the knot now. Married Aquarians involved in tension-filled relationships might decide that this is the time to call it quits. Relationships that are fundamentally sound will alter a bit, ending up with new rules and new expectations.

Underlying flaws in a sales project come to light. If your car and/or communication equipment is defective its flaws will show up now. Best to have them checked out this month to make sure.

After the 20th rest and relax more. Your vitality will return to normal levels next month.

May

Best Days Overall: 1st, 2nd, 9th, 10th, 18th, 19th, 27th, 28th, 29th

Most Stressful Days Overall: 3rd, 4th, 15th, 16th, 17th, 23rd, 24th

Best Days for Love: 1st, 2nd, 7th, 8th, 9th, 10th, 15th, 16th, 17th, 19th, 23rd, 24th, 27th, 28th, 29th

Best Days for Money: 7th, 8th, 11th, 12th, 15th, 16th, 17th, 25th, 26th

As the short-term planets start shifting now into the western hemisphere of your horoscope you are forced to become less 'me-orientated' and more 'other-orientated'. You are becoming more dependent on the good graces of other people for the achievement of your goals and objectives. Thus, the month is confusing to say the least. You have got to deal with a new orientation to life: 50 to 60 per cent of the planets are retrograde, making others more tentative and cautious; and 40 to 60 per cent of the planets are in the element of Earth, which makes people down to earth, pragmatic and less likely to appreciate abstract ideas. This is a good month to take a holiday and get away from it all. You will probably achieve as much on holiday as you would at home or the office. The problem with taking a holiday is that with both Mercury and Jupiter retrograde, travel plans are likely to go awry or get delayed. However, if you allow extra time to get to your destination – and do not schedule connecting flights too tightly – the trip will be successful.

As the month begins your focus is more on the domestic situation than on your career. Again you feel the urge for a move, a renovation or redecoration of the home. The present wiring or telephone lines may not be adequate and you may need to rip them out and replace them. Your wanderlust is very much apparent now after a few relatively quiet months. The sense of caution and prudence in the air, however, conflicts with this wanderlust. Thus you feel inhibited or blocked in your desire to move. You are hesitating. The New Moon of the 17th will clarify things and you will be shown what to do.

Rest and relax more until the 20th. Your vitality will improve dramatically after then. Emotional equilibrium, always important in your health, becomes even more important this month.

Though there are numerous financial opportunities this month, you are rightfully cautious and hesitant. Use this month to review previous investments, purchases and investment strategies. See where you can improve them. Financial opportunities are coming through your partner, the family, siblings, real estate investments, sales and communication projects, and neighbours. But be wary about making long-term financial commitments now – unless you have thoroughly studied the propositions. Be especially alert about anything that you do not completely understand. Lack of understanding either your investment vehicle or the risks involved always increases your risk.

Your love life is stormy until the 10th or so. Compromise is the solution.

June

> Best Days Overall: 5th, 6th, 14th, 15th, 24th, 25th
>
> Most Stressful Days Overall: 12th, 13th, 19th, 20th, 26th, 27th
>
> Best Days for Love: 5th, 6th, 14th, 15th, 19th, 20th, 24th, 25th, 26th, 27th
>
> Best Days for Money: 3rd, 4th, 7th, 8th, 12th, 13th, 22nd, 23rd

With personal, financial and career issues on hold for a while – and there seems little you can do on an objective level to speed things up – you may as well have some fun this month. By all means attend parties and go out to night-clubs, concerts and places of entertainment. This is a good month to explore your personal creativity and to deal with children. Those of you already in the creative or performing arts have a banner month. Income from these activities will increase.

You tend to be more speculative this month, and while

gambling activities are favourable never wager more than you can afford to lose.

Forty to 60 per cent of the planets in Air Signs – your own element – this month. This is a good signal for you, indicating that people are now more interested in ideas, communication and intellectual pursuits. They become less 'earthbound' than they have been and more attuned to the realm of ideas. They can see possibilities that are intangible. For those of you into sales and marketing – and many of you are – this is a successful month. Release that ad campaign or mail-shot or newsletter now. With this much Air around you feel lighter and more comfortable. People tend to talk too much now – including you – so mind your phone bill. Your normal need for space – both intellectual and physical – is increased this month. Avoid cramped quarters with low ceilings. Spend more time out-doors. Your wanderlust is very much activated but caution is still called for.

Your love life is much improved this month. First off, you are more interested in love now – though singles are unsure about commitment. Your love needs now are fun- and pleasure-orientated. You want things light, free and non-committal. You are attracted to the playboy/playgirl type. Performers and creative artists allure you. You enjoy people with a childlike attitude. But after the 21st you want to serve and be served in practical ways. You want someone more serious and work-orientated. The workplace becomes a source of romance. Bosses are likely to fall in love with their employees. Co-workers are alluring. Cupid is cunning in achieving his ends after the 21st.

July

Best Days Overall: 2nd, 3rd, 11th, 12th, 21st, 22nd, 30th, 31st

AQUARIUS

Most Stressful Days Overall: 9th, 10th, 16th, 17th, 24th, 25th

Best Days for Love: 2nd, 3rd, 4th, 5th, 11th, 12th, 14th, 15th, 16th, 17th, 21st, 22nd, 26th, 27th, 30th, 31st

Best Days for Money: 1st, 4th, 5th, 9th, 10th, 19th, 20th, 28th, 29th

With five planets retrograde right now and with most of your life on hold you might as well socialize and have some fun this month. Loosen up, let go, have a good time as you ponder your future moves. All the short-term planets (with the exception of the Moon – for half of the month) are now in the western sector of your chart. Though you are still very much 'me-orientated', you are less so this month than you have been of late.

Your partner is less keen to cater to your every whim right now and you will be forced to compromise his or her interests with your own. Your partner asserts his or her desires very strongly now, while you are temporarily less assertive. Singles are dating more, attending more parties and in general finding more romantic opportunities. Places of entertainment, casinos, resorts, concerts and nightclubs are the likely meeting grounds. The work that you have done in previous months on your image is now paying off. You are noticed and appreciated by the opposite sex.

Though finances are still a bit slow this month, there are some interesting financial surprises coming to both you and your partner. The Full Moon of the 1st and the New Moon of the 15th bring happy financial surprises – also wealth ideas – from your personal work, co-workers or employees. The Full Moon of the 30th increases your personal possessions and personal earning power. Speculations are favourable and money comes to you through your unique creativity and family connections.

Your health is good this month though your self-esteem is not what it should be. Rest and relax more after the 22nd.

Your ability to achieve work goals and to please your employer is creating new career opportunities, but behind the scenes. Employers do not know quite what to do with you yet, or where to put you. Examine all offers carefully and do not accept a career proposal that you do not completely understand. Get all the details down and analyse your risks.

August

Best Days Overall: 7th, 8th, 9th, 17th, 18th, 19th, 26th, 27th

Most Stressful Days Overall: 5th, 6th, 12th, 13th, 14th, 20th, 21st

Best Days for Love: 3rd, 4th, 10th, 11th, 12th, 13th, 14th, 20th, 21st, 23rd, 24th, 28th, 29th

Best Days for Money: 1st, 2nd, 5th, 6th, 15th, 16th, 24th, 25th, 28th, 29th

The short-term planets are still in the western sector, now enlivening your social life and enhancing your social charisma. Temporarily, you are called to put others ahead of yourself. Personal desires, educational interests and financial affairs still seem on hold, but your career is opening up nicely. The career trend – for many years to come – is networking. Networking fosters your career goals and, in many cases, *is* your career. You are creating the career that truly makes you happy now. You are in a unique position to do this, but you need to work on removing obstructions (whether outer or from within yourself) to career success, weeding out friends or causes that are blocking your career progress – and focusing, like a laser beam, on those friends in a position to help.

Your love life sparkles and you are a social star this month. You shine because you allow your spouse or lover to be a star – this is 90 per cent of the art of romantic success. Love becomes much more physical and passionate after the 23rd. You can create further harmony with your partner by fostering and supporting his or her financial goals after the 23rd. You still need to adapt yourself to your partner's desires.

Remain cautious in finances. After the 23rd use spare cash to reduce debt and long-term obligations rather than to invest. Earnings improve after the 23rd through the co-operation of your partner and through social connections. Investors are interested in your projects this month but, as mentioned earlier, study everything carefully before committing. Debts are easily paid and easily made.

This is not one of your best health months, so rest and relax more. Your vitality improves slightly after the 23rd. Those of you who have health problems might jump too quickly into extremist – all or nothing – measures, such as surgery. Get further opinions. Metaphysical healing methods might prove more potent this month. Even if you must see a conventional doctor after trying alternative measures, the ultimate remedy is likely to be less drastic. Purity of diet and happy social relationships seem stronger than any medicine.

September

Best Days Overall: 4th, 5th, 14th, 15th, 23rd, 24th

Most Stressful Days Overall: 1st, 2nd, 3rd, 9th, 10th, 16th, 17th, 29th, 30th

Best Days for Love: 1st, 2nd, 3rd, 8th, 9th, 10th, 11th, 12th, 18th, 21st, 22nd, 23rd, 27th, 28th

Best Days for Money: 1st, 2nd, 11th, 12th, 20th, 21st, 25th, 26th, 29th, 30th

The planets are still in the western sector of your chart, empowering your social life, making you realize personal limits and making you more dependent on the good graces of others. This is not the time for undue self-assertion or power struggles. Put others first and your own needs will be met in due course.

Your love life is basically happy and filled with potential. Thoughts of marriage and romance are in the air. Love is both romantic and physical this month. Perhaps it is a bit too serious – almost obsessive – until the 23rd. But this is brief. Your love life widens and becomes 'lighter' after the 23rd. Singles admire partners who can help them transform their situation; help them break bad habits and addictions; help them to re-invent themselves. There is a delight in exploring the dark side of both your partner and yourself. After the 23rd singles are more attracted to educated, refined, professorial types. They want to be able to learn from their partner, and vice versa.

Those of you already in a relationship need to be patient with your partner until the 23rd. He or she seems overly critical and perfectionist. But this phase passes and your partner becomes more romantic and tolerant after the 23rd.

The lunar eclipse of the 26th deals rather kindly with you, Aquarius. It brings changes in your spiritual life, in your attitude to charities and in the hierarchy of charitable organizations to which you belong. Flaws in a current charitable project or organization are revealed to you now so that you can re-evaluate your position. Definitely have your communication equipment – phones, faxes, modems – and your car checked out this month. Preventative maintenance can save you money.

Your health is good all month but gets especially great after the 23rd. Elective surgery should be avoided from the 4th to the 26th.

October

Best Days Overall: 1st, 2nd, 11th, 12th, 20th, 21st, 29th, 30th

Most Stressful Days Overall: 6th, 7th, 13th, 14th, 26th, 27th

Best Days for Love: 1st, 2nd, 6th, 7th, 8th, 9th, 11th, 12th, 18th, 19th, 20th, 21st, 27th, 28th, 31st

Best Days for Money: 9th, 10th, 18th, 19th, 22nd, 23rd, 26th, 27th, 29th

The ride to your goals may be a bit bumpy this month but it is moving forward nevertheless. Ninety per cent of the planets are moving forward by the end of the month, signalling action, achievement and progress. Your Ruling Planet (Uranus) at long last moves forward after many months of backwards motion. The wanderlust is upon you again and you do not really need a solar eclipse to egg you on.

The solar eclipse of the 12th opens up educational opportunities for many of you. It brings long-term changes in your educational status. Many of you will either begin new studies now or terminate them. You are forced to choose one way or the other. Your marriage or partnership is thrown into a brief crisis as your partner is redefining his or her personality and personal desires. Your partner has some problems with siblings now. Changes in your marital status (or the status of a business partnership) occur this month. The Cosmos does not allow either you or your partner to sit on the fence. Singles must either move forward or terminate a current relationship. Marrieds in an unhappy relationship will have to make hard choices. Financial matters are very much a consideration in these choices. Unexpected expenses or flaws in a current investment force a necessary correction in your financial attitudes and strategies. Hard financial decisions have to be made. A sibling, too, faces a crisis in marriage or a current relationship. Happily, the solar eclipse is making nice aspects to you so the changes occurring are likely to be pleasant and not too disruptive. Moreover, disruptions will tend to work in your favour – in your best interest.

Your health is good until the 23rd. After that rest and relax more. Your partner should take a reduced schedule on the 11th, 12th and 13th.

Push your career after the 23rd. Seek favours from the government or bosses then as well. Authorities in general (but especially males) are kindly disposed to you then.

November

Best Days Overall: 7th, 8th, 16th, 17th, 25th, 26th

Most Stressful Days Overall: 2nd, 3rd, 4th, 10th, 11th, 23rd, 24th, 30th

Best Days for Love: 1st, 2nd, 3rd, 4th, 7th, 8th, 10th, 11th, 16th, 17th, 18th, 19th, 27th, 28th, 30th

AQUARIUS

Career success could trigger the wanderlust in you again.
Perhaps it forces a move or a change in your personal
appearance. You have got to balance your need for personal freedom (doing whatever you want to do when you
want to do it) with the demands of your career. At present
they pull you in different directions. The New Moon of the
11th is bringing you all the information you need to
achieve career objectives. Watch how it comes to you – at
times through the chance remark of a stranger, or from a
newspaper headline taken out of context, or through a
dream, or through cloud formations. The ways are infinite
but the information is coming to you. When it comes to
career activities you have acute, superhuman faculties
working for you now.

Overall you are still in a period for winding down activities. Finish up old projects, pay off debts, clean house, get
rid of old possession that you do not need.

Rest and relax more until the 22nd. After then your
vitality increases tremendously. The period after the 22nd is
overall much happier, more optimistic, much freer than
before then. Until the 22nd you are more serious – you are
conscious of your duties and responsibilities. They call to
you and you must deal with them. Afterwards you get to
do what you love most – socialize, communicate, teach and
learn. New friends come into your life after the 22nd –
good-quality friends at that. They help your career (and
some of them come as a result of your professional status)
and are themselves more prominent and powerful.

Love is pursuing you, singles. The powerful and the
prominent take a romantic interest in you. You like power
and authority in a partner now. Your lover needs to be
careful about being too controlling – but this is temporary.

A more egalitarian approach is the likely result. Singles find romantic opportunities in the pursuit of their career objectives, and after the 22nd through groups and organizations.

Finances are improving every day. Career success leads to pay-rises and other financial opportunities. Your net worth increases this month. Your partner or lover is very generous on the 17th and 18th.

December

Best Days Overall: 5th, 6th, 13th, 14th, 22nd, 23rd

Most Stressful Days Overall: 1st, 7th, 8th, 20th, 21st, 27th, 28th

Best Days for Love: 1st, 7th, 8th, 9th, 10th, 15th, 16th, 17th, 18th, 19th, 27th, 28th, 30th, 31st

Best Days for Money: 2nd, 3rd, 11th, 12th, 15th, 16th, 20th, 21st, 30th, 31st

A happy and socially-orientated month – just the way you like it. You are involved with friends, groups, group activities, seminars and communications. The general tone and mood of the month is optimistic and jovial. With Venus in your Career House and with most of the planets above the horizon your career is still your dominant priority. Good career progress is being made; bosses, elders and superiors are favourably disposed towards you.

Your 11th House of Fondest Hopes and Wishes is very powerful this month and the planets there are basically well aspected. Your dearest aspirations come to pass – or are at least progressing. As you fulfil one set of 'fondest hopes and wishes' you find new and bigger ones coming to take their place. It is an endless and eternal process. This is the month to formulate – to specify and outline – the dreams closest to your heart.

You are still very restless – perhaps even more so than in previous months. The nomad in you is active. The urge to travel, move and change is very strong. There is a great big world out there and you want to explore it and find your place in it. Opportunities to fulfil your wanderlust come through friends and groups.

Your health is good all month and friends are showing you how to enhance it even further.

Love is free, friendly and non-constricting now. Love is seeking you ardently – through your friends and through social organizations to which you belong. After the 21st love becomes more spiritual and altruistic. Both you and your beloved are self-sacrificing when it comes to love. You are both willing to give up everything for true love. After the 21st singles should keep details about a current romance secret. No one needs to know what is going on. Others will be involved in a clandestine affair – for the short term. Psychics and astrologers have important romantic information and guidance for you.

Your finances are improving day by day. Important financial windfalls come after the 21st – and these go way beyond just the normal Christmas or holiday presents you receive. These have to do with long-term financial growth. Your financial intuition is especially powerful after the 21st. Look to your dreams and hunches for guidance.

Pisces

ℋ

THE FISH
*Birthdays from
19th February
to 20th March*

Personality Profile

PISCES AT A GLANCE

Element – Water

Ruling Planet – Neptune
   Career Planet – Jupiter
   Health Planet – Sun
   Love Planet – Mercury
   Money Planet – Mars
   Planet of Home and Family Life – Mercury

Colours – aqua, blue-green

*Colours that promote love, romance and social
harmony* – earth tones, yellow, yellow-
orange

Colours that promote earning power – red, scarlet

Gem – white diamond

Metal – tin

Scent – lotus

Quality – mutable (= flexibility)

Qualities most needed for balance – structure and the ability to handle form

Strongest virtues – psychic power, sensitivity, self-sacrifice, altruism

Deepest needs – spiritual illumination, liberation

Characteristics to avoid – escapism, keeping bad company, negative moods

Signs of greatest overall compatibility – Cancer, Scorpio

Signs of greatest overall incompatibility – Gemini, Virgo, Sagittarius

Sign most helpful to career – Sagittarius

Sign most helpful for emotional support – Gemini

Sign most helpful financially – Aries

Sign best for marriage and/or partnerships – Virgo

Sign most helpful for creative projects – Cancer

Best Sign to have fun with – Cancer

Signs most helpful in spiritual matters – Scorpio, Aquarius

Best day of the week – Thursday

Understanding the Pisces Personality

If Pisceans have one outstanding quality it is their belief in the invisible, spiritual and psychic side of things. This side of things is as real to them as the hard earth beneath their feet – so real, in fact, that they will often ignore the visible, tangible aspects of reality in order to focus on the invisible and so-called intangible ones.

Of all the Signs of the Zodiac, the intuitive and emotional faculties are the most highly developed in the Pisces. They are committed to living by their intuition and this can at times be infuriating to other people – especially those who are materially, scientifically or technically orientated. If you think that money or status or worldly success are the only goals in life, then you will never understand a Pisces.

Pisceans have intellect, but to them intellect is only a means by which they can rationalize what they know intuitively. To an Aquarius or a Gemini the intellect is a tool of knowing. To a well-developed Pisces it is only a tool by which to *express* knowing.

Pisceans feel like fish in an infinite ocean of thought and feeling. This ocean has many depths, currents and sub-currents. They long for purer waters where the denizens are good, true and beautiful, but they are sometimes pulled to the lower, murkier depths. Pisceans know that they do not generate thoughts but only tune in to thoughts that already exist; this is why they seek the purer waters. This ability to tune in to higher thoughts inspires them artistically and musically.

Since Pisces is so spiritually-orientated – though many Pisceans in the corporate world may hide this fact – we will deal with this aspect in greater detail, for otherwise it is difficult to understand the true Pisces personality.

There are four basic attitudes of the spirit. One is outright scepticism – the attitude of secular humanists. The second is an intellectual or emotional belief, where one worships a far-distant God figure – the attitude of most modern church-going people. The third is not only belief but direct personal spiritual experience – this is the attitude of some 'born-again' religious people. The fourth is actually unity with the divinity, intermingling with the spiritual world – this is the attitude of yoga. This fourth attitude is the deepest urge of a Pisces, and a Pisces is uniquely qualified to perform this work.

Consciously or unconsciously, Pisceans seek this union with the spiritual world. The belief in a greater reality makes Pisceans very tolerant and understanding of others – perhaps even too tolerant. There are instances in their lives when they should say 'enough is enough' and be ready to defend their position and put up a fight. However, because of their qualities it takes a good deal of doing to get them in that frame of mind.

Pisceans basically want and aspire to be 'saints'. They do so in their own way and according to their own rules. Others should not try to impose their concept of saintliness on a Pisces, because he or she always tries to find it for him- or herself.

Finance

Money is generally not that important to Pisces. Of course they need it as much as the next person, and many of them attain great wealth. But money is not generally a primary objective. Doing good, feeling good about oneself, peace of mind, the relief of pain and suffering – these are the things that matter most to a Pisces.

Pisceans earn money intuitively and instinctively. They follow their hunches rather than their logic. They tend to be generous and perhaps overly charitable. Almost any kind of misfortune is enough to move a Pisces to give. Although this is one of their greatest virtues, Pisceans should be more careful with their finances. They should try to be more choosy about the people they lend money, so that they are not being taken advantage of. If they give money to charities they should follow it up to see that their contributions are put to good use. Even when Pisceans are not rich, they still like to spend money on helping others. In this case they should really be careful, however: they must learn to say no sometimes and help themselves first.

Perhaps the biggest financial stumbling block for the Pisces is general passivity – a *laissez faire* attitude. In general Pisceans like to go with the flow of events. When it comes to financial matters, especially, they need to be more aggressive. They need to make things happen, to create their own wealth. A passive attitude will only cause loss and missed opportunity. Worrying about financial security will not provide that security. Pisceans need to go after what they want tenaciously.

Career and Public Image

Pisceans like to be perceived by the public as people of spiritual or material wealth, of generosity and philanthropy. They look up to big-hearted, philanthropic types. They admire people engaged in large-scale undertakings and eventually would like to head up these big enterprises themselves. In short, they like to be connected with big organizations that are doing things in a big way.

If Pisceans are to realize their full career and professional potential they need to travel more, educate themselves more and learn more about the actual world. In other words, they need some of the unflagging optimism of the Sagittarius in order to reach the top.

Because of all their caring and generous characteristics, Pisceans often choose professions through which they can help and touch the lives of other people. That is why many Pisceans become doctors, nurses, social workers or educators. Sometimes it takes a while before Pisceans realize what they really want to do in their professional lives, but once they find a career that lets them manifest their interests and virtues they will excel at it.

Love and Relationships

It is not surprising that someone as 'other-worldly' as the Pisces would like a partner who is practical and down to earth. Pisceans prefer a partner who is on top of all the details of life, because they dislike details. Pisceans seek this quality in both their romantic and professional partners. More than anything else this gives Pisces a feeling of being grounded, of being down to earth.

As expected, these kind of relationships – though necessary – are sure to have many ups and downs. Misunderstandings will take place because the two attitudes are poles apart. If you are in love with a Pisces you will experience these fluctuations and will need a lot of patience to see things stabilize. Pisceans are moody, intuitive, affectionate and difficult to get to know. Only time and the right attitude will yield Pisceans' deepest secrets. However, when in love with a Pisces you will find that riding the waves is worth it because they are good, sensitive people who need and like to give love and affection.

When in love, Pisceans like to fantasize. For them fantasy is 90 per cent of the fun of a relationship. They tend to idealize their partner, which can be good and bad at the same time. It is bad in that it is difficult for anyone in love with a Pisces to live up to the high ideals set.

Home and Domestic Life

In their family and domestic life Pisceans have to resist the tendency to relate only by feelings and moods. It is unrealistic to expect that your partner and other family members will be as intuitive as you are. There is a need for more verbal communication between a Pisces and his or her family. A cool, unemotional exchange of ideas and opinions will benefit everyone.

Some Pisceans tend to like mobility and moving around. For them too much stability feels like a restriction on their freedom. They hate to be locked in one location forever.

The Sign of Gemini sits on Pisces' 4th Solar House (of Home and Family) cusp. This shows that the Pisces likes and needs a home environment that promotes intellectual and mental interests. They tend to treat their neighbours as family – or extended family. Some Pisceans can have a dual attitude towards the home and family – on the one hand they like the emotional support of the family, but on the other they dislike the obligations, restrictions and duties involved with it. For Pisces, finding a balance is the key to a happy family life.

Horoscope for 1996

Major Trends

Last year (1995) was a serious, work-orientated year. Those of you who worked hard and disciplined yourselves, who went the extra mile, prospered and achieved new career highs. Many of you achieved new heights of power and prestige. This year is going to be less serious, less burdensome and more socially-orientated. Where in 1995 you worked hard to manifest your fondest hopes and wishes, in 1996 these come to pass with greater ease. After April when Saturn leaves your Sign you will feel better physically – with more energy and vitality. Your self-esteem is increased. You are more able to pursue your career and financial goals without having to do things that you hate or dislike.

Your career continues to be important in 1996 and for many years to come. By the time Pluto leaves your Solar 10th House of Career you will have made a complete transformation of your public image and persona. Finances also become important in 1996. The self-discipline that you have learned in the past two years will now be applied to your financial life – your spending and investment habits.

But perhaps the major long-term change that happens in 1996 occurs in your spiritual life, as Uranus makes a major move from Capricorn into Aquarius. New spiritual powers and abilities come to you. You are more experimental with them. You have greater control of your inner life than you have ever had and you begin to discern a science behind the apparent ambiguity of the great inner kingdoms. Your philanthropic activities – always important in your life – change from purely monetary to giving of yourself intellectually, the sharing of knowledge and information. You find that you can help charitable organizations through action and service.

Health

Your overall health and vitality are vastly improved in 1996. True, Pluto still makes stressful aspects to you (especially those of you born early in the Sign) but Saturn starts to move away from your Sign in April. You will feel that heavy physical and emotional burdens have been magically lifted. You have become accustomed in the past two years to carrying these burdens; now that they are gone you feel bouncier, more optimistic and more energetic. You have developed stronger muscles and suddenly there is less weight to carry.

Where in the past two years you have developed attitudes of stoicism and perhaps denial of personal pleasures and desires, in 1996 – towards the end of the year – you start to experience the good life again. Be careful, though, not to undo all the good – the weight loss and physical purity – that you have achieved in the past two years.

More good health news: Your 6th House of Health is not especially active this year, showing that – for most of you – health is not a big or urgent priority. This does not mean that you start ignoring your health or start taking undue health risks, but that health is stable and requires little extra attention.

Keep in mind that though your overall health trend is positive there will be periods of lesser and greater vitality. This is in the nature of things and is caused by the movements of the fast-moving, short-term planets, as detailed in your monthly forecasts (below).

The Sun is your Health Planet – a good one to have. When it waxes – in the northern hemisphere from 21st December to 21st June – you tend to feel stronger and more vital, and to have more healing ability. When it wanes – in the northern hemisphere from 21st June to 21st December – you feel less energetic and have less innate healing ability. Diets designed to build up the body, to add weight and muscle, are best started from the winter solstice to the summer solstice. Diets designed to help you lose weight or to cleanse the body are best begun when the Sun is waning, from the summer solstice to the winter solstice.

The health of a parent (or parental figure) could be improved through cleansing and purification regimes. This is a year to bring up hidden and unknown pockets of toxins (and potential secret diseases) and get rid of them. Surgery tends to be decided upon too quickly. Let your parent get second opinions and explore alternatives. He or she wants to transform the image and redefine the personality, but this should be done the way nature does it – from within. An elective, cosmetic-type surgery is also likely. Again, this comes from a desire to regenerate and renew the image. On the positive end, this parent receives deep, new knowledge in health matters and shows good persistence in the pursuit of good health.

The health of your siblings, though basically good, undergoes brief upheavals due to two eclipses in their House of Health. These eclipses bring potential problems to the surface for ultimate resolution. In fact if the sibling has been having a health problem the eclipses will probably signal a clearing of it. But if the sibling has hidden health problems they will be revealed this year.

If your spouse has a health concern this is the year for him or her to try the new, the unexplored and the unconventional. Standard, traditional therapies seem like a waste of time. New and high-tech therapies beckon – bio-electronic or energy medicine seem especially favourable. Your partner's attitudes to health seem erratic. One philosophy is embraced one day and another the next. Ideas about health are also erratic – your spouse swings from feelings of ultimate well-being one day to utter panic the next. Your partner is learning that health is as much a state of mind as anything else. As your partner rides your health roller-coaster he or she will attain a position above and beyond these opposite extremes. He or she will identify less with either positive or negative health moods and centre in on the Ultimate Health – changeless and eternal – that lies within and that is unaffected by any material circumstance or condition. This is a place and a consciousness well worth seeking.

Home and Domestic Life

You are much more concerned with outer achievement and the pursuit of ambitions than you are with the daily domestic routine this year, Pisces. You seem content to let family relations continue to maintain the status quo. Your 4th House of Home and Family Relationships is not especially active, thus you are free to shape this area as you will. The

Cosmos pushes you neither one way nor the other. But, if you are married, a move or major renovation of the home could come as a result of pressure from your spouse. Your spouse is more focused on the domestic life and family issues than you are. Moreover, your spouse seems to be disconnecting him- or herself from burdensome family relationships. You seem neutral to all this and will probably go along with his or her decisions.

Be patient with your spouse this year. He or she is exploring deep psychology and working hard to change emotional patterns. He or she is really digging into the psyche this year – fishing out all kinds of messy stuff. Some of it is good, too. When this process is complete he or she will have a new set of feelings and emotions and new emotional patterns. If temper tantrums come up during this process – and they will – understand that you are not the target, though you might feel that you are. Your spouse is merely raw and letting off steam.

Those of you with older children will probably see major changes in their domestic situation this year as two eclipses occur in their domestic Houses. Moves or reorganizations are likely. Weaknesses in their present home will come to the surface for correction, elimination, or to be escaped from completely by moving house.

The parent (or parental figure) who is changing his or her image will probably want to move or renovate the home as a part of this image change. The truth is that he or she feels very cramped in the present condition. Yet a move might not be called for – the space that exists could be used more efficiently.

Your in-laws (brothers- or sisters-in-law) will probably have a series of domestic changes this year. There is a long-term restlessness in them. Their search for the ideal home will be an ongoing process for seven years or so.

Love and Social Life

Though your 7th House of Love and Marriage is relatively inactive this year, there will be improvements in your marriage and social life as Saturn moves off in April and you become less stiff, less serious, less cold and aloof. Your partner or spouse warms up to you more. You have been difficult to live with these past two years. It is not that you have gone out of your way to be cold, aloof and separate, but that people have perceived you this way. You projected these energies unconsciously. Watch the change in how you are perceived after April. You will be less intimidating to others and they will be more likely to approach you for friendship. It is as if you created barriers around yourself for protection – or to allow yourself space to pursue outer objectives. You emphasized your 'separateness' and guarded your space zealously. Now the barriers are gone.

If your marriage has survived these past two years, credit should really go to your partner who hung in there under great duress.

If you are single you are more popular with the opposite sex this year – and though you probably will not marry you will have more romantic opportunities than last year. Your inactive 7th House fosters the status quo – that is, singles tend to stay single, marrieds to stay married.

The main expansion in your social life comes with new friends and acquaintances rather than in the romantic realm. You are meeting new and prominent people. The pursuit of career success makes you socialize more and mix with those who can be of help to you. You meet these kinds of people on a friendship level rather than on a professional level. You become friendly with your bosses and superiors and mix with them socially, and in general get to know them on another plane. Friends are favourably disposed to you and create – or lead you to create – new career opportunities.

You are more involved with groups, professional and social organizations this year. Friendship seems more interesting – and less stressful – than romance. Friendship gives freedom, romance restricts your style.

Singles working towards a third marriage are likely to marry this year. It is not a whirlwind kind of affair, but something that starts slow and takes time to mature. Give this new relationship time. The other person seems like a corporate, managerial type.

Those of you with children of marrying age are also likely to be attending a wedding this year. Your children are involved in something serious, committed and long term. Many of who are reading this have grandchildren of marriageable age – be patient this year. The status quo is likely. Married grandchildren are likely to stay married and singles are likely to stay single. The marriage of a parent (or parental figure) is in crisis this year. Drastic changes are occurring. Survival of the relationship is chancy and entirely up to them.

Career and Finance

These are two very important areas in 1996 and for some years to come. Ever since Pluto moved into your Career House in 1995 you have been focused on career objectives – 'career-driven' is perhaps a better word – even fanatical. Those Pisceans born earlier in the Sign are experiencing this sooner than those of you born later in the Sign – but all will, in the coming years, experience this.

This Pluto drive is superhuman. As you focus and persist you become aware of the various blockages that obstruct your career goals. You do not go around these fences or blocks the way you normally would, but plough right through them – eliminating them where possible. Some of these blockages are psychological and to do with your attitude – these will be most in your power to correct and you should work on correcting them. For example, if you have a narrow vision of your potential or feel that you are not worthy to rise to the heights, know that you are and that the Cosmos desires your success. Other blockages appear as conditions, circumstances and people. As time goes on these will be removed from your path very naturally. Shake-ups in the corporate structure will bring opportunities to you. Takeovers affecting your company are likely – and these too provide opportunities for you. You will even benefit if the company you work for goes bankrupt. You know how to turn disasters into opportunities.

Superiors seem in the mood for downsizing and cutting employees and costs, yet they look favourably upon you.

Your focus and dedication are going to bring you great public and professional recognition as time goes on. But the road is stormy. Your focus is your salvation.

Financially, too, this is an interesting year. With Mars as your Money Planet you like 'quick money' and short-term gains. And though you are cosmically called to develop financial fearlessness and aggressiveness, this year you need to be careful about overplaying these tendencies. Caution, stability and the long-term view are called for. Avoid 'get-rich-quick' schemes like the plague. Avoid speculative tendencies. Focus on investments and purchases that have good long-term value. Buy less but buy quality. If you buy a car, do not look so much at its style and price but at its resale value many years down the road. This is a year – regardless of your age – to think about retirement and what your income will be later on in life. You younger Pisceans can merely spend some time visualizing your ideal financial situation later on in life. It would not hurt either to put some excess cash away now for later on in life. The younger you are and the sooner you begin to do this, the more your investment will grow. Older Pisceans will have to take more practical steps in these areas, such as cutting present expenses so as to invest more in retirement and pension funds and the like. The long-term view is your salvation this year.

Saturn going through a person's Money House often indicates a need to apply system, order and discipline to financial affairs – both in the spending and in the earning. Are you wasting time on projects that bring in little profit and waste a lot of time? This is the year to evaluate these things and do something about them. Where do the bulk of your earnings come from? Focus and expand on these areas. Living within a realistic budget will not hurt you, either, though you generally dislike doing so. Remember that a realistic budget is not meant to deprive you, but merely to guide you. It is common sense – logic – applied to expenses. And since you tend to be an impulse-buyer this can be a big help to you.

On a psychological level Saturn's move through your Money House produces a feeling of 'tightness, lack and limitations'. But this is not what Saturn is trying to do. This is merely a financial 'wake-up call' to make needed changes.

A parent (or parental figure) prospers greatly this year. This parent has more financial freedom to pursue intellectual interests. The income of your partner is more or less stable. Two eclipses in your partner's Money House indicate that short-term upheavals will force financial remedies and long-term improvement.

Self-improvement

Improve your career prospects by joining groups, social and professional organizations. Make friends who are also seeking career advancement and who empathize with your goals. These activities are highly successful in 1996.

Improve your finances in the way described above. Less speculation and more of a long-term perspective will save you most problems. As an intuitive person who likes to flow with events, applying system, method and order to your financial affairs will at first be difficult, but it is time for you to gain some conscious control (rather than intuitive control) over your earnings and investments.

Improve your spiritual life – always important to you – by taking a more scientific, innovative approach to meditation and philanthropy. Explore some of the new tapes and meditation programmes on the market. Also share your technical expertise or scientific knowledge with a charitable organization – this could help them more than mere money. You also might find that the best way to help the poor and the unfortunate is through educating them rather than merely giving them 'things'.

Improve relations with a parent (or parental figure) by understanding his or her need for radical change. These changes do not come easy – often they come through explosions. When you understand where these things come from, you will be more tolerant and more able to help these changes along.

Month-by-month Forecasts

January

Best Days Overall: 5th, 6th, 14th, 15th, 23rd, 24th

Most Stressful Days Overall: 2nd, 3rd, 10th, 11th, 16th, 17th, 18th, 29th, 30th, 31st

Best Days for Love: 2nd, 3rd, 10th, 11th, 12th, 13th, 14th, 19th, 20th, 23rd, 24th, 27th, 28th

Best Days for Money: 1st, 10th, 11th, 12th,

13th, 19th, 20th, 21st, 22nd, 25th, 26th,
27th, 28th, 29th, 30th, 31st

Most of the planets are clustered in the east and above the horizon of your chart this month, Pisces. Thus you are self-directed, have much initiative and are focused on outer, career goals. You have great power to create your own career conditions this month and the world will more or less have to adapt to you. If they do not you can go it on your own.

Your major interest this month centres on friendships, group activities and social and professional organizations. These are interesting for many reasons. For one thing, they help your career. For another they help your spiritual life and further your spiritual quests. And, last but not least, these activities are important for your 'bottom line'. In fact a major financial opportunity – or bonanza – comes through friends around the 5th.

This is a month for making your fondest hopes and wishes come true – in terms of your career, romance and finances. It is a month during which you seek overall happiness and make the moves needed to attain it. The happiness that you seek is more than just money, fame and romance. It is a kind of integrated happiness that includes all these things but is yet more than that. You will start to get a taste of it this month – and this year. For this quest is blessed by the Cosmos now.

Though the past two years has not been your best health years, January is an 'up' period in this area. You really will not feel fully yourself until April when Saturn moves out of your Sign, but you are rallying right now. Enjoy.

Though singles are romantic this month – especially after the 15th – and attractive to the opposite sex, serious commitments are on hold. Mercury's retrograde (backward motion) from the 9th to the 30th suggests caution about jumping into any serious new relationships. Date and enjoy, but withhold on commitment until Mercury starts going forward on the 30th.

Though you should only speculate with a fraction of your holdings – a harmless amount – the Full Moon of the 5th does bring speculative luck.

February

> Best Days Overall: 1st, 2nd, 11th, 12th, 19th, 20th, 28th, 29th
>
> Most Stressful Days Overall: 6th, 7th, 13th, 14th, 26th, 27th
>
> Best Days for Love: 1st, 2nd, 6th, 7th, 13th, 14th, 16th, 17th, 21st, 22nd, 26th, 27th
>
> Best Days for Money: 6th, 7th, 8th, 9th, 10th, 15th, 16th, 19th, 20th, 21st, 22nd, 23rd, 24th, 25th, 28th, 29th

With 90 to 100 per cent of the planets (most of which are moving fast forward) still in your eastern sector this month you are unusually aggressive, wilful, self-directed and independent. It is a month of great progress and achievement and you are at the controls, beholden to almost no one. It is up to you now. Take the bull by the horns and go after what pleases you. The conditions you create now are the ones you will live with for a while.

For most of the month you are involved in your spiritual life and in charitable activities – one of your favourite places to be, by the way. Your normally strong ESP is now even stronger. Your dream life is vivid – and until the 15th a bit combative. You are making war on the inner dimensions with foes within yourself and from the collective past. Mars

– the genius of War – assures that success is ultimately yours.

Mars is also your Money Planet. Its move through your 12th House indicates that you are giving not only time and energy but money to charitable causes; that your dream life includes financial guidance; that astrologers and psychics are important in the attainment of financial goals. Mars makes you socially conscious about your investments and makes you want to avoid industries or companies that you perceive as 'polluters' or unfair to workers, minorities and the like. Mars indicates that great financial fears need to be overcome before your financial goals are met – and Mars will flush them to the surface so that you can eliminate them.

By the 19th your focus starts to shift to the body and personal pleasures. Athletes do particularly well after the 19th. Even non-athletes perform above their norm. You are imbued with a more aggressive spirit and probably do not realize your own strength – avoid arguments and rows. You will probably win, but that is not the point. You will regret later the verbal and/or physical damage that was caused.

Your love life is not particularly prominent though there are numerous sexual opportunities. Early in the month you want friendship from your lover. You want things light, free, uncommitted. After the 15th you want spiritual communion and spiritual harmony with the beloved. You become more altruistic and self-sacrificing in love – and you attract these kinds of lovers into your life.

March

Best Days Overall: 9th, 10th, 17th, 18th, 26th, 27th, 28th

Most Stressful Days Overall: 4th, 5th, 11th, 12th, 24th, 25th

PISCES

Best Days for Love: 1st, 2nd, 3rd, 4th, 5th,
9th, 10th, 13th, 14th, 17th, 18th, 22nd,
23rd, 29th, 30th

Best Days for Money: 4th, 5th, 9th, 10th,
13th, 14th, 17th, 18th, 19th, 20th, 22nd,
23rd, 29th

The planets are still very much in the eastern sector of
your chart, making you 'me-orientated', independent, self-
directed and concerned with your own personal interests.
Uncharacteristically so, it might be added. Even your normally strong spiritual and metaphysical focus is eclipsed by
corporeal needs and desires. This, the birthday month for
many or you, is one of your strongest 'personal pleasure
periods' in 1996. There are strong urges for good food, good
wine, good sex and all the other sensual delights known to
humanity. Normally it might be necessary to caution you
about over-indulging, but with Saturn in your Sign for over
two years perhaps you need some excess. You have been
much too stoic and self-denying lately.

Your health is excellent all month and you have all the
energy you need to achieve whatever pleases you. Those of
you who are involved in athletics excel this month. Even
those of you who are non-athletes do better than usual.
This is the month to buy nice clothing, jewellery and personal accessories. Go to that expensive hair-stylist (whose
fees you have always considered outrageous and prohibi-
tive) and have your hair done. Buy a comfortable chair for
your room. Care for and indulge yourself physically. As
you love yourself you find that you draw love from others.
Married Pisceans find that your partner is more appreciative
and more eager to please.

In spite of your self-centredness – perhaps because of it –
this is a wonderful love month. You are not running to parties but parties are running to you. You are not pursuing

love but love pursues you. Romance is physical and passionate this month. Singles have live-in or quasi live-in loves now.

After the 20th the focus turns to earnings and investments. People may consider you a bit rash in both your spending and investment style, but you do not see it that way. Your financial confidence is so strong that to you what you are doing does not seem risky. There is good financial success. Money is earned through the co-operation of co-workers. Those involved in health fields – and a disproportionate number of you are – gain more patients and clients now. Partners are supportive. Social contacts are like money in the bank now – the wealth of friends is seen as another form of affluence. Interest income and/or dividends are increased. Enjoy.

April

Best Days Overall: 5th, 6th, 13th, 14th, 23rd, 24th

Most Stressful Days Overall: 1st, 2nd, 7th, 8th, 20th, 21st, 28th, 29th

Best Days for Love: 1st, 2nd, 3rd, 7th, 8th, 9th, 11th, 12th, 18th, 19th, 20th, 21st, 28th, 29th, 30th

Best Days for Money: 1st, 2nd, 7th, 8th, 9th, 10th, 16th, 17th, 18th, 19th, 20th, 25th, 26th, 27th, 29th

Not only are the two eclipses this month signalling long-term change, but Saturn leaves your Sign this month – for good. You perceive the upheavals and changes in an optimistic way. It is as if the Cosmic Dramatist is creating a new scene, shifting the actors around and changing the back-drops so that a new act can begin.

Your health is vastly improved this month, as is your optimism.

The lunar eclipse of the 3rd occurs in your 8th House of Transformation and brings changes in your sexual attitudes, creative life and in relations with children. An inheritance or insurance payment you are supposed to get is perhaps not as large as you thought – something comes up to block, reduce or delay it. But this is short term. The upheaval will resolve itself in due course. Your partner's income seems to take a drop – or perhaps an unexpected expense comes up that diminishes his or her 'bottom line'. Your partner's financial flaws are revealed so that they can be corrected. These flaws could involve certain particular investments or involve your partner's general investment philosophy and strategy for earning money.

The solar eclipse of the 17th affects the workplace and your job – and perhaps money earned through your job. Perhaps there is a cut in wages or you are asked to work fewer hours. Perhaps you are shifted temporarily to a job that pays less. These disappointments either lead you to a new company at better pay or, over time, to a better job within the same company. Employers are likely to lose employees during this period. Expensive improvements or renovations will have to be made to the workplace as hidden flaws come to light. But you can handle all these things, and when the dust clears you will be in a new and better work/workplace pattern.

Finances are the main focus of the month. Though your wealth will increase do not ignore the investment flaws that the eclipse is likely to uncover. Greater profits seem to involve greater risks which you may not be aware of.

May

> Best Days Overall: 3rd, 4th, 11th, 12th, 20th, 21st, 22nd, 30th, 31st
>
> Most Stressful Days Overall: 5th, 6th, 18th, 19th, 25th, 26th
>
> Best Days for Love: 1st, 2nd, 7th, 8th, 9th, 10th, 15th, 16th, 17th, 18th, 19th, 25th, 26th, 27th, 28th, 29th
>
> Best Days for Money: 7th, 8th, 13th, 14th, 15th, 16th, 17th, 25th, 26th

The universe slows down this month, Pisces, and so do you. There is nothing wrong with this *per se*, and you can use this constructively, but it feels eerie and strange.

Every major area of your life – love, finance, career and personal desires – needs to be reviewed, re-evaluated and perfected. The delays that are going on in these areas gives you the rare opportunity to do this.

This is the month to review past investments, investment strategies and your general investment philosophy. Keep the things that are good and get rid of what is bad. Prudence and conservatism should guide your investment philosophy and your spending. Those of you living from paycheque to paycheque may find things more difficult this month, as payments could be delayed. But your mystical approach to life – which others consider a problem – is your salvation. Your supply is from the Source, from the Spirit, and this is where your trust must be in these times. Regardless of outer conditions you have a spiritual supply for every need. Only a Pisces can understand fully what this means.

You know that your 'bottom line' can be increased through better advertising and marketing efforts, but do not rush into these things yet. Plan them for the next month or so – get everything ready and put it into action in a few months' time.

Stay loose and detached in love as well. Give a current love or your spouse plenty of space and let him or her review and re-evaluate the relationship. This is a necessary process now. Be especially careful of how you communicate with your lover, friends or business partners this month. Do not assume that they will understand what you really mean. Spell everything out. Mercury's retrograde from the 3rd to the 27th increases the probability of miscommunication and could make an already difficult situation even worse. This applies to superiors, bosses, parental figures and those involved with your career as well.

Your health is excellent until the 20th, but after then rest and relax more.

June

> Best Days Overall: 7th, 8th, 16th, 17th, 18th, 26th, 27th

> Most Stressful Days Overall: 1st, 2nd, 14th, 15th, 22nd, 23rd, 29th, 30th

> Best Days for Love: 3rd, 4th, 5th, 6th, 12th, 13th, 14th, 15th, 22nd, 23rd, 24th, 25th

> Best Days for Money: 3rd, 4th, 9th, 10th, 12th, 13th, 14th, 22nd, 23rd, 24th, 25th

The fast-moving, short-term planets (with the exception of the Moon for part of the month) are now at the bottom half of your horoscope, forcing you to deal with family and domestic issues that you have been ignoring. The slow-moving, long-term planets are still very much at the top half, so over the long term your career is the main focus and you should not lose sight of it. But this month you can safely relax your attention on career issues and focus on the home and family. Those of you who want to move, buy or sell a house, mend fences with the family, embark on psychological therapies, buy or sell furniture for the home, redo, renovate or remodel, should do so now. You are getting plenty of cosmic assistance in these areas – including the New Moon of the 15th which is going to clarify further what you need to do domestically. You might think that you need to move but you may really need a rearrangement of your present home. You may think that you need to assert yourself with a family member but what may really be called for is friendly persuasion. Let the New Moon guide you. It is ready, willing and able to do so.

Over the next two years you are learning important financial lessons. You are seeing that you cannot just spend indiscriminately and that you have to place realistic limits on these things. You have a more pragmatic, realistic attitude towards money and this trend continues this month. You are spending on the home and perhaps on real estate. Financial good comes through your family and through opportunities created by your family. Financial ideas come through your family as well. Writers earn money by writing about day-to-day life. Salespeople should use images from everyday domestic life to sell their products. Sales and marketing projects go well. Your mood becomes more important in your financial life now as Mars moves through your 4th House of Domestic Life. In a bad mood you are likely to make bad financial decisions. You tend to spend and buy according to your mood. You perceive yourself rich or poor depending upon your mood. Thus, make sure you are in a balanced, positive mood before making important purchases or financial decisions. Sleep on things and see how you feel about them the next day. Your financial intuition is exceptionally strong when your mood is balanced.

July

Best Days Overall: 4th, 5th, 14th, 15th, 24th, 25th

Most Stressful Days Overall: 11th, 12th, 19th, 20th, 26th, 27th

Best Days for Love: 2nd, 3rd, 4th, 5th, 11th, 12th, 14th, 15th, 16th, 19th, 20th, 21st, 22nd, 26th, 27th, 30th, 31st

Best Days for Money: 1st, 2nd, 3rd, 6th, 7th, 8th, 9th, 10th, 11th, 12th, 19th, 20th, 21st, 22nd, 28th, 29th

The lull in your career activities continues and the short-term planets indicate that you should get your personal and emotional life in order now. Domestic issues and psychological therapies go well now. Mend fences with family members and spend some quality time with them. Make it a point to have some fun now. If possible take some holiday time. Go to a resort and just relax. You need to get your 'joy batteries' recharged, and the New Moon of the 15th is going to show you how to do this.

Your health and personal creativity are very strong now. Those of you involved in the creative arts receive a financial windfall through these activities. You sell your work for higher-than-expected prices; or you get a creative idea that will earn you money and prestige later on. Financial speculations are more favourable this month as well – remember, though, not to speculate with more than you can afford. Basically you are in one of your 'personal pleasure peaks' of the year.

Your finances are going well. Interest and dividend income should start to increase after the 2nd as Venus starts going direct. Money comes to you through sales and marketing activities, real estate investments, family connections, and perhaps through one of your parents. Your ability to discern short-term financial trends makes you a shrewd trader this month. You are spending more on the home and family and perhaps redecorating your home – buying new furniture, accessories and the like.

Your love life, too, seems very happy. You look for partners with a sense of fun about them. Romance is supposed to be fun – another game, not to be taken seriously. Flirtation is another form of amusement to you – like a video game or sporting event. When a relationship starts to get too serious – or if there are any burdens or responsibilities involved – you start to get cold feet. But this attitude is temporary. After the 16th you become more dutiful in love. You serve and expect to be served by your partner or lover. Until the 16th you are attracted to playboy/playgirl types; afterwards you are attracted to people with a work ethic and who nurture through healing.

August

Best Days Overall: 1st, 2nd, 10th, 11th, 20th, 21st, 28th, 29th

Most Stressful Days Overall: 7th, 8th, 9th, 15th, 16th, 22nd, 23rd

Best Days for Love: 5th, 6th, 10th, 11th, 15th, 16th, 20th, 21st, 25th, 26th, 28th, 29th

Best Days for Money: 1st, 2nd, 3rd, 4th, 5th, 6th, 10th, 11th, 15th, 16th, 20th, 21st, 24th, 25th, 28th, 29th, 30th, 31st

PISCES

The retrograde of Neptune along with the concentration of short-term planets in the western sector of your chart indicate that this is not a month for power struggles or undue self-assertion. Go with the flow, adapt yourself to others, put others ahead of yourself and the desires of your heart will come to pass.

Relations with friends are tentative and cautious this month, but romance blooms. Singles have more romantic opportunities. Your social confidence and charisma are strong. Those already involved in a serious relationship are likely to marry or get a proposal this month. (Even if the relationship is not that serious there is talk of marriage now.) Your lover or partner seems assertive and demanding but this does not bother you. Romantic opportunities come from various sources – friends, organizations to which you belong, the workplace, parties and social gatherings. Co-workers, health care professionals and employees are particularly alluring. Romance is expressed through service and through concern for your partner's health. After the 26th love becomes more physical and passionate.

Though your financial life is on hold, some of the pressure is easing because of Saturn's retrograde. You enjoy both the way that you earn money and the fruits of your earnings more this month. Though you feel more speculative now it would be best to avoid gambles during this period. Focus more on your creativity. This is a good time to redecorate, refurnish and re-accessorize your home. Your aesthetic sense is unusually good right now. Family members and people you knew in childhood have interesting financial propositions for you. Your partner becomes more wealth-orientated after the 26th but there is some rough going ahead. He or she needs to work a lot harder than normal.

Your health is satisfactory until the 23rd, but after that rest and relax more. Remember that you cannot please others and fulfil social obligations if you yourself have no energy.

Recharge your batteries first, then use this power to further your social goals and the needs of your partner.

September

> Best Days Overall: 6th, 7th, 8th, 16th, 17th, 25th, 26th
>
> Most Stressful Days Overall: 4th, 5th, 11th, 12th, 18th, 19th
>
> Best Days for Love: 4th, 5th, 8th, 9th, 11th, 12th, 18th, 19th, 20th, 21st, 27th, 28th, 29th, 30th
>
> Best Days for Money: 1st, 2nd, 7th, 8th, 11th, 12th, 18th, 19th, 20th, 21st, 27th, 28th, 29th, 30th

With Neptune (your Ruling Planet) still retrograde and with most of the planets in the western sector of your horoscope this is not a month for power struggles and egocentric behaviour. Adaptability and versatility – which you are good at – are key to handling the month.

Social affairs continue to be very important if a bit confusing. Singles have marriage very much in mind now, but it should not be entered into while Mercury is retrograde – from the 4th to the 26th. Relationships need time to mature. The people you are meeting now – and you are meeting many – are not sure where they fit into your scheme of things. Neither are you sure where they fit. Time and the New Moon of the 12th will clarify things. A current relationship seems to go backward instead of forward. Someone you rejected in the past, or perhaps did not pay attention to, now becomes more interesting to you. You review and re-evaluate your social and romantic choices.

The lunar eclipse of the 26th creates some upheavals in both your career and financial life. A career change – or shake-up in the corporate hierarchy – causes you to fear about earnings. Perhaps an unexpected expense comes up or the stock-market throws a scare your way. Financial and investment flaws are revealed, causing you to take corrective actions. It all works out in the end and your finances will be stronger than ever before, although in the short term it may look a bit frightening. From the 23rd until late December try to channel spare cash into reducing your debts and expenses. Wealth-building investments are more favourable after the New Year. Financial support and opportunity come from siblings and co-workers. Money is earned through work and practical service this month. Earnings seem stronger because your ability achieve work goals is greater. In spite of your career changes there is forward progress taking place – either within the same company or somewhere else.

Rest and relax more until the 23rd. Your vitality improves after then.

October

Best Days Overall: 4th, 5th, 13th, 14th, 22nd, 23rd, 31st

Most Stressful Days Overall: 1st, 2nd, 9th, 10th, 16th, 17th, 29th, 30th

Best Days for Love: 8th, 9th, 10th, 11th, 12th, 18th, 19th, 20th, 21st, 27th, 28th, 31st

Best Days for Money: 6th, 7th, 9th, 10th, 16th, 17th, 18th, 19th, 24th, 25th, 26th, 27th

The universe moves forward this month, Pisces, and so do you. Progress is being made in almost every area of your life. Your good comes to you through others.

The main challenge right now is to balance and harmonize your financial interests with those of your partner, and both of these with your social needs and goals. Friendship sometimes demands financial sacrifice but do not overdo it. Do what you are able to do. Give from your abundance and from not what you need in order to survive.

Your love life is active and happy. Singles meet serious new love prospects, and current relationships become even more romantic. Marriage is on your mind for a while. But will it last? Your social charisma is strong and your social judgement acute now. Selections you make now are likely to be good. Until the 4th love is romantic and flowery. Afterwards it becomes more physical, passionate and tempestuous. You are more single-minded in love – focused on one person and perhaps overly possessive. You see jealousy as a sign of love and caring, but really it is a danger to love.

The solar eclipse of the 12th adds some spice and challenge to what is essentially a happy month. It forces you to move forward on personal purchases and changes to your image. It creates a disruption at work and perhaps a job change. Those of you seeing a health practitioner suddenly change your treatments – or even the practitioner. Important career choices must be made as the status quo is no longer tenable. Some of you will take off in an entirely new career direction – not just a new job. A parent moves and otherwise changes his or her lifestyle.

You are very much involved in making money for others – for your partner, or for shareholders. But do not completely ignore your own financial interests either.

Your health is good all month but becomes especially so after the 23rd. Before the 23rd work on re-inventing yourself – on breaking negative habits and/or addictions.

Pay off bills and reduce debt. Work on getting rid of the unnecessary from your life.

November

> Best Days Overall: 1st, 10th, 11th, 18th, 19th, 27th, 28th
>
> Most Stressful Days Overall: 5th, 6th, 12th, 13th, 25th, 26th
>
> Best Days for Love: 1st, 5th, 6th, 7th, 8th, 10th, 11th, 16th, 17th, 20th, 21st, 27th, 28th, 30th
>
> Best Days for Money: 5th, 6th, 14th, 15th, 20th, 21st, 23rd, 24th

You are in one of the happiest periods of your year right now, so enjoy. Take opportunities to travel and educate yourself, as these pursuits will pay off in career terms later.

Spiritual and philosophical illumination is yours if you want it. Your ESP and psychic abilities – always strong – are even stronger this month. Writers achieve success with publishers this month. People in the travel business also do well.

Your health is excellent until the 22nd, after which you should rest and relax more. Career and financial demands are taking up most of your energy then.

Your love life is interesting this month. Love is down to earth, practical and sensual. You are unusually aggressive in romance this month. Aggressiveness pays off until the 22nd, but after that creates some problems – for one you may actually get what you want and then have to deal with the consequences. The tendency is to jump into relationships too quickly now. You are in a 'love at first sight' kind of phase. Love decisions are instantaneous and you have difficulty taking no for an answer. On the positive side you are developing a social fearlessness. You perceive (correctly) that fear is the greatest obstacle to love and happiness. The conquest of social fears and inhibitions (the fear of rejection mostly) seems more important to you than the actual relationship. The feeling of conquest – of winning the favour of someone who appears lukewarm – is also a factor in love this month.

Love is important on a financial level as well. Money comes to you through social contacts and with the support of partners. You consider an abundance of friendships and social good will to be as much of an asset as your stock portfolio or money in the bank (and you are right). Your social grace and charm contribute as much to your 'bottom line' as financial acumen and judgement. Be careful, though, not to treat your friends, spouse or partner as material assets that you can manipulate, or to become overly possessive of them. This feeling of 'ownership' could inhibit and diminish these 'assets'.

December

Best Days Overall: 7th, 8th, 15th, 16th, 25th, 26th

Most Stressful Days Overall: 2nd, 3rd, 9th, 10th, 22nd, 23rd, 30th, 31st

Best Days for Love: 1st, 2nd, 3rd, 7th, 8th, 11th, 12th, 15th, 16th, 17th, 20th, 21st, 27th, 28th, 30th, 31st

Best Days for Money: 2nd, 3rd, 11th, 12th, 18th, 19th, 20th, 21st, 30th, 31st

This month 80 to 90 per cent of the planets are moving forward and most of them are above the horizon of your chart.

Great progress is being made – especially in career matters. Though family and domestic issues are important, family members support your career aspirations. You are just as ambitious for family members as you are for yourself. You want emotional harmony and domestic tranquillity for others as much as for yourself. A pay-rise, promotion or other public honour is coming now. But do try to rest and relax more. You seem more concerned about a healthy career than in your own physical well-being.

The planets have now shifted eastward in your chart, making you less socially-orientated and more 'me-orientated'. This trend will continue now for the next six months or so. As this planetary shift continues you become more interested in pleasing yourself than in pleasing others, more interested in creating your own conditions than in adapting to existing conditions. Every day you are becoming more independent and in control of your own destiny.

It seems that the Cosmos has ordained that you shall first attain your career pinnacles before you can attain true and lasting happiness. If you had attained happiness earlier you would always have wondered whether career success – the glitz and glamour of the outer life – could have made you even more happy. Now you see that it cannot. Happiness comes from other things – from good friends, from associating with people of like mind, from intellectual expansion and from being properly integrated into the larger whole. These benefits you will begin to experience after the 21st.

Continue to wind down financial activities until the 21st. Pay off debts, cut useless expenses and become leaner and trimmer financially. After the 21st – but really from next month – you can begin sowing financial seeds into investments, bank accounts and the like.

Mars in your House of Marriage indicates an aggressiveness towards romance. Mercury (your Love Planet) is retrograde, however. Thus you are in two minds this month. One part of you wants to rush into relationships and sweep the object of your desire off his or her feet; the other part counsels caution. The solution? Make haste slowly. Go after what you want but do not commit to anything serious just yet.

Of further interest...

Your Chinese Horoscope 1996

*What the Year of the Rat
holds in store for you*

Neil Somerville

The ancient art of Chinese astrology is being rediscovered
in the West and has proved a highly accurate system of
character analysis and prediction. Neil Somerville's annual
best-selling guide, now in its ninth year, will introduce you
to the 12 signs of the Chinese zodiac, as well as explaining
which of the five elements governs your sign, what your
ascendant is and what lies ahead for you in 1996.

The Year of the Rat, the first of a new 12-year cycle,
promises major political and social changes. It will be a year
of opportunity and economical growth. Neil Somerville
gives both a global forecast for the 12 months and detailed
advice on how each sign can get the best from the year.
Find out how you can make the most of your opportunities
– in business, finance, love and relations with others.

What does the Year of the Rat have in store for you?

Chinese Love Signs

*Are you a sensual horse, an amorous goat
or a seductive snake?*

Neil Somerville

In this fascinating new book about the 12 signs of the
Chinese zodiac, best-selling author Neil Somerville looks at
the personalities of each sign, how they relate to each other
– and how they react when in love.

Chinese Love Signs will guide you toward the sign which will
bring you the most happiness and the perfect love match. It
will also show how you can make the most of relationships
with friends, business associates and your children. You will
discover many intriguing aspects of your personality and
your strengths and weaknesses will become clear.

This intriguing book makes compelling reading and
contains a wealth of revealing information!

Rising Signs

Discover the truth about your personality

Sasha Fenton

The sign of the zodiac rising on the eastern horizon as you were born – your rising sign – reveals details about your outer personality and how it masks what is underneath: your looks, actions and outward behaviour may all be determined by this sign. And, being based on the actual *time* of birth, it is a far more personal indicator of character than the more general sun sign.

Here Sasha Fenton shows how to find your rising sign and explains how it applies to you. In addition, she examines decanates, the modifying 'thirds' of the zodiac signs, and their subsidiary effects on the horoscope.

Rising Signs will enhance your understanding of astrology, of yourself and of those around you.

I Ching

The shamanic oracle of change

Translated by Martin Palmer, Jay Ramsay, with Zhao Xiaomin

For more than 3,000 years the *I Ching* has been used as a source of guidance, divination and inspiration that directly addresses the heart of the human condition. However, until now the oracle's cryptic symbolism has obscured the dramatic historical event that gave rise to this great work.

The authors of this new, beautifully designed translation have not only returned to the earliest meaning of the Chinese characters but also to original source of the oracle: to the shaman seated on a cloudy mountain top in Shensi province. Through painstaking research and an astounding feat of detective work, they have uncovered an epic period in Chinese history, a momentous conflict that gave rise to the *I Ching*. Here they tell this long-forgotten story and present the *I Ching* itself, with all its timeless wisdom.

Step by Step Tarot
Terry Donaldson

Step by Step Tarot is a course aimed at demystifying Tarot reading. It will have an equal appeal for both the beginner and the more experienced student. Whether you feel that you are psychic or have a more down-to-earth interest, this book will give you the training you need to start working with the Tarot. If you have been studying the subject but do not feel confident enough to read for other people, this is an ideal book to help you develop your skills.

The workbook guides you through a practical course that is very easy to use. It gives helpful advice on choosing the right pack and learning the individual meanings of the cards.

Terry Donaldson has over 20 years' experience as a Tarot reader and teacher, having trained over 1,000 people. He is the founder and director of the London Tarot Centre.

YOUR CHINESE HOROSCOPE 1996	1 85538 450 7	£4.99	☐
CHINESE LOVE SIGNS	1 85538 405 1	£4.99	☐
RISING SIGNS	0 85030 751 1	£4.99	☐
I CHING	1 85538 416 7	£12.99	☐
STEP BY STEP TAROT	1 85538 431 0	£6.99	☐

All these books are available from your local bookseller or can be ordered direct from the publishers.

To order direct just tick the titles you want and fill in the form below:

NAME: _____

ADDRESS: _____

_____

_____ POSTCODE: _____

Send to: Thorsons Mail Order, Dept 3, HarperCollins*Publishers*, Westerhill Road, Bishopbriggs, Glasgow G64 2QT.
Please enclose a cheque or postal order or your authority to debit your Visa/Access account—

CREDIT CARD NO: _____

EXPIRY DATE: _____

SIGNATURE: _____

– to the value of the cover price plus:
UK & BFPO: Add £1.00 for the first book and 25p for each additional book ordered.
Overseas orders including Eire: Please add £2.95 service charge.
Books will be sent by surface mail but quotes for airmail despatches will be given on request.

24 HOUR TELEPHONE ORDERING SERVICE FOR ACCESS/VISA CARDHOLDERS – TEL: 041 772 2281.